Philosophical Essays

Philosophical Essays

ANTONY FLEW

EDITED BY JOHN SHOSKY

ROWMAN & LITTLEFIELD PUBLISHERS, INC.
Lanham • Boulder • New York • Oxford

ROWMAN & LITTLEFIELD PUBLISHERS, INC.

Published in the United States of America
by Rowman & Littlefield Publishers, Inc.
4720 Boston Way, Lanham, Maryland 20706

12 Hid's Copse Road
Cumnor Hill, Oxford OX2 9JJ, England

British Library Cataloguing in Publication Information Available

Library of Congress Cataloging-in-Publication Data

Flew, Antony, 1923–
    Philosophical essays / Antony Flew ; edited by John Shosky.
        p. cm.
    Includes bibliographical references and index.
    ISBN 0-8476-8578-0 (alk. paper). — ISBN 0-8476-8579-9 (pbk. : alk. paper)
    1. Philosophy. 2. Analysis (Philosophy). I. Shosky, John. II. Title.
B1626.F573P48   1997
192—dc21   97-27642
                                                                      CIP

ISBN 0-8476-8578-0 (cloth : alk. paper)
ISBN 0-8476-8579-9 (pbk. : alk. paper)

Printed in the United States of America

♾™ The paper used in this publication meets the minimum requirements of American
National Standard for Information Sciences—Permanence of Paper for Printed Library
Materials, ANSI Z39.48–1984.

Antony Flew in his study, Reading, United Kingdom, November, 1995. (photo courtesy of Kathryn Jo Ottman)

CONTENTS

INTRODUCTION

JOHN SHOSKY

INITIAL MEETING

I first heard Tony Flew lecture in 1983. I was a graduate student in philosophy on a summer semester program at the University of London's Chelsea College, sponsored by the Institute of Anglo-American Studies. The organizers of this program, James Halsted and Woody Hannum, brought in Sir A.J. Ayer, Lord Quinton, Elizabeth Anscombe, Martin Hollis, Alan Ryan, and Kenneth Minogue, among others, to lecture to us on the topics in "Modern British Philosophy." Each lecturer had two hours to present a topic of personal choice. Then, after a vigorous question and answer session, the lecturer and the students would often adjourn to a nearby pub, such as the Black Bull or the Wheatsheaf, for lunch and beer. That is when we would take a full measure of our visiting lecturers. How would they hold up under the intoxication of philosophy and ale?

Some refused this trial by fire, notably Professor Ayer, who probably thought that we were lightweights, both intellectually and in terms of party endurance (compared with him we were). Some proved highly fascinating up close. Especially I am thinking of Professor Anscombe, who matched us Guinness for Guinness, all the while offering profound insights into Wittgenstein and the direction of contemporary philosophy.

One of our last lecturers was Flew. He gave a spirited defense of linguistic philosophy, telling us that linguistic philosophers were "Real

McCoy"[1] philosophers who shared much with Plato and Aristotle's approach and method. Flew punctuated the air in that lecture hall with precise prose, rapid changes of volume and rate, significant pauses for emphasis, and even some facial mugging to make sure we did not miss a vital point. All of us were enchanted and intentionally prolonged the question period because we did not want the lecture to end. When we were finally thrown out of the lecture hall, David Askman, Gordon Smith, Elizabeth Stolpe, Woody Hannum and I raced Flew over to the Wheatsheaf. As we sat down, Flew surveyed the place and said "I'll have something wet," which in this case meant a pint of Heineken. Then, in that loud and rollicking pub, Flew mesmerized us with tales of Gilbert Ryle, J. L. Austin, and Ludwig Wittgenstein, and offered reminders to read important pieces by J. J. C. Smart, David Pears, Richard Swinburne, John Wisdom, and John Searle, all the while displaying elegant taste in beverages. Flew also was the teacher, listening to us, finding out about our own work, inquiring whether we had looked at a certain book or considered a salient viewpoint.

The camaraderie, the whizzing exchange of ideas, and the steady rate of patronage at the bar produced my most cherished memory of the summer. I had someone take a picture of all of us that day, and it now hangs in my office, a constant reminder of all that is good and vital about philosophy.

The next day, fully recovered from our afternoon at the pub, I raced to Foyle's bookstore on Charing Cross Road and bought *Thinking About Thinking* and *Logic and Language, II.* I immediately devoured them both and became a great admirer of Flew's work.

FLEW AT AMERICAN UNIVERSITY

Years later, I was pleased to invite Flew to lecture at the American University in Washington, D.C. He came over on several occasions from Bowling Green, Ohio, where he was Distinguished Research Fellow in the Social Philosophy and Policy Center, Bowling Green State University. His "Logic of Mortality" was the annual Bishop Hurst Lecture in Philosophy in 1987. During a visit in 1992 he also was kind enough to sit on my dissertation committee, offering insights on Bertrand Russell and Wittgenstein that turned my defense into a seminar about the depth of Russell's achievements and

---

[1]   I first heard Flew use this phrase in a lecture before the Institute for Anglo-American Studies, Chelsea College, University of London, June 1983.

Wittgenstein's influence on Russell in the fateful year of 1913. Over the years, Flew has lectured at American University on six different occasions, most recently in February, 1997. We were always pleased to have someone of his stature and scholarship on our campus.

FLEW'S CAREER

From his early career at Oxford, and now as professor emeritus of philosophy at the University of Reading, Flew has been a leading voice in philosophical scholarship for more than forty years. Flew is one of the most important interpreters of David Hume.[2] He is one of the most recognized advocates for university instruction in critical thinking.[3] Like Russell before him, Flew has worked tirelessly to make philosophy accessible to larger audiences.[4] Flew has also been a serious advocate of free speech, greater individual choice, market-drive economies, the right to die, racial harmony, educational reform, and the elimination of dogmatic/theocratic government policies. As he recently demonstrated in the first series of Prometheus Lectures,[5] philosophy can be successfully applied to a wide range of current issues, providing insights into solutions and helping citizens and policy-makers avoid dangerous mistakes.

Flew may be widely known for his work on political, theological, or sociological issues. But I believe that Flew's greatest achievements may lie in his application of linguistic philosophy to traditional philosophical problems. Michael Dummett and others have taken Flew to task for being the high priest of the "cult of ordinary language."[6] Dummett sees Flew as a 'publicist'[7] for

---

[2] See *Hume's Philosophy of Belief*, London: Routledge & Kegan Paul, 1961. Out of print since 1990, Thoemmes Antiquarian Books of Bristol currently has plans to reprint this book. See also Flew's *David Hume: Philosopher of Moral Science*, Oxford: Blackwell, 1986.

[3] See *Thinking Straight*, Buffalo: Prometheus, 1977 and *Thinking About Social Thinking*, Oxford: Blackwell, 1985. A second edition of the latter book was published in the United Kingdom by Fontana Press in 1991, although it is now out of print there. However, the second edition is still available in the United States from Prometheus Press.

[4] See *Philosophy: An Introduction*, Buffalo: Prometheus, 1980, and *An Introduction to Western Philosophy*, Indianapolis: Bobbs-Merrill, 1971, Revised Edition, 1989.

[5] *Atheistic Humanism: The Prometheus Lectures*, Buffalo: Prometheus, 1993.

[6] Michael Dummett, "Oxford Philosophy," *Truth and Other Enigmas*, Boston: Harvard, 1978, p. 432. This is a chapter on ordinary language philosophy, making the point that Flew has selectively "nominated" philosophers as part of this movement when they have nothing in common except a dislike of Bertrand Russell. While this is a strange argument by Dummett, it highlights

a school of philosophy that never really existed. Dummett echoes a comment made by several American philosophers, that they went to Oxford looking for a linguistic philosophy movement and failed to find it.

But such a movement did exist. Austin, Ryle, and others believed that attention to language could tell philosophers much about the world and about ourselves. The use of linguistic and argumentative techniques could reveal hidden problems in philosophy. Pseudo-problems could also be exposed and swept away. In his own work, Flew surely has demonstrated the value of linguistic philosophy in addressing traditional philosophical problems in epistemology, theology, and ethics. Unfortunately, many of Flew's important philosophical and linguistic articles were hard to find, and some out of print. That is why it was so important to compile this particular set of essays.

FLEW'S METHODOLOGY

Perhaps for those readers unfamiliar with Flew, I should add a few words about his approach to philosophy. At the beginning of *An Introduction to Western Philosophy*, Flew argues that "there can be, has been, and ought to be progress in philosophy."[8] That is a surprising contention from a late twentieth century philosopher. In an era of deconstruction, post-structuralism, skeptical pragmatism, and other nihilistic intellectual movements, Flew optimistically, and unfashionably, is a "real McCoy, old time philosopher." He believes that philosophy should boldly pursue the truth, and through the faithful employment of rational thinking, help improve the human condition. Flew is no ivory tower

---

a major complaint against Flew and other linguistic philosophers, that they have worked at the periphery of philosophy and not tackled the "great questions." The first two chapters in this book, "Oxford Linguistic Philosophy" and "Philosophy and Language" are a direct refutation of that mistaken, bizarre view.

I should note that Flew informed me personally and by letter that his two essays on linguistic philosophy were not originally intended as direct refutations of Dummett, *per se*. Rather, they were intended to address concerns expressed by others. However, they do work to answer Dummett's charge. Flew stated in a letter dated November 7, 1996 that "I have never read Dummett on 'Oxford Philosophy.' When I do I shall perhaps discover why he believes that the philosophers I have 'nominated' are/were united by a dislike of Russell. I for one certainly was opposed to (Russell's) policy of unilateral nuclear disarmament. But I doubt that all the other nominees agreed with me. In any case this was nothing to do with Russell's work as a philosopher." (letter used by permission.)

[7] *Ibid.*, p. 431.

[8] *An Introduction to Western Philosophy*, p. 18.

philosopher; for him, knowledge must lead to action. That is why I admire Flew so much.

Several common and interwoven threads run through Flew's body of work. First, influenced by Sir Karl Popper, Flew believes that the scientific method can never produce unassailable knowledge about the world. There can never be enough instances of confirmation to allow for certain justification. One falsifying instance can be used to defeat a theory, meaning that all previously confirmed theories merely await falsification.[9] Like Popper, Flew believes that "what must disqualify a theory, or a theoretician, as unscientific is, rather, that it, or he, refuses to allow for any things which if they were to occur, would constitute falsification."[10] We do have some indication as to how the world works, but this information is provisional. It can only be the best we have, so far. Scientific knowledge is not eternal and unchallengeable. The demarcation of falsification would eliminate all reductive theories, such as Marxism, Freudianism, materialism, idealism, and empiricism. The falsification challenge has devastating consequences for many theological beliefs. Of course, the philosophical merits of Flew's position could be, and have been, vigorously discussed. But one vital lesson Flew draws from the debate is that no person, political party, religious sect, corporate entity, philosophical movement, or scientific discipline could ever, or will ever, possess unchangeable truth. Therefore, philosophy and politics must form common cause to craft an unrestricted marketplace of ideas. The best way to test a theory is to allow for its examination against all other competing theories, leaving room for further and continuous examination in the future. Free thought is essential to knowledge and progress.

Second, the marketplace of ideas should be accompanied by a free economic system. Flew embraces Friedrich Hayek and Milton Friedman, and rejects the abysmal centralized, planned economies in communist countries. For Flew, people must be allowed to make the choices best suited to their individual needs, and the economy should be allowed to meet those needs, unless doing so would violate the inalienable rights of others. Like Adam Smith, Flew would leave the decisions of investment and disinvestment to those "who have the greatest possible individual interest in getting them right."[11] Free-market prices transmit information, provide incentives to adopt the least costly methods

---

[9] See Chapters 1 and 3 of *Thinking Straight*. Also, for Popper's own views, consult *The Logic of Scientific Discovery*, New York: Harper Torchbooks, 1965.

[10] *Ibid.*, p. 55.

[11] *Atheistic Humanism*, pp. 235-6.

of production and the most valued use of scarce resources, and determine the passive distribution of earned income. While government has a role in establishing a safety net for those in need, and for tempering the excesses of free markets, Flew would have the government stay out of the marketplace as much as possible. He would agree with Hayek, that planned economies and collectivism are "the road to serfdom."[12] Free-market choice must be co-existent with individual choice in all aspects of our culture, including the right to determine the end of one's own existence.

Finally, we must avoid indoctrination and abdication of rational thought.[13] Reason must not take flight when faced with the pressures of conformity and group-embraced irrationality. Flew maintains that in any argument between a religious believer and an atheist, the presumption lies with atheism. He reminds the critical thinker that "if it is to be established that there is a God, then we have to have good grounds for believing that this is indeed so. Until and unless some such grounds are produced we have literally no reason at all for believing; and in that situation the only reasonable posture must be either the negative atheist or the agnostic."[14]

Not surprisingly, Flew is a humanist. He is willing to place limited trust in our rationality. He rejects overarching, all-knowing dogmatic claims. He is an ardent, committed free-market lobbyist. He values individual freedom and choice. He finds theological explanations unconvincing and often threatening to the liberties of others. Armed with engaging, entertaining, and energetic prose, Flew has fought for freedom of thought, freedom of choice, and the freedom to reject the chains of irrational and unwarranted authority. He has sought all of this -- not to be rebellious, cantankerous, or irritating. Flew is far from an intellectual "gadfly". Rather, the underlying goal is to produce a more understanding, compassionate, and tolerant culture. For Flew, humanism is more than "a rejection of all religious beliefs," and the "insistence that we should be exclusively concerned with human welfare in this . . . the only world."[15] He would agree with A. J. Ayer, that humanists believe that "the only sound basis for a sound morality is mutual tolerance and respect:

---

[12] See F. A. Hayek, *The Road to Serfdom*, Chicago: University of Chicago, 1944.

[13] In all fairness, I must admit my enormous admiration for Flew on theological topics, even though I am a Roman Catholic and surely one of the people to whom his comments are addressed. Religious zealots are a danger to the division between church and state. They embody the very irrationality that is so frighteningly evident in so many countries of the world.

[14] "The Presumption of Atheism," *God, Freedom and Immortality*, Buffalo: Prometheus, 1984, p. 22.

[15] *A Dictionary of Philosophy*, Second Edition, London: St. Martin's, 1979, p. 153.

tolerance of one another's customs and opinions, respect for one another's rights and feelings, awareness of another's needs."[16] Flew's work in philosophy has sought to make our world more sane, free, and secure.

CONTENTS OF THIS VOLUME

There are eleven essays in this volume. Granted, another editor could have probed Flew's work and come up with a completely different set of essays. But I trust that there will be little doubt as to the importance, quality, value, and brilliance evident in the essays that are included here. Flew has been one of the most prolific and influential philosophers of the second half of this century. These essays indicate the range, depth, and power of his continuing legacy.

The first essay, "Oxford Linguistic Philosophy," is a discussion of the development of linguistic philosophy under the direction of Gilbert Ryle and J. L. Austin. This essay is published for the first time in this collection. It demonstrates the philosophical genesis of this movement and the applications of linguistic philosophy to traditional philosophical problems. As Flew shows, the movement owed much to G. E. Moore, Bertrand Russell, Ludwig Wittgenstein, and the logical positivists. Linguistic philosophy itself influenced much of contemporary philosophy.

The second essay is "Philosophy and Language." This is simply one of the most influential and powerful statements of the promise and limitations of linguistic philosophy. It has only been available in Flew's *Essays in Conceptual Analysis*, originally published in 1953 and long out of print.[17] A word of warning: when I have used it in my own classes, I have found that students may become confused by the structure and subheadings of the article. I suggest that readers pay very close attention to the outline of the argument, the difference between criticisms and responses, and the importance of the paradigm case argument at the end. Properly examined, this article is one of the finest examples of philosophical argumentation in the English language.

Perhaps Flew's best-known essay is "Theology and Falsification." It is his most famous work in philosophy. This piece has been widely anthologized

---

[16] A. J. Ayer, "Introduction," *The Humanist Outlook*, London: Pemberton, 1968, p. 10.

[17] "Philosophy and Language," *Essays in Conceptual Analysis*, Flew (ed.), London: Macmillan and Company, 1963, pp. 1-20. This book was reissued by Greenwood Publishers in 1981. It has long been out of print in the United Kingdom.

since its publication in *University*.[18] It is perhaps the most anthologized essay in philosophy. It is also extremely short (only 1,000 words), making the case that endless amending of meaning with propositions not only can make the proposition untestable, but at some point will render it completely meaningless.[19]

The next essay is "Against Indoctrination."[20] It is now almost impossible to find. It was included in several collected works on humanism in the late 1960s and early 1970s, most of which are now out of print.[21] This essay is an outstanding discussion of how philosophy can be used to undermine those who would like to think our thoughts for us.

One of Flew's first publications was "Locke and the Problem of Personal Identity."[22] It outlines Locke's contribution to the subject of personal identity, attacks Locke's proposed solution, and examines how Locke was misled into offering this mistaken answer. This essay was included because it is one of the best expositions of the problem of personal identity, which has been a central question of philosophy since the time of Descartes, if not before.

Flew is well known as a commentator on Hume, having published numerous articles and two books on Scotland's enduring philosopher. Flew has also edited a series of Hume's works for Open Court Press. "Private Images and Public Language" was originally written as part of Flew's *Hume's Philosophy of Belief*.[23] It is considered a classic discussion of Hume's view of sense images and how we build a shaky edifice of beliefs upon this data.

In my view, one of the very finest critical comments on Hume is "What Impressions of Necessity?," a version of which was given by Flew at American

---

[18] "Theology and Falsification," *University*, Volume 1, Number 1, 1950. The page numbers are unknown. Most scholars first saw this essay five years later, in *New Essays in Philosophical Theology*, Flew and Alasdair MacIntyre (eds.), London: Student Christian Movement Press, 1955, pp. 96-98.

[19] There is a longer, Silver Jubilee version of "Theology and Falsification" in Flew's *God, Freedom, and Immortality*, pp. 71-80.

[20] A version was originally published as "What is Indoctrination?," *Studies in Philosophy and Education*, 1966, pp. 281-306. See the next note for publication information on the version used in the present collection.

[21] For example, the version used in the present collection is "Against Indoctrination" in *The Humanist Outlook*, pp. 79-97.

[22] "Locke and the Problem of Personal Identity," *Philosophy*, Vol. 26, 1951, pp. 53-68.

[23] "Private Images and Public Language," first appeared in *Hume's Philosophy of Belief*, London: Routledge and Kegan Paul, 1961, pp. 18-52. The version found here was used by Alexander Sesonske and Noel Fleming in their *Human Understanding: Studies in the Philosophy of David Hume*, London: Wadsworth, 1965, pp. 34-59.

University in 1989.[24] Here Flew explicates a misunderstood concept in Hume, demonstrating a consistency that is often overlooked.

In many respects, philosophy began with Socrates and Plato. And all philosophers still struggle with central questions raised by them. In "Responding to Plato's Thrasymachus,"[25] Flew analyzes Plato's position on justice in the *Republic*. In recent years, Flew has written widely on the topic of justice, and this application of his views to the much-studied passage in the *Republic* is a major contribution.

Flew is also well-known for his vigorous, sustained, and uncompromising advocacy for human freedom. In "Communism: The Philosophical Foundations,"[26] Flew presents a fair, yet devastating attack on the philosophical work of Marx and Engels, and shows how those ideas were tragically flawed.

When my friends in the Bertrand Russell Society learned of my interest in compiling Flew's philosophical essays, several lobbied for "Russell's Judgment on Bolshevism."[27] Strictly speaking, this is not a work of philosophy. Rather, this essay is an attempt at philosophical history, discussing how one of the most important philosophers of the twentieth century rejected what came to be known as the "war communism" then practiced in the former Soviet Union. Flew shows why Russell, initially much-disposed to embrace the Russian experiment, found Bolshevism politically and philosophically fraudulent. I should probably add that this essay contains some dated material and references, since it was written well before the disintegration of the Soviet Union.

A recent essay, "Stephen Hawking and the Mind of God,"[28] examines the brilliant and best-selling physicist's search for a cosmological foundation for God.

Finally, in an Afterword, Flew discusses his life and philosophical positions in "A Philosopher's Apology." This essay was written especially for this collection.

A special note about editing this volume. I have had to reconcile various formats and styles. My rule of thumb was to follow Flew's original

---

[24] "What Impressions of Necessity?," *Hume Studies*, Volume 18, Number 2, November 1992, pp. 169-177.

[25] "Responding to Plato's Thrasymachus," *Philosophy*, Volume 70, 1995, pp. 436-447.

[26] "Communism: The Philosophical Foundations," *Philosophy*, Volume 66, 1991, pp. 269-282.

[27] "Russell's Judgment on Bolshevism," *Bertrand Russell Memorial Volume*, George Roberts (ed.), London: Allen and Unwin, 1979, pp. 428-454.

[28] "Stephen Hawking and the Mind of God," *Cogito*, Spring 1996, pp. 55-60.

punctuation, spelling, and footnotes. I have tried to standardize the punctuation without changing the meaning. Spelling retains the original British versions employed by Flew. The footnotes are from the original publications, unless otherwise noted. The difficulty of reconciling single and double quotation marks has been resolved by using the single quotation mark for words and titles, and the double marks for actual quotations. This seems to be the preferred use by Flew. Yet, after all of the editing, scrubbing, and proofreading by Flew, Katie Kendig, Sylvia Rolloff, Lynn Weber, and myself, there are probably a number of inconsistencies from chapter to chapter, which may reflect the different styles used for the original publications. Also, after working out various differences with Professor Flew, I then had to conform to the printing format used at Roman & Littlefield.

ACKNOWLEDGMENTS

I would like to thank Professor Flew for all of his help in preparing this volume. He has been most patient and kind. I should add that I have enjoyed our many recent discussions at American University and in Reading, again over beer. Professor Flew gave permission for reprinting all of these essays. Additional copyright permission was given by St. Martin's for "Philosophy and Language," the editor of *Philosophy* for "Locke and the Problem of Personal Identity," "Responding to Plato's Thrasymachus," and "Communism: The Philosophical Foundations," the editor of *Hume Studies* for "What Impressions of Necessity," Routledge for "Russell's Judgment on Bolshevism," and the editor of *Cogito* for "Stephen Hawking and the Mind of God."

I must also thank Jon Sisk, Michelle Harris, Jennifer Ruark, Robin Adler, and Lynn Weber at Rowman & Littlefield for their encouragement and support.

David Rodier, chairman of the Department of Philosophy and Religion at the American University, provided much personal encouragement and necessary advice. I would also like to thank my friends and colleagues in the department for allowing me the honor of teaching at American University, especially Charles White, Harold Durfee, and the late Roger Simonds. American University President Benjamin Ladner has created an increasingly favorable intellectual environment for scholarship.

I also greatly benefited from many conversations about this book with Bob Barnard, Paul Summers, Cliff Henke, Matt Peterson, Jeff Cothran, Dennis Burke, John Renaud, Mitchell Haney, David Rafferty, Cheri Lemley, and, especially, Elizabeth Stolpe. In fact, Elizabeth is an unbroken thread to Flew, going back to 1983. She and I have shared a common interest in Flew for 15 years, the entire length of our close friendship.

Kathryn Jo Ottman addressed many of the technical computer/word processing problems in preparing this book. She also captured Flew on film in his study. Her photograph of Flew is found at the beginning of this collection.

Austin Shepherd and Bertram W. Collier of Roncalli Communications, both full of advice and enthusiasm, were also of great assistance.

Catherine Kendig and Sylvia Rolloff, two of our talented graduate students in the Department of Philosophy and Religion at American University, assisted in the research, selection, typing, editing, and proofreading of these essays. Many thanks to both of them. Thanks also to Janet Caffo, Rachel Levine, Melessa Gentry, Kellene Kennedy, and Andrew Easton in our department for their help.

CHAPTER 1

OXFORD LINGUISTIC PHILOSOPHY
(1996)

In the United Kingdom since the Second World War the most distinctive philosophical development, and hence the development most likely to be of interest to a wider public, occurred in the first twenty or so years immediately after that war. This development was centred in the University of Oxford, which had then and still has by far the largest philosophy department in the country. By common consent the leading figures were John Austin and Gilbert Ryle. Both were inspiring and devoted teachers who laboured to foster young talent. From all over the English-speaking world, philosophers and would-be philosophers came to sit at their feet, and at the feet of such then up and coming juniors as R. M. Hare and Peter Strawson.

When it was not confused with the Logical Positivism of the Vienna Circle, propagated in English by the young A. J. Ayer's brilliant *Language, Truth and Logic* in 1936, what these people came to study was by outside commentators customarily characterized as 'Oxford linguistic philosophy' or 'the philosophy of ordinary language'. There was an implicit and sometimes explicit contrast between these 'linguistic philosophers' -- thought to be somehow narrowing or trivializing what should be a broad and elevated endeavour -- and such splendid, real, old-time philosophers as Plato and Aristotle, Descartes and Hume. Those classical philosophers were, it was assumed, and their true contemporary successors would be, it was suggested, not at all concerned with anything so workaday and commonplace as language; and least of all with anything so exoteric and universally familiar as its ordinary, everyday, untechnical manifestations.

But philosophical disagreements about words -- unlike personal preferences for the monosyllables 'car' and 'lift' over the polysyllables 'automobile' and 'elevator' -- cannot properly be dismissed as insubstantial and *merely* verbal. Nor, since they are about concepts rather than the particular vocables employed to express those concepts on some particular occasion, are such disagreements peculiar and exclusive to one particular natural language. When, for instance, Plato's Socrates in the *Laches* or the *Theaetetus* asked "What is courage?" or "What is knowledge?" it would be quite wrong for a translator to refuse to translate the final words of these interrogative sentences -- as if Socrates had been mentioning rather than using the original Greek words; words which, of course, were in his day as ordinary and untechnical as are their equivalents in our own time and places.

The relevant contrast is, therefore, not an antithesis between the great and glorious true philosophers and their degenerate, pseudo-philosophical epigoni. Instead the difference which matters is that between, on the one hand, those who are constantly even obsessively aware that and why philosophers need to be concerned with elucidations of meanings and, on the other hand, those who are not aware of and would perhaps even deny this essential involvement, and who most certainly are not similarly obsessed. The philosophical concern with language is a concern with the meanings of words, with their communicational functions, with the jobs which they are employed to do. It is in pursuit of this interest that the 'linguistic philosopher' asks both how meaning, use and usage are connected; and how certain key words could be and necessarily are given the meanings which they have been given. For, as Austin once famously maintained and as we are about to show, "there is gold in them thar hills."

I

The *use* of a word, the task which that word is put to work to fulfill, is not at all the same thing as the *usage* of that word, the sorts of occasion upon which that word is uttered -- whether in speech or writing or however else. But although use and usage are thus entirely different they are nevertheless inseparably connected. No word can be said to have a use as a word save in so far as some language group or sub-group gives it a use and recognizes as correct the usage appropriate to that use. For the sounds which we use as words are all, intrinsically and prior to the emergence of any relevant linguistic conventions, almost equally suitable to do any linguistic job whatever. Whereas a knife, say, could not be used, or even misused, as a tent, the English word 'knife' might have been given any other use, or none at all.

The question "How would you teach the meaning of that (sort of) word?" can be of crucial philosophical significance. For there are some (sorts of) words and expressions the meaning of which can only be explained by reference to actual examples of the kind of objects or situations or whatever to which those (sorts of) words and expressions are used to refer. Wherever some (sort of) word or expression of which this is true is an element of the common language of some set of people, any scepticism about the existence or occurrence of referents for that (sort of) word or expression has to be altogether groundless. For would-be skeptics could not even understand expressions of their skepticism without pre-supposing the known existence or occurrence of those referents!

II

So consider, as a first example, how this 'linguistic approach' makes possible the development of a decisive refutation of radical Cartesian scepticism. There is a remarkable and profoundly revealing sentence in the first part of the final section of Hume's *Enquiry Concerning Human Understanding*. In it he takes absolutely for granted as incontestably established the radically sceptical position which Descartes reached in the second paragraph of Part IV of *A Discourse on the Method*: "These are the obvious dictates of reason; and no man who reflects, ever doubted, that the existences which we consider, when we say 'this house' or 'that tree', are nothing but perceptions in the mind, and fleeting copies or representations of other existences, which remain uniform and independent" (XII [i]).

Certainly this statement expresses something which has been fundamental for that whole philosophical tradition which began with *A Discourse on the Method*; namely that what and all that we can be immediately aware of in perception must be our private sense data and not any sort of object in the (public) external world. Once we approach such a statement with the insight that usage determines use, it becomes immediately obvious that what Hume maintains that "no man, who reflects, ever doubted," stands truth on its head. For, if we are to have a language in which we can communicate, and know that we can communicate with one another -- as here and everywhere Hume himself rightly assumes that we can have, and do have -- then it must be possible, as of course it is, for us to give meanings to our words by reference to public objects, and to confirm that other people are giving the same meanings to the same words by observing that their usage of these words is the same as ours. If everyone's usage of every word they employed referred only to experiences private to each individual; then, even if *per impossibile* they could all have their individual and necessarily private languages, these would equally necessarily contain no common vocabulary. So there could be no communication between one person and another. "No man who reflects" could ever discover that others reflected to the same effect!

According to Hume when we say, 'this house' or 'that tree', we are using these words to refer to "nothing but perceptions in the mind, and fleeting copies or representations of other existences, which remain uniform and independent." Most emphatically, we are not. Actual verbal usage determines that the use of these expressions is to refer to meanings which can only be explained by reference to actual examples of the kind of objects or situations or whatever to which those (sorts of) words and expressions are used to refer to public objects. Such objects do indeed remain, at least in the short run, more or less uniform; and they are independent, in the sense that, unlike our (private) experiences, they do not cease or move away with our deaths or departures. If Hume's account were right, then every attempt to converse about this particular actual house or that particular actual tree would leave the would-be conversationalists at cross-purposes. Each would by the hypothesis be confined to talking; not about this (public) house, or that (public) tree; but about his own (private) house sense-datum, or her own (private) tree sense-datum.

The truth is that, if we are to be able to discuss even our several sense-data, then this can only be done if and in so far as the words we use in picking out and describing these sense-data can be given their meanings by reference to public ongoings. They must have a usage on certain public occasions, and not others, if they are to have a use and hence a meaning in a public interpersonal language. How, for instance, could I know that you mean the same as I mean by the words 'yellow sense-datum', if I were not in a position to confirm that you describe as yellow (roughly) the same public objects as those which I so describe; if, that is to say, I could not know that your usage and hence your use of the word 'yellow' is (substantially) the same as mine?

The consequences of these considerations about the presuppositions of an interpersonal language are of the last importance. They show that we cannot start where Hume wanted us to start and then, as a conversing collective of the learned, proceed to wonder: whether, like Descartes, to deduce the public world from private premises; or, whether, like Berkeley, to suppose that it does not even make sense to speak of such a world; or, whether, with Hume himself and later Kant, to conclude that it is impossible for us to know things-in-themselves. For if only one of us is in a position to know that there are others with whom he can converse, then he is by the same token in a position to know that there is a public world; a world, as Hume put it, "of other existences which remain uniform and independent." For without that public world, and knowledge of it, there could be no known and public usages; and hence no known and public uses, and hence no known and public language for the conduct of the conversations of a distinction which Hume and his contemporaries would have had no hesitation in making, either the learned or the vulgar.

III

In Book II of his *Paradise Lost* John Milton, the English Dante, describes how in Pandemonium a small party of Devils withdrew to a hilltop and, proceeding at a correspondingly elevated level of abstraction:

> Reasoned high
> Of providence, foreknowledge, will and fate;
> Fixt fate, free will, foreknowledge absolute
> And found no end, in wandering mazes lost.

If anyone quoted this to a 'linguistic philosopher' the response would surely be that they "found no end, in wandering mazes lost," precisely because they insisted on reasoning high; that they should at least have begun by studying the usages and hence the uses of 'free will' and of other logically associated words and expressions. Such, as Austin so characteristically said, should be, if not "the be-all and end-all," at any rate least the "begin-all" of "sober philosophy."

At the beginning of his account 'Of Liberty and Necessity' in Section VIII of *An Enquiry Concerning Human Understanding* Hume was scandalized to discover that a controversy "canvassed and disputed with great eagerness since the first origin of science and philosophy" had, as he put it, "turned merely upon words." It should by now be clear that a philosophical concern with words is not with 'mere words' but only and necessarily with words as the expressions of concepts. Hume's complaint here is, therefore, wrong-headed. It is as wrong-headed as the notorious, and notoriously philistine Logical Positivist dismissal of philosophical problems as 'pseudo-problems' for no better reason than that they are philosophical and conceptual rather than empirical and scientific. It is as wrong as Kant's consequent attack in his second *Critique* on Hume's treatment here as "a petty word-jugglery"; or as Hume's own further comment here on the tendency "for philosophers to encroach upon the province of grammarians, while they imagine that they are handling issues of the greatest importance and concern."

The point is that the suggested solution which Hume proceeded to outline depends, fairly explicitly, upon recalling, with the help of simple concrete examples, just what the ordinary, non-technical use of the word 'free' actually is; and that it is not its ordinary job (not what it ordinarily means), not yet part of its ordinary job (not yet part of what its employment implies), to attribute to actions unpredictability in principle. The moral correctly drawn is, given that this is indeed what correct usage is and hence what the word means, that it is not after all contradictory to say of some action: both that it was performed of the agent's own freewill: and that it could have been predicted that the agent would so act. For the ordinary opposite of to act of one's own freewill is to act under compulsion, not to act predictably. So it is agents, not their wills, which may be either free or not free.

A further moral, not drawn by Hume, is that the most fundamental questions here are about not freedom but agency. To bring this out, and in so doing to make it still clearer that and how investigations of the usages and uses of words are essential to philosophy, consider two common and crucial phrases, 'he had no choice' and 'she could not have done otherwise'. The great temptation is to construe these phrases literally. But the truth, as we can clearly see just so soon as we attend to the established usages and the uses determined by those usages, that when ordinarily we say that he had no choice or she could not have done otherwise we are not denying, rather we are presupposing that the agent was truly an agent who did have a choice between at least two entirely possible courses of action (or inaction). The point is this: not that the persons in question had literally no alternatives, and hence in this respect were not agents at all; but that they had no tolerable alternatives, no alternatives which they could reasonably have been expected to choose.

To enforce this point consider two dramatic illustrations. The first is that of Martin Luther at the Diet of Worms: "Here I stand. I can no other, So help me God." What of course Luther was saying, and saying in perfectly correct albeit, it seems, often philosophically misleading German, was this: not that he was helpless in the grip of a sudden paralysis, that he was hearing words come from his own mouth as if they were spoken by another person; but that all the many alternative courses of action which had been or were now open to him -- such as having run away before the Diet opened or recanting here and now -- were, to him, altogether unacceptable.

The second illustration is drawn from a fictitious yet perhaps now equally famous source, the film *The Godfather*. Remember the mafioso who said: "I made him an offer which he could not refuse: I said that within thirty seconds I was going to have either his signature or his brains on that sheet of paper." Once again, a moment's thought shows us that the recipient of such an offer remains still an agent in the matter, and hence in the more fundamental senses both did have a choice and could have done otherwise. Though he acts under overwhelming compulsion, nevertheless he does act. In this his case is quite unlike that of the person who is simply gunned down from behind, or that of the person whose hand is forced across the paper by the main force of stronger hands.

Hume presented his treatment 'Of Liberty and Necessity' as a "reconciling project." As such it has to be rated a failure, since the pretended reconciliation depended upon introducing and employing what he proudly presented as a new conception of necessity but what was in fact no more than a conception of unnecessitated regularity. Suppose now that we want to try to dispose of suggestions that we are all always somehow inexorably necessitated to behave in whatever ways we do behave, that we are never agents choosing between the two or more courses of action which are open to us; that we are indeed never agents, creatures who must always have been able to act in ways other than those in which they did act. Then the most promising move is to ask how the key concepts of inexorable necessity and of being able to do otherwise can be acquired.

Let us start by taking a hint from the seminal chapter 'Of Power' in Locke's *Essay Concerning Human Understanding*, noting by the way that for present purposes voluntary inaction is a special case of action. "Everyone," he argues, "finds in himself a power to begin or forbear, continue or put an end to several actions" and from "the consideration of the extent of this power . . . which everyone finds in himself, arise the ideas of liberty and necessity" (II [xxi] 7). A little later Locke provides two illustrations:

> We have instances enough, and often more than enough, in our own bodies. A man's heart beats, the blood circulates, which t'is not in his power . . . to stop; and therefore in respect of these [movements] where rest depends not on his choice . . . he is not [an agent]. Convulsive motions agitate his legs, so that though he will it never so much, he cannot . . . stop their motion (as in that odd disease called *chorea Sancti Viti*,) but he is perpetually dancing; he is . . . under as much necessity of moving as a stone that falls or a tennis-ball struck with a racket (II [xxi] 11).

These two passages equip us to develop ostensive definitions of two sorts of bodily movements. Going deliberately with rather than against the grain of modern English usage, let those bodily movements which can be either initiated or inhibited at will be labelled 'movings' and those which cannot 'motions'. Certainly it is obvious that there are plenty of marginal cases. Nevertheless, so long as there are far, far more which fall unequivocally upon one side or the other, we must resolutely and stubbornly refuse to be prevented from labouring this absolutely fundamental and decisive distinction by any such diversionary appeals to the existence of marginal cases.

Contemplation of this fundamental distinction and of what it is which it distinguishes should be sufficient to show, first, that all of us have the most direct, and the most inexpugnably certain experience: not only both of physical (as opposed to logical) necessity and of physical (as opposed to logical) impossibility; but also both, on some occasions, of being able to do other than we do do and, on other occasions, of being unable to behave in any other way than that in which we are behaving.

So it would seem that it is only in terms of the same fundamental distinction between movings and motions that we can establish and explicate the even more fundamental concept of action. An agent is a member of a kind of creature which, precisely and only in so far as they are agents, can and cannot but make choices: choices between alternative courses of action both or all of which are open; real choices, notwithstanding both that sometimes by choosing one or even any of these open alternatives the agent will incur formidable costs. And, furthermore, the nerve of the distinction between the movements involved in an action and those which constitute no more than items or partial components of necessitated behaviour just is that such behaviour is necessitated, whereas the senses of actions not merely are not but necessarily cannot be.

Once we are seized of these insights, we become ready to recognize that there is no way in which creatures neither enjoying nor suffering experiences of both these two contrasting kinds could either acquire for themselves or explain to others the crucial and fundamental concepts of physical necessity and of physical impossibility, of action and of being able to do other than we actually do.

Now, if none of the key and contrasting notions could be explained, acquired or understood by creatures neither enjoying nor suffering such experiences, then that fact must constitute an objection of overwhelming and decisive force against any doctrine of universal, physically necessitating, determinism; at any rate if that doctrine is to be construed as implying that none of us could ever do other than we actually do. For in that construction it implies that concepts which, it has here been contended, can only be explained by references to their actual applications nevertheless have no actual application; which is absurd.

IV

Those still inclined to challenge this contention and to maintain that it is certain or even possible that all our behaviour is necessitated and that we could none of us ever behave in any way other than that in which we do behave have a challenge to face. They must excogitate their own alternative accounts of how the notions of physical necessity, of physical impossibility, of agency, and of being able to do otherwise can be acquired and understood by creatures who, by the hypothesis, have no experience of being subject to physical necessities, of confronting physical impossibilities, of being agents, and of being themselves able to do other than they do. Maybe this challenge can, after all, be met. Maybe. But, until and unless it is met, and met convincingly, the prudent philosopher is bound to adopt the archetypical attitude of the man from Missouri. Notoriously, if his reluctance to believe is to be overcome, he has to be shown.

CHAPTER 2

PHILOSOPHY AND LANGUAGE
(1953)

I propose to attack a miscellany of popular misconceptions, trying incidentally to illuminate various possibly puzzling practices.[1] A very typical passage from Aristotle's *Nicomachean Ethics* will serve as a text:

> We must also grasp the nature of deliberative excellence and find whether it is a sort of knowledge, or of opinion, or of skill at guessing, or some thing different from these in kind. Now it is not knowledge: for men do not investigate matters about which they know, whereas deliberative excellence is a sort of deliberation, and deliberating implies investigating and calculating. But deliberation is

---

[1] This paper was originally commissioned by the Philosophical Quarterly as a cross between a survey of work of a certain sort published since the end of the Second German War and an *apologia pro philosophia nostra contra murmurantes*. Hence it was to a quite exceptional degree both polemical in tone and burdened with footnotes. For this reprinting the tone has been softened and the burden lightened a little. But the former is considerably sharper and the latter very much heavier than they would be if I had been writing now and for this present purpose. [Editor's note: This footnote by Flew refers to the version which appeared in *Essays in Conceptual Analysis*. This is the version used for this present collection. I have included it, although the self reference is to the 1963 publication of this essay.]

23

not the same as investigation: it is the investigation of a particular subject [i.e. conduct]. Nor yet is it skill at guessing: for this operates without conscious calculation, and rapidly, whereas deliberating takes a long time. . . . Correctness cannot be predicated of knowledge, any more than can error, and correctness of opinion is truth (Bk.VI, ch.ix: 1142 a 32 ff.).

Objections: (i) 'But imagine that a man knew that there was a body buried in his back garden, and nevertheless joined with the police in their investigations: would that not be investigating a matter about which he already knew?'

(ii) 'But surely it is sometimes all right to speak of erroneous knowledge: as when sarcastically I say: "He knew the winner of the two-thirty: but he knew wrong"?'

Replies: (i) 'No, it would in his case, but not that of the police, only be *pretending* to investigate, a matter of "investigating" (in inverted commas, making the protest that this is a bogus case of investigation). To anyone who knows that the man knows that the body is there, and yet sincerely persists in saying that that man is investigating, and not pretending to investigate or "investigating" (in snigger quotes): what else can we say but "You just do not know the meaning of the word 'investigate'"?'

(ii) 'You are quite right, of course: but your exception is one which, properly understood, only helps to reinforce Aristotle's thesis. For the whole sarcastic point of the use of the expression "knew wrong" and of saying "he 'knew'" (in that sniggering inverted comma tone of voice) depends absolutely on the (logical) fact that "He knows p" entails "p"; that it is incorrect to say "He knows p" unsarcastically if you or he to your knowledge have reason to doubt p.[2] And, again, if anyone has reason to doubt p (or, still better, knows not p); and yet sincerely and unsarcastically insists "He (there) knows p": what else can we say but "Either you do not know the meaning of the word 'know'

---

[2] See J. L. Austin's classic 'Other Minds' in *Logic and Language*, Series II, Antony Flew (ed.), Blackwell, Series I, 1951, Series II, 1953. Austin's famous essay also may be found in his *Philosophical Papers*, Oxford, 1961. I shall use *LL*, I and *LL*, II as abbreviations for *Logic and Language*, First and Second series, respectively. I apologize for the frequency of these references: but those willing to look up some of the articles mentioned here will presumably be glad to reduce the number of volumes with which they have to deal; while certainly no one will wish to have repeated anything I have said before. [Editor's note: I have followed this convention for this essay only.]

and are ignorantly misusing it; or else you have your own peculiar use for the word which I wish you would explain and try to justify"?'

Notes: (i) It is appropriate to build our basic example here upon a passage of the *Nicomachean Ethics,* since most of the *avant-garde* of Oxford philosophy since the war (Austin, Hart, Hare and Urmson, for instance) are soaked in this book, and there is a very strong analogy between their work and it.

When someone like Ryle says 'We don't say' or 'We can't say' or uses any of the semi-equivalent expressions of the material mode of speech; and we can think of occasions on which we might and do intelligibly and not incorrectly say precisely what he says we cannot say: it is a good rule to consider whether these exceptions do not in fact actually reinforce the point he is really concerned to make, or whether, if not, they are really relevant to it, involving the same use of the word. No one is infallible, and certainly not Ryle in this matter, but we should allow for the fact that a self-contradictory or otherwise logically improper expression may get a piquancy precisely as such; and can thus acquire a use, a point, which depends entirely on the fact that it is a misuse, and is thus parasitical on the logico-linguistic rule to which it is an exception. 'He knew but he knew wrong', 'bachelor husband', and 'the evidence of my own eyes' all get their piquancy in this way.

(A) 'But Aristotle was not concerned with *mere words*: whereas your replies to objections involve nothing else.' A closer look at the example will show that and how this antithesis is here crucially misleading. The replies are not about words in the way in which protests at the replacement of 'men (and women)' or 'people' by '(male and female) personnel' are about words.[3] Nor do they concern English words to the exclusion of equivalents in Greek or Chocktaw. Nor do they even concern words as opposed to non-verbal signs doing the same jobs. (Consider the camp-fire version of 'Underneath the spreading chestnut tree', of which our late King was so fond, in which gestures replace some of the words.) Rather they are about the *uses* of certain words, the *jobs* they do, the *point* of employing them: their *meanings*, and the *implications* which they carry.

Thus it would be no more necessary to mention the particular English words 'investigate' and 'know' in translating the replies into another language than it is to mention Greek in rendering Aristotle's argument from the Greek. Though English-speaking philosophers sometimes speak of correct or standard English this must not be mistaken to imply that they are concerned with English

---

[3] "God created personnel in his own image" (Sir Alan Herbert).

as opposed to other languages (usually: but see (B) below).[4] The replies, like Aristotle's theses and the objections to them, are all equally concerned with logic as much as with language. The whole enquiry is logical rather than philological, an examination of the 'informal logic'[5] of two workaday concepts. Hence the fashion for expressions such as 'the *logic* of (our) language', '*logic* and language', 'the *logic* of "probable"', 'the *logical* behavior of "God"-sentences', and even '*logical* geography' is not necessarily just a pointless irritating fad; though nothing we have to say will do anything to justify 'The Logic of British and American Industry' or 'The Logic of Liberty' when used of enquiries neither in the linguistic idiom nor even conceptual.

(B) This suggests why philosophers given to talking about correct English "seem to take little account of the existence of other languages whose structure and idiom are very different from English . . . but which seem equally if not more capable of engendering metaphysical confusion."[6] Being, like their colleagues, concerned with conceptual matters, their protests against the misuse of English are not primarily motivated by a concern for correct *English* as opposed to faultless Eskimo. But the matter should not be allowed to rest there. The existence of other natural languages whose structure, idiom, and vocabulary are not completely congruent with those of our own is philosophically relevant in at least three ways.

(i) They provide concepts not available in the stock of our language group. Notoriously there are in all languages words untranslatable into English: no English words, that is, have precisely the same use. And many of the concepts concerned are of philosophic interest: either directly in themselves; or indirectly because it is necessary to master them in order to understand some philosopher who used or discussed the concept in question.

(ii) Different languages offer different temptations. J. S. Mill must have been beguiled into his disastrous argument from what is in fact desired to what is in morals desirable by the 'grammatical' analogy between English words like 'audible' and 'visible' and the English word 'desirable'.[7] (There might be a language in which there was no such morphological analogy between a class of words meaning 'able as a matter of fact to be somethinged' and one meaning

---

[4] Cf. L. J. Cohen, 'Are Philosophical Theses Relative to Language?' in *Analysis*, 1949.

[5] G. Ryle, 'Ordinary Language', *Philosophical Review*, 1953. This is also found in his *Collected Papers*, Vol. II, Hutchinson, 1971.

[6] *Philosophical Quarterly*, 1952, p. 2 (top).

[7] *Utilitarianism* (Everyman), p. 32 (bottom): Mill argues from this morphological analogy, explicitly. Though even here it is doubtful if this was more than the occasion for a mistake, the true cause of which was the quest for a 'scientific ethics'.

'ought as a matter of value to be somethinged'.) The misconstruction of 'infinity' as being the word for a gigantic number is made attractive by the morphological analogy between the expression 'to infinity' and such expressions as 'to one hundred'. If we always said 'for ever' or 'indefinitely' instead of 'to infinity', and if 'aleph-nought' did not happen to sound like a word for a colossal number, then this temptation would disappear.[8] It has been said that it is hard to make Hegel's dialectic plausible or even intelligible in English for the lack of any word with ambiguities parallel to those of the German *aufheben.*[9] Kant, in a significantly phrased passage, noted:

The German language has the good fortune to possess expressions which do not allow this difference [between the opposites of *das Ubel* and *das Bose*] to be overlooked. It possesses two very distinct concepts, and especially different expressions, for that which the Latins express by a single word *bonum.*[10]

While the Greek way of forming abstract noun substitutes from the neuter of the definite article and the adjective does something, though not of course very much, to explain the attractions for Plato of the Theory of Forms.[11]

(iii) The existence of natural languages with radically different logical characteristics gives the opportunity for logical explorations of ways of thinking far more diverse than those embraced in most of these singly: for, as it were, logico-linguistic travel, which can broaden the mind and stimulate the imagination and so provide benefits of the sort which alert people are able to get from physical travel.

Consider, for example, the analogy between the recognition of the legitimate existence of non-Euclidean geometries which helps to undermine rationalist hopes of a quasi-geometrical deductive system of knowledge about the world based on self-evident necessary premises; and the realization that there actually are natural languages to which the subject-predicate distinction can scarcely be applied, which are not saturated with the concept of cause, and which provide words to pick out different differences and likenesses from those

---

[8] See *Proceedings of the Aristotelian Society*, Supp. Vol. XXVII, pp. 42-3 and 47-8, for a recent example of this howler and its criticism.

[9] T. D. Weldon, *The Vocabulary of Politics*, Pelican, 1953, p. 107.

[10] *Critique of Practical Reason*, trans. T. K. Abbott, 1909, p. 150.

[11] For some of the many more worthy attractions see D. F. Pears, 'Universals', in *LL*, II. For Aristotle's battle against the temptations of this idiom, in which he had to express his definition of goodness. see the early chapters of *Nicomachean Ethics.*, Bk. I.

which English, and indeed most European languages, are equipped to mark. To realize this is to discredit ideas that the subject-predicate distinction must be inextricably rooted in the non-linguistic world,[12] that the notion of cause is an indispensable category of thought,[13] and that language must reflect the ultimate nature of reality.[14] Of course, it is theoretically possible to imagine other conceptual systems and categories of concept.[15] But this is excessively difficult, as witness the calibre of some of the philosophers who have assumed or even asserted contingent, though perhaps admirable, characteristics of their particular languages to be necessities of thought. In any case there is actual material waiting to be studied,[16] and there is much to be said for the use of real, as opposed to imaginary, examples in philosophy. It can add vitality to discussion and help to break down the idea that philosophical training and philosophical enquiry can have no relevance or value in the world outside our cloistered classrooms.

(C) The *use* of a word is not the same as, though it is subtly connected with, the *usage* of that word. The former (see above) is language-neutral: if we enquire about the *use* of 'table' then we are simultaneously and equally concerned with the *use* of 'tavola' and other equivalents in other languages; with, if you like, the concept of table. The latter is language-specific: if we enquire about the *usage* of 'table' then we are concerned with how that particular *English* word is (or ought to be) employed by those who employ that word, and not 'tavola'.

But the two are crucially related. No word could be said to have a use except in so far as some language group or sub-group gives it a use and recognizes as correct the usage appropriate to that use: for the sounds we use as words are all, intrinsically and prior to the emergence of any linguistic

---

[12] This point was originally made by Sayce; and reiterated by Russell, *Analysis of Mind*, George Allen and Unwin, 1921, p. 212.

[13] See articles by D. D. Lee mentioned below, though her interpretation of Trobriand thought is disputed.

[14] See *Republic*, 596 A 6-8 for a suggestive admission: "We have been in the habit, if you remember, of positing a Form, wherever we use the same name in many instances, one Form for each many."

[15] Cf. the 'language games' of Wittgenstein, imaginary truncated languages used as diagrams in *Philosophical Investigations*, Blackwell, 1953, and the 'Newspeak' of George Orwell's *1984*, Harcourt, Brace and Jovanovich, 1949, Appendix.

[16] See *LL*, II, p. 3: to the references given there in the second note can be added D. D. Lee in *Psychosomatic Medicine*, Vol. XIII, 1950, and in *The Journal of Philosophy*, 1949.

conventions about them, almost equally suitable to do any linguistic job whatever. Whereas a knife, say, could not be used, or even misused, as a tent, 'glory' might have been given the use we have, in fact given to 'a nice knock-down argument'.

The *uses* of words depend subtly on the correct *usages* of words. Humpty Dumpty can only be accused of *misusing* 'glory' because the accepted, standard, correct *usage* of Lewis Carroll's language group was radically different from Humpty Dumpty's private usage. It was perverse, ill-mannered, misleading, and endangered the possibility of linguistic communication, thus wantonly and without explanation to flout the linguistic conventions. (No doubt, like contemporary "prophets of a new linguistic dispensation,"[17] he regarded such linguistic conventions as "preposterous restrictions upon free speech."[18]) Furthermore, as academic philologists[19] and people concerned with maintaining and increasing the efficiency of the English language[20] (and others) have often urged, what is *correct* usage of any language group depends ultimately upon *actual* usage. It is because *use* depends on *correct usage* while this in turn depends ultimately upon *actual usage* that changes in actual usage can enrich or impoverish the conceptual equipment provided by a language. If a new usage is established by which a new use is given to a word, a use not previously provided for, then to that extent the language concerned is enriched.[21] Whereas if an old usage whereby two words had two different uses is replaced by a new one in which one of them loses its job to become a mere synonym of the other, then similarly there is a proportionate impoverishment. Since the actual usage of any language group or sub-group is never in fact completely static, both processes are usually going on, and together constitute a considerable part of the history of the language. ('The history of language . . . is little other than the history of corruptions': Loundsbury was writing as a grammarian, but the same is true from a logical point of view; though 'corruption' must be taken as value-neutral here.)

To come at the matter from a new angle: consider how the historical

---

[17] *Philosophical Quarterly*, 1952, p. 12.

[18] *Ibid.*, 1952, p. 2.

[19] To the point here would be references given by P. L. Heath, *Philosophical Quarterly*, 1952, p. 2, *n.*

[20] See Sir Alan Herbert's *What a Word!* Sir Ernest Gowers' *Plain Words* and *ABC of Plain Words*, etc. [Editor's note: Publication information unavailable.]

[21] This point is developed by F. Waismann in his 'Analytic-Synthetic', and stressed to a point at which some might complain that it encouraged anarchic Humpty-Dumptyism. See *Analysis*, 1950, Vol. X ff.

theologian studies the concept of *nephesh* in Israel. He has and can have no other method but the examination of the occurrences of the word *'nephesh'* in his texts: the attempt to discover from a survey of usage what was its use, what job this word did in the vocabulary of the people who employed it. Or, again, consider how Professor H. J. Paton objects decisively to the translation of *abgeleitet* as 'deduced' because "an examination of Kant's usage will show that it seldom or never means this."[22] Or consider how the cryptographer tries to discover the meaning of an unknown element in a code. He has and can have no other method but a similar examination of its occurrences, hoping by a study of usage to hit upon its use, its meaning. Appeals to *use* and *usage* in creative philosophy can be regarded as a belatedly explicit application of the tried and necessary methods of the historians of ideas.

Before passing to section (D), various minor points: First, 'linguistic conventions' here means those by which we use 'pod' rather than 'pid' or 'nup' to mean pod; and so forth. Second, 'language group or sub-group' is not here a precise expression. It is intended to cover the users of recognized languages, of their dialects, of jargons and private languages of all kinds, down to and including individuals who develop terminologies private to themselves and their readers and interpreters, if any. Our point is one about the presuppositions of linguistic communication. Third, not all features of the usage of a word will be relevant to questions about its use: that the personal pronouns 'I', 'he', and 'she' are subject to radical morphological transformation in other cases is of concern to Fowler, but not to the philosopher; for their use would be unaffected if usage were to send these transformations the way of other unnecessary case-indications. But this is a matter for caution, for it is hard to be sure without examination what will turn out to be relevant: Fowler would be concerned with the spread of the usage which makes 'contact' a transitive verb; but perhaps this change also subtly affects the notion of contact.[23] Fourth, it is possible for people to communicate, in a way which depends partly on words (or other conventional signs), in spite of misusing many of the words (or other conventional signs) they employ: for the intelligent appreciation of context (in the widest sense) can do much to compensate for such deficiencies. But to the precise extent to which it needs to, communication is thereby not depending upon words (or other conventional signs). Fifth, this stress on *use* derives

---

[22]   *The Categorical Imperative*, p. 134, *n*.

[23]   On the analogous difficulty of knowing in advance the 'logical breaking strains of concepts' see Ryle's Inaugural, *Philosophical Arguments*, Oxford, 1945. This lecture is also in his *Collected Papers*, Vol. II, Hutchinson, 1971.

mainly from Wittgenstein: the idea is present unexploited in the *Tractatus Logico-Philosophicus:* "In philosophy the question 'For what purpose do we really use that word . . . ?' constantly leads to valuable results"[24]; and it became the slogan 'Don't ask for the *meaning,* ask for the *use'* in the early thirties after his return to Cambridge.[25] The explicit concern with correct *usage* as the determinant of *use* seems to derive mainly from J. L. Austin.[26]

(D) Notoriously there is often a gap between actual and correct usage. It is possible for some usage which is (even much) more honoured in the breach than the observance to be one which defaulters are prepared to acknowledge as correct, mainly because certain people and reference books are recognized as generally authoritative: there is still, in Britain at any rate, no question as to what is the correct usage of such non-technical logical terms as 'refute', 'imply', and 'infer', but it seems most unlikely that the actual usage of the majority even of first-year university students conforms with it. The gap is of the greatest importance to anyone who wishes to understand "what is at the bottom of all this terminological hyperaesthesia, and all the whistle-blowing and knuckle-rapping and scolding that goes along with it."[27]

(i) It enables a piece of 'logical geographizing', telling us only what most of us in a way know, making no distinction not already provided for in familiar words, to be an exercise in precisification of thought and in improvement of usage for all those who work through it: and not merely for those, like the students mentioned above, whose word training has been conspicuously deficient. Consider the effects of describing the differences and analogies between *threats, promises,* and *predictions;* to draw example from a recent Oxford examination paper. Though often such examinations of present correct usage will show that we need not only to bring our actual usage more into line with correct usage, but also to go further by suggesting improvements. As Austin said: "Essential though it is as a preliminary to track down the detail of our ordinary uses of words, it seems that we shall in the end always be compelled to straighten them out to some extent."[28]

---

[24] Routledge and Kegan Paul, 1922, 6.211. See also 3.328, 3.326, and 5.4732i.

[25] See the *Philosophical Investigations,* especially *ad init.* for his own account of the reasons for this maxim.

[26] See M. Weitz, 'Oxford Philosophy', *Philosophical Review,* 1953: and *Proceedings of the Aristotelian Society,* Supp. Vol. XVIII, for Austin's first characteristic publication. Austin's essay is also in his *Philosophical Papers,* Oxford, 1961.

[27] *Philosophical Quarterly,* 1952, p. 5 (top).

[28] 'How to Talk' in *Proceedings of the Aristotelian Society,* 1952-3, p. 227. This essay is also in his *Philosophical Papers,* Oxford, 1961.

(ii) It gives ground for hope that philosophers, including always and especially ourselves, who misuse or tolerate the misuse of certain words and expressions,[29] or who give or accept incorrect accounts of their *rationes applicandi*, may be led by suitable attention to their correct usage and actual use to realize and remedy their mistakes. This phrase *ratio applicandi* is modeled deliberately upon the *ratio decidendi* of the lawyers: the principle under which all previous decisions can be subsumed and upon which, as the fiction has it, they were in fact made. For just as it is perfectly possible to make decisions consistent with such a principle without having actually formulated it: so it is possible, and even usual, to be able to apply a word correctly in unselfconscious moments, without being able to discern its ratio applicandi, or even to do so when positively in error about it; though of course anyone making such a mistake will have some inclination to misuse the word.

(iii) But it also makes it possible to misrepresent present *correct* usage as nicer, more uniform, and more stable than it in fact is: "the assumption being that the necessary rules and regulations are *already* embodied in ordinary parlance, requiring only inspection, or the production of a few trivial examples, to make clear what is allowable and what is not."[30] To do this is especially tempting perhaps for philosophers in strong reaction against the contempt shown by many of their mathematically minded colleagues for the rich and subtle instruments provided by all but the most beggarly of the natural languages to those willing and able to use them with care and skill (see (v) below). The extent to which the 'logical geographers' have in fact succumbed has perhaps been exaggerated; but it is well to be on guard.

(iv) It is this alone which makes it possible to speak at all of *misuses*. When philosophers are attacked for misusing an ordinary, or even an extraordinary, word this is rarely an "attempt to convict perfectly respectable philosophers of illiteracy, or of the perpetration of ungrammatical gibberish," but rather "what is complained of is not lack of *grammar*, even [*sic*] in the textbook sense, but incoherence or absence of meaning" (my italics); even though some (like Wittgenstein who perhaps discovered it) given to pressing "the familiar and overworked analogy between logical and grammatical rules"[31] occasionally omit the prefix 'logical' where the context makes it clear that it is *logical* grammar that is at issue. The point is, usually, that the philosopher

---

[29] For some subtle and very important examples of a sensitivity to ordinary correct usage see G. J. Warnock's *Berkeley*, Pelican, 1953, especially chaps. 7-10.

[30] *Philosophical Quarterly*, 1952, p. 6.

[31] *Ibid.*

under attack has somehow been misled into misusing a word in a way which generates paradox, confusion, and perplexity. Hume was scandalized that a controversy "canvassed and disputed with great eagerness since the first origin of science and philosophy" had "turned merely upon words."[32]   But the skeleton solution he suggested depended, fairly explicitly, upon recalling to mind with the help of simple concrete examples, just what the ordinary use of the word 'free' actually is: and that it is not its ordinary job (not what it ordinarily means), nor yet any part of its ordinary job (nor yet part of what it implies), to attribute to actions unpredictability in principle.[33]   If this is so then it is not contradictory to say that some action was both predictable and performed of the agent's own free will: always assuming, of course, that the key words are being used in their ordinary senses.   And in any case complaints about 'pseudo-problems',[34] 'a petty word-jugglery',[35] or the tendency "for philosophers to encroach upon the province of grammarians, and to engage in disputes of words, while they imagine they are handling controversies of the deepest importance and concern"[36] all miss the point.   For Hume is broaching a conceptual solution to a philosophical problem, which cannot thereby lose whatever importance it may have had before.

Such a brief outline example may suggest facile crudity: "a very simple way of disposing of immense quantities of metaphysical and other argument, without the smallest trouble or exertion."[37]   This is inevitable perhaps in the terse cartoon simplicity needed in incidental illustrations but the suggestion could scarcely survive: *either* an examination of such contributions to the free-will problems as R. M. Hare's 'The Freedom of the Will',[38] W. D. Falk's 'Goading and Guiding',[39] and H. L. A. Hart's 'Ascription of Responsibility and Rights';[40] *or* an awakening to the fact that no one has asked to be excused from dealing with whatever arguments may be deployed in support of such

---

[32] *Enquiry Concerning Human Understanding*, Section VIII, pt. i.

[33] His views had been substantially anticipated: by Hobbes, *Leviathan*, chap. xxi, and in his pamphlet *Of Liberty and Necessity*; and no doubt by many others long before.

[34] See *LL*, II, pp. 5-6, for an attack on this once popular misdescription of philosophical problems; Ryle, *Concept of Mind*, Hutchison, 1949, p. 71 (top), lapses by writing "largely spurious problems."

[35] Kant, *Critique of Practical Reason*, trans. T. K. Abbott, 1909, p. 188.

[36] Hume, *Enquiry Concerning the Principles of Morals*, App. iv.

[37] *Philosophical Quarterly*, 1952, p. 1.

[38] *Proceedings of the Aristotelian Society*, Supp. Vol. XXV.

[39] *Mind*, 1953.

[40] *LL*, I.

philosophers' misuses. (We give these examples because they are concerned with the problem we have chosen as an illustration: but of course the rest of this book provides many others.) Perhaps Kant was discouraged from recognizing the merit in Hume here by Hume's own misleading talk about mere words as well as by the aggressive way in which he misrepresented a good start as the end of the affair. Certainly we find Kant two pages later very grudgingly conceding part of Hume's point, but insisting that at any rate *transcendental* freedom cannot thus be reconciled with scientific determinism.[41]

(v) After so much has been said about misuses and misconstructions, it must be mentioned that interest originally directed at the uses of words only inasmuch as this brought out what were misuses and misconstructions, is sometimes, by a familiar psychological process, partly diverted to the study of use for its own sake. Before suggesting that, however psychologically understandable, such interests do not become a philosopher in his working hours we should cast our minds back to Aristotle and reflect whether all his studies of the concepts of moral psychology were in fact wholly directed to some ulterior end even within philosophy; or, more generally, ask ourselves whether an interest in concepts is not one of the things which makes a philosopher.

But whatever are the rights and wrongs about ulterior and ultimate ends and whatever the jurisdictional proprieties, disputes about these here turn out to be largely unnecessary. For in elucidating the ordinary uses (as opposed to philosophers' suspected misuses) of some of the rather limited range of words around which our controversies tend to cluster,[42] it has been noticed that the conceptual equipment provided by ordinary (here opposed particularly to technical) language is amazingly rich and subtle; and that even the classical puzzles cannot be fully resolved without elucidating not merely the formerly fashionable elite of notions but also all their neglected logical hangers-on. In formulating and attacking free will puzzles, philosophers, with the outstanding exception of Aristotle, have been inclined to concentrate on a few ideas: *free will, compulsion, choice, necessity, responsible,* and one or two others. Whereas we have available in our ordinary vocabulary of extenuation and responsibility a great range of notions, which it would be wise to master and

---

[41]   Kant, *Loc. cit.* p. 190.

[42]   See Waismann, 'Language Strata' in *LL*, II, and Ryle, 'Ordinary Language', for suggestions about this clustering.

exhaust before thinking of adaptation or invention:[43] *automatically, by mistake, unintentionally, by force of habit, involuntarily, unwillingly, on principle, under provocation,* to mention a few. Philosophers have tended to ignore all this richness and variety, assuming that it could all be satisfactorily assimilated to a few most favoured notions. But to do this is clumsy and slovenly. For proposals to jettison ordinary language in favour of new-minted terms overlook the crucial primacy of the vernacular: ordinary, as opposed to technical, language is fundamental in the sense that the meaning of terms of art can only be explained with its aid; and it is a perennial complaint against such lovers of jargon as Kant and the Scholastics that this essential work is so often botched, skimped, or altogether neglected. The upshot of all this is that it is improbable that the elucidation of the logic of any term at all likely to engage any philosopher's attention will fail some day to find application to some generally recognized philosophical problem, however 'pure' his own interests may have been. The implied comparison with the pure scientific research, which so frequently finds unexpected and unintended application, is suggestive and, up to a point, apposite. It is to such often seemingly indiscriminate interest in the uses of words that we owe such fruitful logical explorations of neglected territory as R. M. Hare's 'Imperative Sentences',[44] and J. L. Austin on performatory language in 'Other Minds'. Contrast the old 'fetich of the indicative sentence' (Ryle) formulated by Hobbes: "In philosophy there is but one kind of speech useful . . . most men call it *proposition,* and [it] is the speech of those that affirm or deny, and expresseth truth and falsity."[45] If one quoted

Others apart sat on a hill retired
In thoughts more elevate, and reasoned high
Of providence, foreknowledge, will and fate;
Fixt fate, free will, foreknowledge absolute
And found no end, in wandering mazes lost
(Milton, *Paradise Lost*, Bk. II)

---

[43] Not that such adaption or invention may not be called for: see P. D. Nowell-Smith in *The Rationalist Annual,* 1954, for suggestions designed to accommodate the discoveries of psychoanalysis.

[44] *Mind,* 1949, and incorporated with addition and improvements into his *The Language of Morals,* Oxford, 1952.

[45] *The English Works of Thomas Hobbes,* Vol. I, W. Molesworth (ed.), p. 30.

to those who have learnt most from Austin, their reply would be that the Devils in Pandemonium found no end *precisely because* they insisted on 'reasoning high'; that they should have begun with a meticulous and laborious study of the use of 'free will' and all the terms with which it is logically associated. Such an examination, which is certainly no quick and easy matter, is, as Austin has said, if not the be all and end all, at least the begin all of philosophy.

(E)   A derisive brouhaha has been raised about the notion of 'Standard English' -- "Why it should have been thought to deserve consideration as a philosophical principle it is by no means easy to imagine."[46]   Those who have emphasized the frequent philosophical importance of "unexplained and unnoticed distortions of standard English" and "deviations from standard English to which no sense has been attached"[47] have not, of course, been claiming that there is or ought to be an absolute, unchanging, universal, inflexible standard of correctness applicable to all users of the English language, past, present, and to come.   The strange idea that they have seems to derive: partly from failing to appreciate the force of the emphasis of *uses*, etc. (see (A) and (C) above);   partly from a significant though perhaps seemingly trivial misrepresentation, whereby a concern for 'Standard English' is attributed to those who have in fact written 'standard English';[48] and partly from the sheer errors that standards must necessarily be universal, inflexible, unchanging, and absolute.   These last may be dispelled by the reflection that makers of cars may offer fresh standard models yearly, different ones for different markets, and with a standard choice of fittings and colours for each.   About standards such as these there is presumably nothing normative, whereas with standard linguistic usage there certainly is.   For the reasons already given [see (C) *ad init.*], everyone ought in general to conform with the usage accepted as correct by the language group or sub-group of which his linguistic and non-linguistic behaviour makes it reasonable to presume he is, tacitly or explicitly, claiming membership.   This is *not* to say that usage ought to be absolutely rigid, uniform, and static among all users of any language.   That would be to impose an embargo on improvisation and innovation, growth and decay.

It is common enormously to exaggerate the amount of variation in usage which there in fact is.   People often write as if usage were so fluid, irregular, and varied that it must be impossible to say anything about the meaning of any

---

[46]   *Philosophical Quarterly*, 1952, pp. 2 and 3.

[47]   *LL*, I, p. 9.

[48]   Compare *Philosophical Quarterly*, 1952, pp. 2 and 3 with *LL*, I, p. 9, of which it purports to be a criticism.

word, except perhaps as employed by one particular person on one particular occasion. As we have argued above [in (C)] and elsewhere,[49] if this were in fact the case, verbal communication would be impossible. These exaggerations, like the linguists' analogue that different languages are all so very different that there is no equivalent of any word at all in any other language, arise from the understandable and inevitable preoccupation of philologists with differences and changes, and of translators with their more intractable difficulties. They are perhaps encouraged by vested interests, in obfuscation generally, and in the pretence that knowledge of foreign languages is even more important than it actually is.

(F) Ryle has so recently distinguished again between, and redeployed some of the arguments in favour of, the various policies which have sometimes been confused together as 'the appeal to ordinary language' that there is no need here to develop at length their relations and differences.[50] Consider four. First, appealing to the ordinary use(s) of terms to elucidate philosopher's possible misuses. Second, appealing for plain English as opposed to jargon and high abstraction in philosophical prose. Not that anyone is suggesting an embargo on technical terms and abstraction: only a bias against, except where they prove essential. Third, concentrating upon everyday as opposed to technical concepts and their problems. Yet the fact that a large proportion of classical problems centre round such notions as *cause, mistake, evidence, knowledge, ought, can,* and *imagine* is no reason at all for neglecting those which arise from *psi-phenomena, collective unconscious, transubstantiation, economic welfare,* and *infinitesimal.* But whereas (most of) the former group can be tackled with no knowledge other than that minimum common to all educated men, even to understand the latter one must acquire some smattering of the disciplines to which the notions belong. Fourth, a protest 'that the logic of everyday statements and even . . . of scientists, lawyers, historians, and bridge-players cannot in principle be adequately represented by the formulae of formal logic.'[51] Oxford philosophers who incline to all four policies together may be thought of as trying to preserve a balance: between this 'formulizer's dream' that non-formulized language really is, or ought to be replaced by, a

---

[49] See *LL*, II, pp. 8-9: on "the unwitting allies of a revolution of destruction".

[50] 'Ordinary Language', *loc. cit.*

[51] Ryle, *loc. cit.*, p. 184.

calculus;[52] and the Humpty Dumpty nightmare that there is, at least in those parts of it which most concern philosophers, no logic or order at all.

One pattern of argument, a particular application of the first policy, demands special attention. Talk, mainly deriving from Moore, of the Plain Man and his Common Sense, has now been largely replaced by emphasis upon the ordinary uses of words. But many philosophers have been as reluctant to abandon their reasoned paradoxes because they offend the Plain Man in his capacity as arbiter of ordinary language as they were to abdicate in face of Moore's protests on behalf of his common sense. And not without reason. The clue to the whole business now seems to lie in mastering what has recently been usefully named, The Argument of the Paradigm Case.[53] Crudely: if there is any word the meaning of which can be taught by reference to paradigm cases, then no argument whatever could ever prove that there are no cases whatever of whatever it is. Thus, since the meaning of 'of his own freewill' can be taught by reference to such paradigm cases as that in which a man, under no social pressure, marries the girl he wants to marry (how else *could* it be taught?): it cannot be right, on any grounds whatsoever, to say that no one *ever* acts of his own freewill. For cases such as the paradigm, which must occur if the word is ever to be thus explained (and which certainly do in fact occur), are not in that case specimens which might have been wrongly identified: to the extent that the meaning of the expression is given in terms of them they are, by definition, what 'acting of one's own freewill' is. As Runyon might have said: If these are not free actions they will at least do till some come along. A moment's reflexion will show that analogous arguments can be deployed against many philosophical paradoxes.

What such arguments by themselves will certainly not do is to establish any matter of value, moral or otherwise: and almost everyone who has used them, certainly the present writer, must plead guilty to having from time to time failed to see this. For one cannot *derive* any sort of value proposition: from *either* a factual proposition about what people value; *or* from definitions, however disguised, of value terms. This applies to any sort of value: indeed we might distinguish a Special (in ethics) from a General (anywhere)

---

[52] Though there has been a long tradition of this sort of thing, *e.g.*, Leibniz's *characteristica universalis* and similar ideas in his century. Nowadays it is usually a matter of an over-estimation of the philosophic value of the techniques of symbolic logic; found in the Vienna Circle, in Russell, and today particularly prevalent in the U. S. A.

[53] By J. O. Urmson in 'Some Questions Concerning Validity', *Revue Internationale de Philosophie*, 1953.

Naturalistic Fallacy.[54] There is a world of difference between saying that it is reasonable in certain circumstances to act inductively (which is a value matter, one of commending a certain sort of behaviour); and saying that most people regard it as reasonable so to act (which is a factual matter, one of neutrally giving information about the prevalence of that kind of ideal). Thus that too short way with the problem of induction, which tries to *deduce* that induction is reasonable from the premise that people regard it as so or even that they make inductive behaviour part of their paradigm of reasonableness, will not do. It is necessary for each of us tacitly or explicitly actually to make our personal value commitments here. Most of us are in fact willing to make that one which is involved in making inductive behaviour part of our paradigm of reasonableness. But as philosophers we must insist on making it explicitly and after examining the issues. *Mutatis mutandis* the same applies to attempts to derive ethical conclusions simply from what we (as a matter of fact) call reasonable behaviour or good reasons to act; without the introduction of an explicit commitment to accepted moral standards. These must involve versions of the (Special) Naturalistic Fallacy.[55]

To see the power, and the limitations, of the Argument of the Paradigm case is to realize how much of common sense can, and how much cannot, be defended against philosophical paradoxes by simple appeal to the ordinary uses of words; and why.

---

[54] This is the fallacy of trying to *deduce* valuational conclusions from purely factual premises which in its Special form was first named by G. E. Moore.

[55] Compare R. M. Hare, *The Language of Morals*, with S. E. Toulmin, *The Place of Reason in Ethics*, Cambridge, 1950, and see Hare and J. L. Mackie on the latter in *Philosophical Quarterly*, 1951 and *Australasian Journal of Philosophy*, 1951, respectively. T. D. Weldon in *The Vocabulary of Politics*, Pelican, 1953, gives a crisp example of the false move involved, pp. 42-3. I have tried to say something myself about it in 'The Justification of Punishment', *Philosophy*, 1954.

CHAPTER 3

THEOLOGY AND FALSIFICATION
(1950)

Let us begin with a parable. It is a parable developed from a tale told by John Wisdom in his haunting and revelatory article 'Gods'.[1] Once upon a time two explorers came upon a clearing in the jungle. In the clearing were growing many flowers and many weeds. One explorer says: 'Some gardener must tend this plot.' The other disagrees: 'There is no gardener.' So they pitch their tents and set a watch. No gardener is ever seen. 'But perhaps he is an invisible gardener.' So they set up a barbed-wire fence. They electrify it. They patrol with bloodhounds. (For they remember how H. G. Wells's *The Invisible Man* could be both smelt and touched though he could not be seen.) But no shrieks ever suggest that some intruder has received a shock. No movements of the wire ever betray an invisible climber. The bloodhounds never give cry. Yet still the Believer is not convinced: 'But there is a gardener, invisible, intangible, insensible to electric shocks, a gardener who has no scent and makes no sound, a gardener who comes secretly to look after the garden which he loves.' At last the Skeptic despairs: 'But what remains of your original assertion? Just how does what you call an invisible, intangible, eternally elusive gardener differ from an imaginary gardener or even from no gardener at all?'

In this parable we can see how what starts as an assertion, that something

---

[1] *Language and Logic*, Series I, Antony Flew (ed.), Blackwell, 1951.

41

exists or that there is some analogy between certain complexes of phenomena, may be reduced step by step to an altogether different status, to an expression perhaps of a 'picture preference'.[2] The Skeptic says there is no gardener. The Believer says there is a gardener (but invisible, etc.). One man talks about sexual behaviour. Another man prefers to talk of Aphrodite (but knows that there is not really a superhuman person additional to, and somehow responsible for, all sexual phenomena). The process of qualification may be checked at any point before the original assertion is completely withdrawn and something of that first assertion will remain (Tautology). Mr. Wells's invisible man could not, admittedly, be seen, but in all other respects he was a man like the rest of us. But though the process of qualification may be, and of course usually is, checked in time, it is not always judiciously so halted. Someone may dissipate his assertion completely without noticing that he has done so. A fine brash hypothesis may thus be killed by inches, the death by a thousand qualifications.

And in this, it seems to me, lies the peculiar danger, the endemic evil, of theological utterance. Take such utterances as 'God has a plan', 'God created the world', 'God loves us as a father loves his children'. They look at first sight very much like assertions, vast cosmological assertions. Of course, this is no sure sign that they either are, or are intended to be, assertions. But let us confine ourselves to the cases where those who utter such sentences intend them to express assertions. (Merely remarking parenthetically that those who intend or interpret such utterances as crypto-commands, expressions of wishes, disguised ejaculations, concealed ethics, or as anything else but assertions, are unlikely to succeed in making them either properly orthodox or practically effective.)

Now to assert that such and such is the case is necessarily equivalent to denying that such and such is not the case. Suppose then that we are in doubt about what someone who gives vent to an utterance is asserting, or suppose that, more radically, we are skeptical about whether he is really asserting anything at all, one way of trying to understand (or perhaps it will be to expose) his utterance is to attempt to find what he would regard as counting against, or as being incompatible with, its truth. For if the utterance is indeed an assertion, it will necessarily be equivalent to a denial of the negation of that assertion. And anything that would count against the assertion, or which would induce the speaker to withdraw it and to admit that it had been mistaken, must be part of (or the whole of) the meaning of the negation of an assertion. And to know the meaning of the negation of an assertion is as near as makes no

---

[2] *Ibid.*, pp. 10-11.

matter to know the meaning of that assertion. And if there is nothing which a putative assertion denies then there is nothing which it asserts either: and so it is not really an assertion. When the Skeptic in the parable asked the Believer, 'Just how does what you call an invisible, intangible, eternally elusive gardener differ from an imaginary gardener or even from no gardener at all?', he was suggesting that the Believer's earlier statement had been so eroded by qualification that it was no longer an assertion at all.

Now it often seems to people who are not religious as if there was no conceivable event or series of events the occurrence of which would be admitted by sophisticated religious people to be a sufficient reason for conceding 'There wasn't a God after all' or 'God does not really love us then'. We are reassured. But then we see a child dying of inoperable cancer of the throat. His earthly father is driven frantic in his efforts to help, but his Heavenly Father reveals no obvious sign of concern. Some qualification is made -- God's love is 'not a merely human love' or it is 'an inscrutable love', perhaps -- and we realize that such sufferings are quite compatible with the truth of the assertion that 'God loves us as a father (but, of course, . . .)'. We are reassured again. But then perhaps we ask: what is this assurance of God's (appropriately qualified) love worth, what is this apparent guarantee really a guarantee against? Just what would have to happen not merely (morally and wrongly) to tempt but also (logically and rightly) to entitle us to say 'God does not love us' or even 'God does not exist'? I therefore put to the succeeding symposiasts the simple central question: 'What would have to occur or to have occurred to constitute for you a disproof of the love of, or of the existence of, God?'

CHAPTER 4

AGAINST INDOCTRINATION
(1968)

'Give me a child until it is seven.' A Church of England (aided) infant school, in Midlands, three hundred children, excellent church teaching, needs new building. No diocesan funds available. Will anyone who realizes the importance of Church Schools please communicate. Write Box C. 705 The Times, E.C.4. Advertisement in the Personal Columns of *The Times* for August 26th, 1965.

In this paper I first propose, explain and defend a definition of the term *indoctrination*. After that I begin to put this notion to work. The first part is long, and the practically-minded may well become impatient with these philosophical preliminaries. They do nevertheless have a practical point. For it is in this part that I shape the framework within which the whole discussion ought to take place. Once given this right framework clearly appreciated it becomes easy to realize, what I try briskly to indicate in the second part, where the onus of proof really lies, what has to be proved, and what hinges upon success or failure in the attempt to prove it.

In this second part I argue, generally, that indoctrination is presumptively, although not for that reason necessarily also categorically, always wrong; and, in particular, I urge that parents (and others) have no moral right to indoctrinate (or to arrange for other people to indoctrinate), their (or any) children in a religious (or political) creed of the parents' (or anyone else's) choice. From the general conclusion I draw out the general corollary that the onus of proof must lie on the indoctrinator to justify his practices, if he can; and I then indicate how the recognition of this corollary must underline the importance of the

45

sometimes underrated issues of theological epistemology. From the particular conclusion I extract the particular corollary that states -- whatever their duties of toleration -- have no right, much less any duty, to provide -- as ours most lavishly does -- positive support for indoctrination.

In the first part, and to a lesser extent in the second also, I draw on materials which I have already presented within my contributions to a discussion started by Professor R. M. Hare and Mr. John Wilson in a book on *Aims in Education: the Philosophic Approach*, and continued in the journal *Studies in Philosophy and Education*.[1]   But the manner in which these materials are arranged is totally different, and they are here employed for quite explicitly practical purposes.

I

(a) Indoctrination consists in implanting, with the backing of some sort of special authority, of a firm conviction of the truth of doctrines either not known to be true or even known to be false. The classical, albeit imaginary, instance is found in Plato's sponsorship of his 'noble lie . . . a sort of Phoenician tale . . . demanding no little persuasion to make it believable'. Plato proposed that the whole power and authority of his supposedly ideal state -- *The Republic* -- should be deployed 'to persuade first the rulers themselves and the soldiers and then the rest of the population . . .' of the truth of his own deliberately made up Myth of the Earthborn. Plato's 'Socrates' and his interlocutor despair of so indoctrinating the first generation, but believe that it would be possible to persuade 'their sons and successors and other men who come after'.

The object of the exercise is to instill an acceptable, though false, account of the origins of *The Republic*. This is an account of origins which is supposed at the same time to provide an acceptable, though nevertheless strictly unwarranted, justification of the peculiar institutions of that allegedly ideal state. The final comment here of Plato's 'Socrates' is that, allowing that you could only reasonably hope thus to indoctrinate the successors, still "even that would have a good effect in making them more inclined to care for the state and one another."[2]

---

[1]   The book was edited by H. B. Hollins, and published by Manchester University Press in 1964. The relevant issues of the journal, which is sponsored and published by Southern Illinois University at Edwardsville and Carbondale, Illinois, are Vol. IV, No. 3, of 1966 and Vol. V, No. 2, 1967.

[2]   414-415D.

We must not, however, even as we consider this classical example, overlook that in the completely typical case the indoctrinator does believe that his doctrine is true. This is so even where he might reasonably hesitate to claim that, by ordinary and non-sectarian standards, it constitutes an item of knowledge. This does not, of course, even begin to show that such indoctrination is morally unobjectionable. Yet it is, equally obviously, importantly relevant to the entirely different question of the goodness or badness of the intentions of the indoctrinator. For, notoriously, a man may from the best of motives unfortunately do the wrong thing; just as he may chance to do the right thing despite the most evil of intentions.

(b) In explaining and defending the definition proposed we shall be appealing both to the present accepted usage of the term *indoctrination* and to considerations of economy, clarity and utility. Usage seems in this case to be somewhat untidy and even inconsistent; this is only to be expected with a term so emotionally charged and so much a focus of conflict. In so far as there is any such untidiness and inconsistency in the present usage any definition determining a philosophically satisfactory concept of indoctrination must be to some extent prescriptive (or stipulative), as opposed to purely descriptive (or lexical).

Nevertheless, even where and in so far as our definition is intended to prescribe for an improved concept of indoctrination, we have to attend to previous usage: first, because a reformed concept can only be any sort of concept of indoctrination in so far as there really is some substantial overlap between the new and the old use of the term; second, because examination of the existing usage may well reveal subtleties of which the wise reformer will wish to take account; and, third, because (since speech habits are as difficult to break as other habits) it is foolish unnecessarily to try to go against the grain of well-established verbal habits.

(c) The first thing to explain and to justify is the employment in our definition of the word *implanting*, and the inclusion of the clause *with the backing of some sort of special authority*. The point is to exclude from the scope of the concept of indoctrination all cases where one man persuades another of the truth of some doctrine by the straightforward presentation of arguments as man to man. The indoctrinator has always to be in some sort of privileged situation as against those who are being indoctrinated, usually that of teacher to pupil; and certainly not that of one man carrying on a frank, give-and-take, discussion with an equal. Thus Plato's 'Socrates' is the Founder-Teacher-Legislator of *The Republic*, notwithstanding that his role is to be concealed behind his self-made Myth of the Earthborn. Typically it is an educational system which indoctrinates; and the teacher as such is obviously the bearer of a special authority over the pupil. Or, again, a state or private propaganda machine may (and all too probably will) attempt to indoctrinate; and any such machine is necessarily in a privileged position as compared with the individual exposed to its efforts to persuade.

This first restriction of the scope of the concept of indoctrination seems, as we have suggested, to accord with present ordinary usage. Even if it did not, there would be very good reason to prescribe that it should. For without some such limitation the word *indoctrination* is left with no peculiar and useful job to do. It becomes either a ponderous and offensive synonym for *persuasion*, or at best an unnecessary word for persuasion of the truth of a particular class of propositions. But what we want (and have here got) is a special word for such persuasion, backed by advantages which might be (and at least by me are) thought to be improper and unfair.

(d) The second thing in our definition requiring explanation and comment is the word *doctrines*. The employment of this particular word is again quite deliberately restrictive. Not every proposition constitutes a doctrine, although it would be hard if not impossible to specify precisely what propositions do and what do not. In so far as this is so our concept of indoctrination must necessarily be in this direction and to this extent vague. Yet it would be entirely wrong to think that a concept which is in any way imprecise, unspecific or indeterminate must therefore be rejected as useless, or worse than useless. It is, as Aristotle long since insisted, a mark of the educated man to demand only that degree of precision and specification which the particular subject permits and requires.[3]

Although the term *doctrine* is thus admittedly imprecise, the point of using it, and of confining the word *indoctrination* to the implanting of doctrines, can be brought out sufficiently by considering the misuse of the latter term in a very characteristic piece of apologetic for *The Catholic Way in Education*:

> Every educational institution makes use of indoctrination. Children are indoctrinated with the multiplication table; they are indoctrinated with love of country; they are indoctrinated with the principles of chemistry and physics and mathematics and biology, and nobody finds fault with indoctrination in these fields. Yet these are of small concern in the great business of life by contrast with ideas concerning

---

[3] *Nicomachean Ethics*, 1094 B12-28.

God and man's relation to God . . . . the Catholic educator makes no apology for indoctrinating his students in these essential matters.[4]

This is a remarkable and instructive passage. Every statement in it except those of the final sentence is false, and of these the first is most importantly misleading. In effect the author is denying that there is any difference between teaching and indoctrination. For only if this were true would it be correct to say that every educational institution is involved in indoctrination. But there is a difference, and what makes the term *indoctrination* useful is that it is employed to make the distinction. Certainly children are taught the multiplication table. But that twelve twelves are one hundred and forty-four is not a doctrine. Hence to teach this necessary truth cannot be to indoctrinate. Again, children in many other countries are studiously taught to be patriotic. But patriotic affections and inclinations as such, precisely as affections and inclinations, do not presuppose or contain any beliefs. Hence to encourage these affections and inclinations is not essentially and necessarily to implant false or disputatious doctrines. And where the teaching of patriotism is as a matter of contingent fact tied up with the implantation of such doctrines some people do (in my view rightly) find fault with the indoctrination so involved.

What makes a proposition a doctrine is its being in some way ideological, a possible candidate for inclusion in a creed: 'The principles of chemistry and physics and mathematics and biology' do not qualify, whereas assertions 'concerning God and man's relation to God' obviously and paradigmatically do. Some may perhaps find it significant that the author of the passage under discussion temporarily stops employing the word *indoctrination* at precisely the point in his list where for the first time it becomes apt. Certainly we must notice the use which he wants to make of his very proper insistence on the enormous importance of 'ideas concerning God and man's relations to God'. For he proceeds to slide, easily but illegitimately, from this innocuous and noncontroversial general premise to an obnoxious and highly particular conclusion -- that it must be perfectly all right for 'the Catholic educator' to indoctrinate his pupils with his own particular doctrines about 'these essential matters'.

The crucial, but constantly neglected, difference here can best be brought out in terms of the distinction between two totally different, yet too often confounded senses of the curriculum cliche *religious knowledge* ('RK'). In the

---

[4] A. C. F. Beales, *Looking Forward in Education*, A. V. Judges (ed.), Faber and Faber, 1955, p. 84.

first interpretation religious knowledge is knowledge about the religious beliefs which have been, and are, in fact held; and about the religious practices which have been, and are, actually pursued. In this interpretation to allow that there truly is religious knowledge carries no necessary commitment to the highly disputatious proposition that certain religious beliefs are indeed (not merely true but) known to be true; nor does it carry any implications about adopting any of these practices. There is, therefore, nothing in the least incongruous about an atheist humanist claiming to possess religious knowledge in this first sense; and, furthermore, most of us do in fact and consistently support the demand that 'RK' in this sense is so important that it must have a place in the most basic school curriculum, as well as some representation in all universities.

It is the second, totally other, interpretation which is the focus of conflict. In this second interpretation 'RK' consists in some particular set of religious propositions which are taken to be, and are taught as if they were, themselves knowledge; on which assumption it seems appropriate to teach the corresponding practices, not as facts about what some people do, but as practices which the pupil is himself to adopt. It is one thing (and obviously desirable) to know what Roman Catholics, qua Roman Catholics, believe, and do. But it is another and totally different thing to claim and to teach that these beliefs are themselves items of knowledge; and to train your pupils to follow the corresponding practices.

(e) The third and last clause requiring explanation and defence is, *either not known to be true or even known to be false.* To know it is necessary, but it is not sufficient, to believe and to be right. There is, of course, no doubt but that these are both necessary, indeed constitutive, conditions of knowledge. Thus it would be contradictory to claim to know what you also at the same time claim to believe to be false. More interestingly, it is also contradictory to say, without reservation, that someone knew something while you are also maintaining that what he claimed to know was false. Certainly we do intelligibly and pointedly say such things as 'He knew that his horse would win the Two Thousand Guineas, but he knew wrong'. But this genuinely is a rule-proving exception. For had he really known he must necessarily have been right: the whole paradoxical point of saying 'He knew, but he knew wrong', lies precisely in the fact that it is strictly self-contradictory. If he was wrong then he did not really know, but only 'knew' (in inverted commas): just as, if there were no pink rats really there to be seen, the dipsomaniac on his lost weekend can only be said to have 'seen' (in inverted commas), and not truly to have seen, such creatures.

In addition to these first two necessary, constitutive, conditions there is also a third. Properly to know you have to be in a position to know, you must possess sufficient reason for believing. Consider how, when we are exercising the fastidious caution appropriate to a statement upon which a great deal hinges, we may admit to believing that someone is a thief while nevertheless insisting that we are not (yet) in a position to know: 'it is only a hunch, a suspicion'; 'there is no (real) evidence'; and so on. It follows, therefore, that a claim to know may be rebutted, not only by challenging the sincerity of the claimant's belief in what he claims to know, or by showing that the content of his belief is in fact false, but also by showing that he has not got sufficient reason to justify him in claiming to know. If any one of these objections can be sustained then what we have is simply not a full standard case of knowledge proper.

II

(a) There can now, after the elucidations of Part I, be little doubt but that indoctrination must be presumptively (and hence whenever the presumption cannot be defeated also categorically) wrong. For to try to implant a firm conviction of the truth of some doctrine is to teach this doctrine as if it were known truth, whereas it is a constitutive condition of indoctrination that the doctrines involved are either not known to be true or known to be false; and to do this is misrepresentation. Again, to indoctrinate a child is to deprive it, or at least to try to deprive it, of the possibility of developing into a person with the capacity and the duty of making such fundamental life-shaping judgements for himself, and according to his own conscience; and if anything is an assault on the autonomy and integrity of the human person this is it. (One might say that it was paradoxical were it not so much what one wryly expects, that, just as the Plato who elsewhere in *The Republic* insists that a high value must be placed on truth advocates the implantation of a 'noble lie', so those who are hot for Christian indoctrination commend their own God on other occasions for his desire to create not automata but free creatures.)

To say that something is presumptively wrong is to say that it is always categorically wrong, unless some overriding consideration makes it all right in the particular circumstances. To say that something is categorically wrong is to say that it just is wrong, either absolutely in all circumstances, or at any rate in the circumstances in question. Take lying for example. This is always at least presumptively wrong. But it may (and by most moralists would) be allowed that there are other still more urgent moral claims, which may sometimes override the obligation not knowingly to assert what is false. Hence there may be (and surely are) some circumstances where to tell a lie not merely is not categorically wrong but is even positively obligatory.

Thus the first thing which now, thanks to our long preparations, comes out very clearly is that the indoctrinator (like the liar) has a presumption to defeat. It is up to him to vindicate himself by showing: either that the doctrines in question are known to be true, and hence that strictly he is not indoctrinating at all; or that there are overriding moral reasons why those beliefs should be so implanted notwithstanding that they cannot be rated as actually known truths. That this initial framework conclusion is indeed worth establishing begins to become clear when we notice how common and how respected is the assumption that parents (or alternatively states) have a moral right to arrange for the indoctrination of their (or the nation's) children in whatever religious (or political) doctrine they as parents (or states) (or as parents to be) may choose. If once it is appreciated that indoctrination must be presumptively wrong, any such assumption becomes very hard to defend. For unless it is in some way drastically qualified it is surely impossible to appeal to the goodness of the ends achievable by these presumptively evil means: it would be ridiculous to suggest that good results would follow from indoctrination in any set of doctrines which any parent (or any state) might happen to favour!

The only apparent alternative would be to argue that parents (or states) are indefeasibly entitled to do what they like with their own; and that it is for this reason that indoctrination, though always presumptively wrong, is not categorically wrong when sponsored by parents (or states). Such servile notions of absolute property rights in human beings certainly are found in, and are perhaps essential to, theist religions: it is, for instance, urged that God, because He is our Creator, has not just total power over but unlimited legitimate claims upon us; and Christian theologians have frequently endorsed the objection to suicide of certain slave-holding Greek philosophers, that it is wrong because it violates God's property rights in his creatures. But this is not a line of argument which we are likely to meet in the present context. Hence it can safely be left to condemn itself.

(b) It is, therefore, clear: both that it must be presumptively wrong to (try to) implant in children a firm conviction of the truth of doctrines either not known to be true or known to be false; and that, if this presumption is ever to be defeated, it will have to be defeated, not by any general appeal to the rights of parents (or states), but by arguments referring to particular cases or to one particular case. So let us come to cases.

There can be no doubt, though there often is an extreme reluctance frankly to acknowledge, what is overwhelmingly the most extensive and important case in Britain, and indeed generally in the English-speaking world. It is, obviously, religious indoctrination, especially that most whole-hearted and successful form effected in Roman Catholic schools. These schools were of course determinedly founded, and are stubbornly maintained, precisely and only in order to produce indoctrinated Roman Catholics. Since nowadays it seems to be thought to be bad form for any non-Catholic to assert this manifest fact I quote a statement from a Catholic source: "Our basic philosophy must not only be a part of education but must be the core and centre of it, and every subject in the curriculum must be considered expressly as an instrument for making that philosophy prevail in the formation of children's character and beliefs."[5] (The word *philosophy* here can be taken as being synonymous with our *ideology*.)

If the indoctrinator is to vindicate himself against the presumption that his activities are morally wrong, then (as we suggested in the first section of the present part) he will have to show one or both of two things: either that the doctrines which he is implanting are in fact known to be true, and hence that he is not properly speaking indoctrinating; or that the effects of believing these doctrines are so excellent as to defeat any presumption that it is wrong thus to implant them. Confronted by this challenge many apologists (at any rate in Britain) will wish to respond in both ways. Thus it will be argued, or, more likely, simply assumed, that the content of the proposed religious instruction actually is religious knowledge: the employment of the ambiguous and question-begging cliche 'RK' can here be helpfully confusing. But appeal will probably also be made to a piece of the established British conventional wisdom, the falsism that religion is the essential foundation of morality.

(c) Consider now the first of these two contentions in the light of what we have said about the two senses of *religious knowledge* and about the constitutive conditions of knowledge (in I[d] and I[e], above). Obviously we are concerned here only with the second and disputatious sense: the question of indoctrination can hardly arise where (as must often be the case nowadays within the ordinary state schools) Religious Instruction ('RI') consists only in the presentation of religious knowledge in the first sense. The constitutive condition which is crucial here is the third: for a full standard case of knowledge proper the claimant has to be in a position to know, has to have sufficient reasons to justify his claim.

No one who wants to say (as perhaps most contemporary Protestant Christians do) that the fundamentals of his religion belong to the sphere of faith, and who then wants to contrast faith with reason, can at the same time consistently claim that his belief in these fundamentals rates, by ordinarily exacting standards, as knowledge. Nor again will it do (notwithstanding that it is all too often done) for a believer to claim, and for others to allow, that the

---

[5] *Ibid.*

incorrigible intensity of his conviction is by itself sufficient reason for describing his beliefs, whatever these may happen to be, as knowledge. It is, again by the ordinarily exacting standards of everyday life, plain false to concede that he knows unless it is the case his beliefs are in fact true and that he has sufficient reason to warrant his claim to know. We ought surely to be shocked, even if we are too old to be surprised, to see how often people see fit to lower their standards in precisely those areas which are on their own showing the most vital: whether this lowering is a matter of allowing as knowledge what fails to satisfy the constitutive conditions upon which they themselves would elsewhere insist; or whether it is a matter of accepting as sufficient reasons which in a less privileged context certainly would not pass.

If, therefore, this first contention is to be made good it must be by spokesmen who are prepared to maintain that the fundamentals of their religion are indeed known truths, and hence that there are sufficient good reasons to warrant claims to know. Traditionally Roman Catholics have been inclined to claim exactly this. Indeed decrees of the First Vatican Council define as essential and constitutive elements of the Roman Catholic religion the dogmas that it is possible to know of the existence of God by the natural light of human reason, and that it is possible similarly by recognizing the occurrence of endorsing and constitutive miracles to authenticate the genuineness of the Christian revelation.[6] Cardinal Newman was, therefore, exactly 'on the party line' when in his *The Idea of a University* he wrote: "Religious doctrine is knowledge, in as full a sense as Newton's doctrine is knowledge. University teaching without theology is simply unphilosophical. Theology has at least as good a right to claim a place there as astronomy."[7]

This is not the place for a thorough examination of this bold, not to say brazen, thesis; and we disclaim the task here with a better conscience for having ourselves undertaken it elsewhere.[8] Two very relevant points must however be made, briefly. The first is that the upshot of the whole argument of the present paper is to underline the practical import of such issues of philosophical theology: the question whether or not Newman's contention can be made good is seen to bear directly upon major educational decisions.

The second is that such a contention about the epistemological status of the

---

[6] H. Denzinger, *Encheiridion Symbolorum*, 29th Revised Edition, Herder, 1953, §§ 1806 and 1813.

[7] G. N. Schuster (ed.), Image Books, Doubleday, 1959, p. 80.

[8] *God and Philosophy*, Hutchinson, 1966. This book has been reissued as *God: A Critical Enquiry*, Open Court, 1984.

basic doctrines of (Roman Catholic) theology cohabits most incongruously with the famous zeal to catch them young: 'Give me a child until it is seven'. If these doctrines really were epistemologically on all fours with the fundamentals of astronomy, then surely believing parents could afford (as they ought) to wait until their children become of an age to consider the evidence for themselves. But the fact is, of course, that while we need have little fear that if we introduce a mature adult to astronomy he will reject the conclusions of the astronomers as unwarranted or false, everyone (and most especially the indoctrinator) is very well aware that unless you catch them young with religion you are nowadays most unlikely to catch them at all.

Notoriously, it is the exception rather than the rule for adults who without benefit of earlier teaching as juveniles set themselves to examine the evidence for (any set of) religious doctrines to become persuaded that the evidence really is adequate to justify belief; and even of those few who do thus as adults 'see the light', most seem to be converted at periods when there is good independent reason to think that the balance of their minds is disturbed. Of course, this actual unpersuasiveness of the (particular favoured) religious case may (albeit somewhat arrogantly) be attributed to the bigotry and the inbred sin of those who are not persuaded. Nevertheless at the very least it has to be admitted that this absence of actual consensus constitutes a striking negative analogy between the basic propositions of (any positive) theology and the fundamentals of astronomy.

(d) The second possible response, that religion is the essential foundation of morality, often is, and consistently may be, combined with the first. Sometimes, however, it is instead disreputably but equally consistently supported by the cynical claim that, since (as every sensible person is supposed to know) in the sphere of religious belief knowledge is impossible, we are free to believe, and to teach our children to believe, whatever may be most convenient to us, or whatever may be thought most beneficial to society. To this shabby suggestion it should be sufficient to reply: first, that where knowledge is impossible the reasonable man must be convinced of nothing at all, save perhaps that knowledge is indeed impossible, rather than convinced of anything whatever that he or his tutors may have chosen for his credence; and, second, that it reveals a frivolous indifference to truth which I for one would not wish my children to learn, least of all from any example of mine.

By contrast there is nothing similarly shabby about the position of those who, while believing that their own particular religious beliefs do constitute knowledge, then offer as a further reason for instilling them into their wards the statement that, happily, these convictions do also tend to produce morally excellent fruit. What and all that can be said against this further thesis is: first, that in the particular and locally important case of Roman Catholicism the utterly inadequate evidence available points, if anywhere, in exactly the opposite direction; and, second, that any suggestion that religion (any religion?) is essential to morality is certainly wrong.

Again, as with the first response (considered in II[c], above), it is impossible to provide an adequate treatment here. And again we can disclaim the attempt with a better conscience for having ourselves traversed some of this well-trodden ground on another occasion.[9] A very few remarks will have to suffice now. On the first point it ought to be a familiar fact that there seems to be a statistically highly significant positive correlation between delinquency and Roman Catholicism: every study of the religious affiliation of those in prison or in approved schools has revealed that the proportion of Roman Catholics inside is two or three times that in the population as a whole.[10] Nor will it do to say that these delinquent Catholics are those who have been deprived of the peculiar benefits of Catholic schools. For, to quote from a Catholic source, "At the annual meeting of the Catholic Moral Welfare Council, Fr. McCormack said many Catholics tended to shrug off the high percentage of Catholic delinquents by saying these were only nominal Catholics. But . . . figures he had obtained from Catholic approved schools showed that more than 90 per cent of the boys in them had spent from 3 to 10 years in Catholic schools."[11] The proportion of all Catholic children in Catholic schools is about 66 per cent.

Of course, in the present wretched state of the evidence the possibility is certainly not precluded that the real connection is not between delinquency and Roman Catholicism but between delinquency and something else which in Britain, and in the several other countries yielding similar data, just happens to correlate with Catholicism. Yet this is scarcely a promising line for the apologist, since the most obvious alternative suggestions (such as the poverty and the size of the families from which so many delinquents come) are

---

[9] *Ibid.*, Chap. V.

[10] The Home Office, which should of course supply complete statistics, is in fact extremely reticent about religious affiliations; for reasons which we can only, but may easily, guess. But, for instance, A. G. Rose in his *Five Hundred Borstal Boys*, Blackwell, 1964, found 23 per cent Roman Catholics, compared with 8 or 9 per cent in the population as a whole. Mrs. Margaret Knight tells me that she extracted figures for 1957 from the Scottish Home Department, showing that in that year about 40 per cent of all prison and 36 per cent of all Borstal admissions were of Roman Catholics; compared with about 15 per cent Roman Catholics for the whole population of Scotland.

[11] *Catholic Herald*, November 20th, 1964: again my attention was drawn to this passage by my friend and fellow contributor Mrs. Margaret Knight. She also supplied the motto for the whole article.

certainly themselves really connected with Catholicism: he can scarcely afford to boast of the practical effectiveness of Catholic behavioural teaching while at the same time denying that it tends in fact to encourage (at least relatively) large families and hence (at least relative) poverty!

Suppose that we concede (as no doubt we should) that all this is a controversial matter of the interpretation of admittedly insufficient evidence. Still what at least does emerge quite clearly is that it must be utterly outrageous for spokesmen of the immensely successful Roman Catholic education lobby blandly to take it that the salutary effectiveness of their behavioural teaching as a bulwark against delinquency and bad citizenship is so much a plumb obvious established fact as to constitute a major reason why the state should continue, and continually increase, its enormous grants to Roman Catholic schools. For these are schools which, as we have insisted already, are established and maintained as separate institutions precisely and only for the purpose of Roman Catholic indoctrination (II[b], above.).[12]

The general suggestion that religion is essential to morality can be construed in two ways, either as a proposition about a supposed logically necessary connection, or as a claim about some contingent causal relation. As the former, the contention will presumably be that moral concepts logically presuppose the idea of God (presumably because the moral law is taken to be essentially the positive law of a Divine Legislator) and/or that obedience to the demands and precepts or morality somehow does not make sense unless God provides for suitable rewards and punishments for, respectively, compliance and defiance.

To the idea that the moral law is essentially the positive law of a Divine Legislator the most direct and decisive reply is that, on the contrary, it actually is of the essence of morality that it must always make sense to ask of any edict of positive law (the putative positive law of any supposed God not excluded) the further and different question: 'Yes, I know that it is the law. But is it right? Is it a good law?' The different idea that morality somehow can not make sense unless there are rewards and punishments no doubt arises partly from the same mistaken equation of morality with a (rather special) system of positive law. But partly too it arises from a gross confusion of morality with prudence: while prudence cannot dictate any course which conflicts with my own long-term self-interest, morality may; and, notoriously, often does.[13] The

---

[12] See, for instance, Mrs. Margaret Knight's 'Should the State back Religious Education?', in *New Society* for July 21st, 1966.

[13] See, for instance, my 'Must Morality Pay?', in *The Listener* for October 13th, 1966.

conventional wisdom which assumes that morality logically presupposes the idea of God thus exposes itself to the charge of just not knowing what morality is.

(e) Earlier in the present part (II[a] and [b] above) we drew out some general conclusions about the presumptive wrongness of indoctrination; and then applied these to what is in Britain the most important particular case -- religious indoctrination, above all that effected in the Roman Catholic schools. We then proceeded in the next two sections (II[c] and [d]) to consider and dismiss the two sorts of attempt which might be made to defeat this presumption. The upshot therefore seems to be that such indoctrination is not merely presumptively but also categorically wrong. Hence we cannot allow that parents have any moral right to so indoctrinate their children: those who do this or arrange to have this done are doing something which (however pure their intentions and however clear their consciences) is in fact morally wrong. And furthermore, though it might be as wrong as it would certainly be imprudent for the state to try to prevent parents making private arrangements for the indoctrination of their children, it must also follow that the state can have neither a moral duty nor even a moral right either to subsidize such efforts from public funds or in any other way to give positive support to the indoctrinators. It would be elegant and apt to end there, with a final recapitulation of clear-cut conclusions. Unfortunately experience teaches that the protagonists of indoctrination, and particularly Roman Catholics, when confronted with objections such as we have presented, usually respond by accusing their opponents of being, whether openly or covertly, simply advocates of some rival brand of indoctrination.[14] Really it ought not to be difficult to appreciate the difference between: on the one hand, going all out to persuade children that (say) Roman Catholicism is true, or going all out to persuade them that it is false; and, on the other hand, presenting these or other disputatious doctrines to children as disputatious, as issues, that is, about which equally well-informed, honourable, and reasonable men do sincerely disagree, and hence as issues about which they will in due course need to make up their own minds.

Both of the first two alternatives are kinds of indoctrination; and as such I (along with most British humanists) reject both as morally wrong. The second option is an eschewal of all indoctrination; and it is this course which I am

---

[14] See, for instance, the correspondence following Mrs. Knight's article in *New Society* for July 28th, 1966 and August 4th, 1966. In the U.S.A., where state subsidization of parochial schools is constitutionally forbidden, not only Roman Catholics but also enthusiastic Protestant Christians customarily complain that the public schools indoctrinate their pupils with the ideology of scientific humanism.

advocating, and which my wife and I try to follow in our own home with our own children. (As one result our five-year-old daughter recently announced: 'Mummy and Daddy don't believe in God, but Granny and I do; and that's all right!').

The difficulty which so many Roman Catholics seem to find in grasping this surely quite easy distinction, and in appreciating that it refers to a vital difference, may be instructively, and at the time of writing topically, compared with the apparent inability, commonly displayed in the same quarter, to recognize that the Abortion Law Reform Association is working to relax a law which at present (almost always) forbids abortion, not to impose another which would make it (even sometimes) compulsory; and hence the apparent inability to see that all talk of compelling Roman Catholic doctors, mothers-to-be, and so on to act against their consciences is altogether beside the point. It would, I'm afraid, be more charitable than realistic to refuse to recognize in all this any element of unscrupulous and calculating misrepresentation. But another and much larger part of the explanation surely lies in other damaging facts: that an authoritarian Roman Catholic upbringing does little to make the essential concept of a liberal and 'open society' familiar;[15] and hence that Roman Catholics are apt to attribute to others their own zeals, both to indoctrinate the young with favoured doctrines and to enforce their own particular morality with the sanctions of the criminal law.

---

[15]   K. R. Popper *The Open Society and its Enemies*, Routledge and Kegan Paul, 1945, especially Vol. I.

CHAPTER 5

LOCKE AND THE PROBLEM OF PERSONAL IDENTITY
(1951)

I. PREAMBLE

This paper attempts to do three main things. First, it outlines Locke's contribution to the discussion of the problem of personal identity, that is, the philosophical problem of what is meant by the expression 'same person'. Second, it attacks Locke's proposed solution, showing that it is quite irreparably wrong. Third, it enquires how Locke was misled into offering this mistaken yet perennially seductive answer.

II. LOCKE'S CONTRIBUTION

Locke's contribution to the discussion was fourfold. First, he saw the importance of the problem. Second, he realized that the puzzle cases, the "strange suppositions," were relevant. Third, he maintained that 'same' had a different meaning when applied to the noun 'person' from its meaning in other applications. And, fourth, he offered his own answer to the main question of the meaning of 'same person'.

1. Locke saw the importance of the problem. It is important because, "In this *personal identity* is founded all the right and justice of reward and

61

punishment" (*Essay*, II, XXVII, 18).[1] That is to say, it is never fair to blame nor just to punish the prisoner in the dock for murdering his bride in her bath unless the prisoner is the same person as he who did the deed. The same is equally true of the ascription of responsibility at the Last Judgment. Furthermore and even more fundamentally, as Locke clearly saw but never so clearly stated, all questions of survival, preexistence, and immortality are questions of personal identity. The question 'Is Cesare Borgia still alive, surviving bodily death?' is equivalent to 'Is there a person now alive, surviving bodily death, who is the same person as Cesare Borgia?'

But it might still be argued (and certainly would be argued, by those numerous contemporary philosophers who pray, with the Trinity mathematicians, that their subject may never be of any use to anybody) that all that has been proved is that some important questions are or involve questions of personal identity, and that it has not been shown that these questions demand a solution of the philosophical problem of personal identity. Perhaps psychical research can proceed without benefit of any philosophical analysis of 'same person' just as many other sciences proceed satisfactorily with the study of so-and-sos without feeling handicapped by the lack of philosophical analyses of the expression 'so-and-sos'. This analogy is misleading here. For it is precisely the cases studied by psychical researchers and parapsychologists which raise both in them and in everyone who reads of their work exactly those questions of meaning which it is the proper business of analytical philosophy to answer.

When we are presented with stories like that of the 'Watseka Wonder', recorded by William James in Chapter X of *The Principles of Psychology*, we ask whether the patient Lurancy Vennum really was or became the same person as Mary Roff. Someone then is bound to ask what we mean by 'same person', for this is pre-eminently the sort of question where 'It all depends what you mean'. Or take an example from Locke: "I once met with one, who was persuaded that his had been the *soul* of Socrates (how reasonably I will not dispute; this I know, that in the post he filled, which was no inconsiderable one, he passed for a very rational man, and the press has shown that he wanted not parts or learning; . . ." (*Essay*, II, XXVII, 14: italics original). Perhaps this was

---

[1] [Editor's note: Although Flew doesn't identify the particular version of Locke's masterpiece, a good version is P. H. Nidditch (ed.), *An Essay Concerning Human Understanding*, Clarendon, 1975.]

a case which set Locke himself enquiring about personal identity. But for us it is sufficient if we have shown that the puzzle cases which are so characteristic of certain investigations inevitably and rightly raise philosophical questions about the meaning of 'same person'.

2. Locke seems to have been the first to appreciate the relevance of such puzzle cases. They present a challenge. Any solution to the problem must be able to do one of two things. Either it must consist in some sort of definition or set of rules which will enable us to deal with all possible puzzles; either by telling us that 'same person' is or is not correctly applicable; or by hinting to us what further factual information we require before we can know. Or else the solution must explain why the questions raised by the puzzle cases cannot be so definitively answered. Locke himself chose the first alternative, and answered all the puzzles he had invented in the light of his talismanic definition. For instance, he tells us what would decide the puzzle of the man who claimed to have the same soul as Socrates (*Essay*, II, XXVII, 19).

3. Locke maintained that 'same' is systematically ambiguous: "It is not therefore unity of substance that comprehends all sorts of identity or will determine it in every case; but to conceive and judge of it aright, we must consider what idea the word it is applied to stands for" (Essay, II, XXVII, 8). It would not be relevant to discuss this general claim. It is enough to show that Locke is right at least in so far as he is maintaining that there are special and peculiar problems about 'same' as applied to persons. And this can be seen to be the case by the example of Hume, who thought he could solve the problem of the identity of things, but confessed himself completely at a loss as to "the nature of the bond which unites a person."

4. Locke proposed a solution to the philosophical problem. It is that X at time two is the same person as Y at time one if and only if X and Y are both persons and X can remember at time two (his doing) what Y did, or felt, or what have you, at time one. The parenthetical 'his doing' has to go in since, as Professor Bernard Williams has pointed out, "We constantly say things like 'I remember my brother joining the army' without implying that I and my brother are the same person";[2] though it is worth stressing, as Williams does not, that all such utterances do still carry an implicit personal identity claim about the speaker -- the claim that he was himself around and acquiring the information at the time in question. Certainly by making this insertion our reformulation becomes even more obviously exposed to "Butler's famous objection that

---

[2] B. A. O. Williams, 'Personal Identity and Individuation' in *Proceedings of the Aristotelian Society* 1956-57, p. 233. The objection itself is considered more fully in III (1), below.

memory, so far from constituting personal identity, presupposed it." Yet this is not a fault in the reformulation, considered as a representation of Locke's position. For that position actually is wide open to that objection. It is not, as Williams seems to be suggesting, only our present belated insertion which lends colour to it.

A person is for Locke "a thinking intelligent being, that has reason and reflection, and can consider itself as itself, the same thinking thing, in different times and places" (*Essay*, II, XXVII, 11). This is distinguished from the idea of man since, "ingenious observation [*sic!*] puts it past doubt," that "the idea in our minds, of which the sound *man* in our mouths is the sign, is nothing else but of an animal of such a certain form" (*Essay*, II, XXVII, 9: italics supplied); although a very little later we are told that the same idea consists "in most people's sense" of the idea of "a body, so and so shaped, joined to" that of "*a thinking or rational being*" (*Essay*, II, XXVII. 10: italics supplied).

Locke's proposed solution, in his own words, is that: "That with which the consciousness of this present thinking thing *can* join itself, makes the same person, and is one self with it, and with nothing else; and so attributes to itself and owns all the actions of that thing, as its own, as far as that consciousness reaches, and no further; as everyone who reflects will perceive" (*Essay*, II, XXVII, 17: italics original). One must here point out that the word 'consciousness' is not used by Locke clearly and consistently. Sometimes it seems to mean self-conscious, in the tricky and curious sense in which to say that someone is self-conscious is not to say that he is embarrassed. For instance, we read that "a being that . . . can consider itself as itself . . . does so only by that consciousness which is inseparable from thinking . . ." (*Essay*, II, XXVII, 11). Sometimes it seems to be more straightforwardly the consciousness which is the opposite of anaesthesia: for instance, when 'self' is defined as "a conscious thinking thing . . . which is sensible or conscious of pleasure or pain, capable of happiness or misery . . ." (*Essay*, II. XXVII, 17). But in his main statements of his position 'consciousness' is simply equivalent to 'memory', as can be seen from the words, "Could we suppose any spirit wholly stripped of all its memory or consciousness of past actions; as we find our minds always are of a great part of ours, and sometimes of them all . . ." (*Essay*, II, XXVII, 25). In the interests of both clarity and brevity we have used 'remember' instead of 'be conscious of' in our restatements of Locke's central thesis.

III. OBJECTIONS TO LOCKE'S SOLUTION

There are two lines of attack.

1. The first and simpler was classically taken by Bishop Butler in his dissertation *Of Personal Identity*: "And one should really think it self-evident, that consciousness of personal identity presupposes, and therefore cannot constitute, personal identity; any more than knowledge, in any other case, can constitute truth, which it presupposes" (§ 3).[3] It is absurd to say that 'he is the same person' means that 'he can remember that he is the same person'. The absurdity is usually slightly masked, since expressions such as 'I remember doing, feeling, seeing something' do not refer explicitly to the fact that what is remembered is that the speaker is the same person as did, felt, or saw whatever it was.

2. The second line of attack is much more intricate, demanding very careful generalship. The crux is that Locke's criterion is at the same time both too strict in blackballing and too lenient in admitting candidates. Often his definition would not allow us to apply the expression 'same person', where we certainly should think it properly applicable; whereas in other cases Locke's ruling would be that it did apply, when we should certainly judge it not correctly applicable.

Before developing this second attack two distinctions have to be made. Two of the terms in Locke's definition are relevantly ambiguous. 'Can' may be either 'can as a matter of fact' (hereafter referred to as 'can [factual]') or it may be 'can without self-contradiction be said to' (hereafter referred to as 'can [logical]'). There is also a more subtle ambiguity in 'remember', which is best brought out by symbolic examples. 'I know *p*' entails '*p*', whereas 'He said that he knew *p*, and he was not lying' does not entail '*p*'. Similarly, 'I remember *p*' entails '*p*', but 'He said that he remembered *p*, and he was not lying' does not entail '*p*'. For, just as it is possible to be honestly mistaken in a claim to know something, so it is possible to be honestly mistaken in making a claim to remember something. When someone challenges a knowledge claim or a memory claim he is not necessarily, or even usually, challenging the claimant's integrity. He is much more likely to be merely questioning the truth of the proposition said to be known or remembered. And, of course, if the proposition is in fact false this is sufficient to defeat the claim really to know or truly to remember. (Another possibility, mentioned only to be dismissed as here irrelevant, is that the critic is either challenging the adequacy of the grounds available to support the knowledge claim or challenging the implicit claim to have been in the past in a position which qualifies remembering now.) We have, therefore, to distinguish between genuine remembering, which necessarily

---

[3] *Works*, W. E. Gladstone (ed.), Oxford University Press, 1897.

involves the truth of the proposition said to be remembered, and making honest memory claims, which does not.

It is now time and possible to ring the changes on those alternative interpretations of 'can' and 'remember'.

(a) First, taking 'can' as logical and 'remember' as entailing the truth of what is remembered, Locke's definition could be made into a necessary truth, albeit a futile necessary truth. For it is manifestly true, though not an helpful definition of 'same person', that X at time two is the same person as Y at time one if and only if X and Y are both persons and X can (logically) remember at time two (his doing) what Y did, or what have you, at time one. It is manifestly true since for it to be genuine memory the person remembering must necessarily be the same person as the person whose experience or activity he claims to be remembering as his own. On this interpretation what we have is of course not open to attack on the ground that it is too exclusive or too inclusive, only that it is an otiose only too truism.

(b) Second, taking 'remember' in the same way as referring to genuine remembering and 'can' as 'can (factual)', Locke's definition is open to two objections. First, it excludes too much; for we often and rightly want to say that we must have done something or other though we cannot for the life of us remember doing it. We are even prepared to accept full responsibility for such forgotten actions, at any rate provided that they are not too important. Even if they are important, and even if we want to disown or diminish our moral or legal responsibility for them, we are prepared to concede that we are the same persons as did them, unless, mistakenly, we think that personal identity is not merely the necessary but also the sufficient condition of full moral and legal responsibility.

The second objection to the second interpretation is the famous paradox, The Case of the Gallant Officer. This objection seems to have been made first, but in a monochrome version, by Berkeley in the eighth section of *Alciphron* VII. Later it was reproduced by Reid in glorious Technicolor: "Suppose a brave officer to have been flogged when a boy at school, for robbing an orchard, to have taken a standard from the enemy in his first campaign, and also to have been made a general in advanced life."[4] Then, if the young officer could remember the flogging, and the general could remember taking the standard but not being flogged as a boy, on Locke's principles we should have to say that the general both is and is not the same person as the orchard robber. He is not the same (because he cannot now remember the robbery), and yet he is the

---

[4]   *Essays on the Intellectual Powers of Man*, A. D. Woozley (ed.), Macmillan, 1941, 111, 6.

same (because he is the same as the young officer who was in turn the same as the boy thief).

(c) The third possibility is to take 'can' as 'can (logical)' and 'remember' as involving only the making of an honest memory claim. The objection to this is that it will let too much in. This point too was, it seems, first made by Berkeley in the private *Philosophical Commentaries*: "Wherein consists identity of person? Not in actual consciousness; for then I'm not the same person I was this day twelvemonth, but while I think of what I then did. Not in potential; for then all persons may be the same, for aught we know. *Mem*: story of Mr. Deering's aunt. Two sorts of potential consciousness -- natural and preternatural. In the last section but one I mean the latter."[5]

It is surely our present point which Berkeley is making since his preternatural potential consciousness is obviously equivalent to ability to remember in the present interpretations of 'can' and 'remember'. No one seems able to provide any informative gloss on his note: "*Mem*: story of Mr. Deering's aunt." But presumably Berkeley is thinking of something which we should count as a puzzle case, and it looks as if he (unlike Locke's other early critics) appreciated the relevance of such cases.

(d) The fourth possible combination, that of 'can' as 'can (factual)' with 'remember' as involving only the making of an honest memory claim, yields an interpretation open to all three objections made against the thesis in interpretations two and three. First, it leaves too much out, ignoring amnesia. Second, it lets too much in, ignoring paramnesia. Third it is internally inconsistent, being exposed to the paradox of The Case of the Gallant Officer. Since people seem more familiar with amnesia than with paramnesia it is just worth remarking that paramnesia is not just a logical possibility but a real phenomenon. The stock and pathetic example is the British King George IV, who in his declining and demented years 'remembered' his dashing leadership at the Battle of Waterloo; notwithstanding that only a devoutly Lockean, or an unscrupulously flattering, courtier could have pretended that the King must therefore have been present on that decisive field. Vulgar cases are provided daily by those who press forward to claim sincerely but without factual foundation the discredit for committing the latest newsy murder.

3. This completes our direct case against Locke's proposed solution of the main philosophical problem. But here, as in the political trials in less happier lands, the direct case can be rounded off with a sort of confession. For despite

---

[5] *Works*, A. A. Luce & T. E. Jessop (ed.), Nelson and Sons, 1948-57, Vol. 1, p. 6. Entries 200-2: spelling and punctuation slightly modified.

his insistence that "the same consciousness being preserved, whether in the same or different substances, the personal identity is preserved" Locke is nevertheless, reasonably but inconsistently, anxious lest "one intellectual substance may not have represented to *it*, as done by itself, what it never did, and was perhaps done by some other agent . . ." (*Essay*, II, XXVII, 13: italics original).

Locke's anxiety is indeed very reasonable, and as F. H. Bradley said in a slightly different connection: "It may help us to perceive, what was evident before, that a self is not thought to be the same because of bare memory, but only so when the memory is considered not to be defective."[6] But, though reasonable, Locke's anxiety is entirely inconsistent with his official account of personal identity, which requires him to deny that there can (logical) be honest but falsidical memory claims. For if 'being the same person as did that' *means* 'being a person able to remember (his) doing, or being able to be conscious of (his) doing, that' then you cannot consistently say that a person may both be able to remember doing and yet not actually have done some particular thing. (Or, rather, to be absolutely strict, this can be made consistent only by interpreting 'remember' to refer exclusively to genuine veridical memory; thus reducing this whole account of personal identity to vacuity.)

In his desperation Locke falls on his knees: "And that it never is so, will by us, till we have clearer views of the nature of thinking substances, be best resolved in the goodness of God; who as far as the happiness or misery of any of his sensible creatures is concerned will not, by a fatal error of theirs, transfer from one to another that consciousness which draws reward or punishment with it" (*Essay*, II, XXVII, 13). But the assistance for which Locke supplicates is beyond the resources even of Omnipotence. For on Locke's view there could be no sense in his own fear that people might lose or escape their deserts because they remembered doing what they had not in fact done: if anyone can remember doing something then necessarily, according to Locke's account, he is in fact the same person as did that deed. By making this desperate appeal, Locke both tacitly confesses the inadequacy of his own account of personal identity and provides one more example of a phenomenon already all too familiar to the student of religious apologetic -- the hope that the sheer physical power of a postulated God can make contradictions consistent or by itself make utterances to which no sense has been given sensible.

---

[6] *Appearance and Reality*, Swan Sonnenschein, 1893, p. 85.

IV. SOURCES OF TROUBLE

The question now arises how Locke managed to get himself into this confused and catastrophic position. This is a question of very much more than merely antiquarian interest, since in one form or another both that position itself and the mistakes which misled Locke into it seem to have a perennial appeal. One first part of the answer lies in those possibilities of confusion about memory, which we have examined already. (See III, especially III[2], above.)

Second, as we have also seen, Locke uses the word 'conscious' and its associates in several ways. He seems to slide from his definition of 'person' as "a thinking intelligent being, that . . . can consider itself as itself, the same thinking thing, in different times and places," by way of talk of "that consciousness which is inseparable from thinking, and as it seems to me, essential to it," to the eventual conclusion that "and as far as this consciousness can be extended backwards to any past action or thought, so far reaches the identity of that person" (*Essay*, II, XXVII, 11). Here we seem in the first passage to be dealing with the sort of consciousness of self which is not the self-consciousness of embarrassment, in the second with that consciousness which is contrasted with complete unconsciousness, and in the concluding third with a consciousness which is identified with memory.

Third, Locke seems sometimes (like many others since) to have confused the epistemological questions, 'How can we know, what good evidence can we have for, propositions about personal identity' with the inseparable but not identical enquiry, 'What do such propositions mean?' It is the latter which he is supposed to be pursuing. But what he offers would provide a partial answer to the former. Thus when he tells us that on the "Great Day" everyone will "receive his doom, his conscience accusing or excusing him," or that if he could remember "Noah's flood" as clearly as last winter's "overflowing of the Thames" he could no more doubt "that he was the same *self*" who saw both floods, he is clearly answering a question of the first sort; or perhaps one of the subtly but importantly different "How can we convince ourselves" sort (*Essay*, II, XXVII, 22 and 16). But neither sort of question can be identified with that to which Locke's main problem belongs: "in this doctrine not only is consciousness confounded with memory but, which is still more strange, personal identity is confounded with the evidence which we have of our personal identity."[7]

Fourth, as we have seen, Locke defined 'person' as "a thinking intelligent being, that has reason and reflection, and can consider itself as itself, the same thinking thing, in different times and places." Ignoring the possible danger of circularity which lurks in this talk of 'the same thinking thing', the more radical objection must be made that this definition misses the ordinary meaning and use of the term 'person'. We learn the word 'people' by being shown people, by meeting them and shaking hands with them. They may be intelligent or unintelligent, introspective or extraverted, black, white, red, or brown, but what they cannot be is disembodied or in the shape of elephants. Locke's definition would make it a contingent truth about people that some or all of them are either embodied in, or are of, human form. But in the ordinary use of the word 'people', we do actually meet people and shake hands with them; we do not meet the fleshy houses in which they are living or the containers in which they are kept. Nor is it logically possible for cougars (or parrots!) to be people. It is in short a necessary truth that people are of human shapes and sizes; and, not a contingent fact that some or all people inhabit human bodies or are of human form.

This is not to say that all talk of disembodied people (or even parrot people) must always and necessarily be self-contradictory. It may perhaps be that the word 'people' is being used in a radically unusual sense by those who wish to point out an analogy between the behaviour of people and some situations in which no people are present. This is a perfectly respectable method of adding to our language, a method which only becomes dangerous when it is not understood, when it is thought that 'person' in the new sense has the same meaning, the same logical liaisons, as 'person' in the old, familiar sense. Locke himself admitted that his distinction between 'man', which he used in substantially its ordinary sense, and 'person', which he wants to use in a sense which would allow the possibility of disembodiment or embodiment, in different (or even non-human) bodies, is not made in ordinary language: "I know that, in the ordinary way of speaking, the same person, and the same man stand for one and the same thing" (*Essay*, II, XXVII, 15).

But though Locke did unguardedly admit this, he failed to realize how important this admission was and what its implications are. If you use 'person' in a new sense, in a way other than the ordinary, then you wreck your chances of producing a descriptive analysis of 'same person'. And it was this which, most of the time, Locke has to be construed as trying to do: "we must consider

---

[7] Reid, *op. cit.*, III, 6.

what *person* stands for" he tells us, in introducing his definition of 'person'; and he rounds off his account of the meaning of 'same person' with the comment, "as everyone who reflects will perceive" (*Essay* II, XXVII, 11 and 17).

V. PERSONS, UNLIKE MEN, THOUGHT INCORPOREAL

This attempt to make a fundamental distinction between 'same man' and 'same person' demands investigation. Why does Locke want to do it?

1. First, we can find certain nuances of English idiom which might suggest a distinction of this kind. For instance it would be slightly more natural to use 'man' when referring to physical characteristics and 'person' when referring to psychological ones: Charles Atlas and the Army offer to make a new man of you; the Pelman Institute, or your psychoanalyst, is more likely to promise that you would be an altogether different person after a course of their treatment. But this is the merest nuance, for when Robert Browning wrote:

There they are, my fifty men and women
Naming me my fifty poems finished!

he was dedicating a collection of character sketches. A slightly more promising temptation lies in phrases like 'Our Claude is quite a different person since he went away to school.' As we are quite sure that he is really the same boy, the same person, as in fact we should only say someone was quite a different person (in this sense) if we were sure he was the same person (in the ordinary sense), we may become inclined to make our point by saying that the same man may or may not be the same person.

Then again there are in our language, and in many others, the embedded traces of what was once a scientific hypothesis, the hypothesis of possession. This degenerated into a mere alternative idiom through the addition of so many qualifications ('But it is an *invisible* spirit', and so on) that it no longer risked falsification. It thus ceased to be an hypothesis at all. Instead of saying, 'He drove wildly', or 'Why on earth did he do it?' we can say 'He drove like a man possessed' or 'Whatever possessed him to do it?' And this sometime hypothesis and present dead metaphor has even now perhaps not altogether lost its seductive power. Certainly it had not when Locke wrote. For, noticing that we do not punish "the mad man for the sober man's actions" he thought that this, "is somewhat explained by our way of speaking in English when we say such a one is 'not himself', or is 'beside himself': in which phrases it is insinuated, as if those who now, or at least first used them, thought that self was changed;

the self-same person was no longer in that man" (*Essay*, II. XXVII, 20).

2. This suggests a second reason for Locke's distinction between a man and a person. Locke seems to have assumed that there is one single necessary and sufficient condition of moral and legal responsibility. But he notices cases where he does not want to blame or punish someone who in some sense seems to have been the agent who did the wrong or criminal action. For instance, he does not want a madman to be punished for what he did before he went mad; and he does not want to blame people for actions which they simply cannot remember having done. So then, instead of saying that the person in question did do whatever it was but he is not to be held responsible, or at least not fully responsible, because he is now amnesic or insane, Locke distinguishes the man from the person, announcing that the word 'person' is a "forensic term, appropriating actions and their merit" (*Essay*, II, XXVII, 26). This opens up for him the possibility of saying in some troubling case that blame or punishment would be here improper because we have before us only the same man and not the same person as did the deed.

3. The third basis for Locke's distinction between the man and the person was his Platonic-Cartesian conviction that people essentially are incorporeal spirits, and that human bodies in fact are controlled by internal shadow beings in ways similar to, but much less intelligible than, that in which ships are directed by their captains or vehicles by their drivers: "For I presume it is not the idea of a thinking or rational being alone that makes the *idea of man* in most people's sense: but of a body so and so shaped joined to it . . ."; but, though the idea of man thus involves the body as well, the essential person is the thinking or rational being which is not necessarily of human shape or even corporeal (*Essay*, II, XXVII, 10: italics original). Or, again, "if the identity of soul alone makes the same man; and there be nothing in the nature of matter why the same individual spirit may not be united to different bodies, it will be possible that . . . men living in distant ages . . . may have been the same man: which way of speaking must be from a very strange use of the word *man*, applied to an idea out of which body and shape are excluded" (*Essay*, II, XXVII, 7: italics supplied). Which is all very well, but still takes for granted that people are souls; which, presumably, conceivably could thus transmigrate.

This is not the place either fully to characterize or generally to assail the Platonic-Cartesian view of man.[8] But it is worthwhile to devote some space to showing how fundamental and how important this view was for Locke, and

---

[8] For such more thorough treatment see G. Ryle, *The Concept of Mind*, Hutchinson, 1949, perhaps comparing A. G. N. Flew (ed.), *Body, Mind, and Death*, Collier, 1964.

how little inclined he was seriously to question it. For it is a view presupposed by his whole account of personal identity; while the impossibility of that account should itself in turn be seen as one of the most powerful objections against that view of the nature of man.[9]

Locke's first concern in the *Essay* is to prove that we have no surreptitious access to black-market ideas, but are properly confined to getting our supplies through the official channels of post-natal waking experience. He claims at one point: "We know certainly, by experience, that we *sometimes* think; and thence draw this infallible consequence -- that there is something in us which has the power to think" (*Essay*, II, I, 10: italics original). The conclusion of this lamentable argument opens up precisely the possibility which Locke is most concerned to close. For the word 'thinking' is being used in the Cartesian sense, in which to think is to have any sort of conscious experience. Now, if our thinking is done by some possibly incorporeal internal thinking thing, then it becomes natural to ask whether it can do any thinking without our knowledge; whether perhaps it may not sometimes slip out to have some experiences on its own, maybe taking up station for the purpose inside some alien body. All of which suggestions, colourfully presented as the hypothetical doings of Socrates, Castor, Pollux or their several souls are then duly considered by Locke (II, XXVII, 13-15).

Yet the 'infallible consequence' which here sets off these bizarre speculations is not validly drawn. For though we do undoubtedly know that 'we sometimes think' this has not the slightest tendency to show that this thinking is done by 'something in us which has the power to think'. Quite the reverse. The argument derives what little plausibility it has from the tacit assumption that everything we do is done with some special organ. But this is false. We write with our hands, certainly. But we do not decide, or sleep, or fret with special organs of deciding, sleeping, or fretting. It is the same with thinking, both in the ordinary and in the wide Cartesian sense. Thinking, like sleeping and deciding, is an 'affection of the whole man'. It would be pleasant to believe that Locke was beginning to realize this when he wrote: "But whether sleeping without dreaming be not an affection of the whole man, mind as well as body, may be worth a waking man's consideration . . ." (*Essay*, II, I, 11).

4. One aspect of the Platonic-Cartesian view of man deserves special separate mention. It is that it provides something which may plausibly be held both to survive a man's death and to be accountable, on the 'Great Day', for

---

[9] Compare A. M. Quinton, 'The Soul', *The Journal of Philosophy*, 1962, and A. G. N. Flew '"The Soul" of Mr. A. M. Quinton,' *The Journal of Philosophy*, 1963.

his deeds upon earth. Now to be justly accountable, here or hereafter, for a murder you have to be the same person as the villain who did the murder: that is the necessary, though by no means the sufficient, condition of full responsibility. But if you attach the customary sense to 'person', this necessary condition can never be satisfied by anyone who died before the 'Great Day'. For he will simply not exist to be to any degree responsible. He will have died and been buried. Nor can the situation be saved merely by producing an indistinguishable person to stand his trial. For "one thing cannot have two beginnings of existence, nor two things one beginning . . . That, therefore, that had one beginning, is the same thing; and that which had a different beginning in time and place from that, is not the same, but diverse" (*Essay*, II, XXVII, 1).

Locke therefore, committed as he was to beliefs both in immortality and in a just reckoning on 'that Great Day', had a very strong reason (or perhaps it should be called a motive) for insisting that 'person' unlike 'man' may refer to something incorporeal. For while it is immediately obvious that a person in the everyday sense, a person such as we can meet face to face in the streets, (logically) cannot survive bodily death and dissolution, it may perhaps seem at first sight conceivable that a person, in the sense of a series of experiences linked together in some subtle gap-indifferent way, or in the sense of a 'thing which is sensible or conscious of pleasure and pain, capable of happiness or misery', might survive, and be the bearer of responsibility for what that same person (in a new and rather peculiar sense) did 'in the body'. There are appalling difficulties in the logic of such new senses of 'person' and 'same person', which we do not have to discuss here.[10]

Yet it is both relevant and worthwhile to draw attention to Locke's achievement in uncovering some of these difficulties. He himself did not see clearly what, or how great, or how numerous they are. This was partly because he thought he was defining the ordinary sense of 'person'. He therefore saw no difficulty in making a 'disembodied person' (that is a person in some new sense) the same as (and thus possibly accountable for the actions of) some person who had lived at a previous date (some person, that is, in the old sense). Partly again it was because, since he thought he had successfully found in memory what Hume called the "uniting principle, which constitutes a person," he could scarcely be expected simultaneously to realize that memory can only discover and not constitute personal identity (in any sense of 'person'). Partly, finally, it was for the simple reason that this territory Locke had entered was too vast and too difficult for any single explorer to open up immediately.

---

[10]   But see Quinton and Flew, *ibid.*

Locke had to struggle to his insights through a rank growth of baffling terms, such as, 'immaterial substances', 'selves', 'thinking substances', 'rational souls'. The insights which he did achieve are the more remarkable inasmuch as a critic of the calibre of Bishop Butler failed to see that the subject presented difficulties, complaining of the "strange perplexities" that had been raised: "Whether we are to live in a future state, as it is the most important question which can possibly be asked, so it is the most intelligible one which can be expressed in language" (§ 1). Locke, had he lived to read the dissertation *Of Personal Identity*, would have agreed about the supreme importance of the question. But he might, very reasonably, have asked for some solution of those "strange perplexities" of the puzzle cases before being prepared to concede that things really were all quite so straightforward as Butler thought.

5. A fifth source of Locke's unhappy analysis of personal identity lies in his un-Lockean assumption that we can find a definition such that, granted we are provided with all the relevant factual data, we shall be able to say in every actual or imaginable case whether or not the expression 'same person' can correctly be applied. This assumption is mistaken.

(a) Doubt may be thrown upon it in three ways. First, it is unsettling to see the troubles of those who have tried to fulfill such a requirement. Locke offered one such candidate definition, with the unfortunate results already examined. Berkeley, more prudently, refrained deliberately from the attempt. In the *Philosophical Commentaries* he reminds himself "carefully to omit defining of Person, or making much mention of it" (Entry 713). This good advice he resolutely follows throughout his published works, with the significant exception of a passage in the eighth section of Book VII of the *Alciphron*. There he challenges the minute philosophers to, "untie the knots and answer the questions which may be raised even about human personal identity" before requiring "a clear and distinct idea of *person* in relation to the Trinity": a very typical piece of Berkeleian intellectual judo.

(b) Second, this assumption overlooks the possibilities of vagueness, of the marginal cases in which we do not quite know where to draw the line. Most words referring to physical objects are vague in some direction: somewhere there is an undemarcated frontier: somewhere there is a no man's land of indeterminacy: often there is a complete encircling penumbra of perplexity. And this is and must be so because nature has no natural kinds: "God made the spectrum, man makes the pigeonholes." It was Locke himself who launched attack after attack on the superstitions of real essences and natural kinds. It is he himself who points again and again to the specimens which will not fit properly into any available category. It is he who points to the vagueness even of the term 'man'. It is he who draws attention to the changelings who are "something between a man and a beast," he too who tells us the story of the Abbot Malotru who was so monstrous at his birth that "he was baptized and declared a man provisionally." Again it is Locke who insists that "There are creatures . . . that, with language and reason and a shape in other things agreeing with ours, have hairy tails; others where the males have no beards, and others where the females have" (*Essay*, IV, IV, 13 and III, VI, 26 and 22).

Nevertheless, despite all this, Locke never seems to entertain the possibility that 'person', 'rational being', 'soul', 'Immaterial spirit', 'self', and the rest of the words and expressions alleged to refer to the putative and elusive internal population of the body, may be affected in the same way. This failure shows up most strikingly when he argues that no external shape is an infallible sign that there is a rational soul inside: "Where now (I ask) shall be the just measure; which is the utmost bounds of that shape which carries with it a rational soul?" He points out once again "all the several degrees of mixture of the likeness of a man or a brute," and demands: "What sort of outside is the certain sign that there is or is not such an inhabitant within?" Finally he complains: "we talk at random of *man*; and shall always, I fear, do so, as long as we give ourselves up to certain sounds, and the imaginations of settled and fixed species in nature, we know not what . . . . So necessary is it to quit the common notion of species and essences, if we will truly look into the nature of things . . . ." (*Essay*, IV, IV, 16). Yet he himself is all the while assuming as it were a real essence of the rational souls, a fixed species or natural kind of the people who inhabit some, though we cannot always tell which, of these men and near men whom we meet.

(c) Third, since our ordinary language, and the concepts of ordinary language, have been evolved or introduced to deal with the situations which are ordinarily met with, and not with the extraordinary, we may reasonably expect some failures of adaptation when new and unexpected situations arise. And these do in fact occur. The old conceptual machinery breaks down. The old terminological tools fail to cope with the new tasks. These breakdowns are different from the cases in which indecision arises from the vagueness of a term. 'Ship' is perhaps a vague term in that a whole spectrum of similarity stretches between things which are certainly ships, via the things which provoke linguistic hesitation, to other things which are undoubtedly boats. But when a court has to decide whether the word 'ship' in a statute covers flying boats, the difficulty arises: not so much from the vagueness of the term 'ship' (that would imply that the drafting of the statute was bad and could perfectly well have been improved); but from what has been called its open-texture. The concept which we have has in fact evolved to cover the situations that have arisen before or were thought likely to arise, and not the situations which have not arisen and could not have been foreseen. Vagueness could have been removed by prescribing that nothing under so many tons was to count as a ship within the meaning of the act: "To remove vagueness is to outline the penumbra of a shadow. The line is there after we have drawn it and not before." But it is not possible "to define a concept like *gold* with absolute precision, i.e. in such a way that every nook and cranny is blocked against the entry of doubt. That is what is meant by '*open texture*' of a concept."[11] It is this open texture much more than any actual vagueness in use which prevents the definition of 'person'.

By imagining, fully two centuries before the foundation of the Society for Psychical Research, a series of puzzle cases which leave us at a loss as to whether or not to apply the expression 'same person', Locke revealed what he did not himself see, that it is not possible to define the meaning of 'same person' descriptively and at the same time give a definition which will answer all possible problems of application. This is not possible because there is no usage established for many of these unforeseen situations. Therefore no such proper usage can be described. In cases such as Locke produces we can only admit that we don't know what to say: and then perhaps prescribe what is to be the proper usage if such cases do occur or recur. It is not possible to produce even a prescriptive definition which will give absolute security against all possibility of surprise and indecision. Locke produced a definition of 'same person' which enabled him to give an answer to all the puzzle cases which he imagined. Let someone appear who seemed to remember the Noah's flood as clearly and accurately as he remembered last year's overflowing of the Thames. If we accepted Locke's definition, then clearly we could and should say without hesitation that he had been present at Noah's flood: an answer which, assuming that he had been born in this century, would be false. But no prescription can give absolute determinacy. Locke did not, and could not, imagine all the possibilities. Suppose, what is not merely conceivable but imaginable, that a person splits like an amoeba, first into two Siamese twins, then separating into two identical twins. And suppose both twins, call them *A1* and *A2*, can remember all that the original person, call him *A*, could remember before his unfortunate and disruptive experience. On Locke's definition *A1* and *A2* will both be the same person as *A* and yet they will obviously, be different people, just as are identical twins. Clearly we should not know what to say. This

---

[11] F. Waismann, 'Verifiability' in *Logic and Language*, I, Antony Flew (ed.), Blackwell, 1951.

preposterous supposition will serve to show that it is not possible to produce either a descriptive or a prescriptive definition of 'same person' which shall remove every possibility of linguistic perplexity. We can prescribe against vagueness, but then there is always the open texture through which forever threatens the insidious infiltration of the unforeseeable and the unforeseen.

VI. CONCLUSIONS

The search for the talismanic definition which shall solve all possible problems, the search for the real essence of personal identity, was therefore a mistake. Why did Locke make it? It involved, as we have seen, an abandonment of his greatest insight and a betrayal of the glorious revolution he was leading against the superstition of real essences and natural kinds. However, it is just as easy to fail to apply a new discovery consistently as it is to push it to absurd extremes. We smile at the man who tells us: "I'm an atheist now, thank God!" But we all fall into similar inconsistencies. So there is every reason to expect with the notoriously inconsistent Locke what we do in fact find, a failure to see all the implications of, and to apply thoroughly and systematically, his own discoveries.

Then we remember those long struggles that had to be fought, and which still drag on in some intellectual backwoods, before the doctrine of evolution was allowed to include, without reservation, our own species. We remember the bitter rear-guard actions, arguing for a special creation for this one most favoured species. We can see still in Rome the final forlorn hope to save the special creation of souls to inhabit the bodies which have at last been conceded to be the most recent results of the evolutionary process. In the light of all this, it no longer seems surprising that Locke, living two centuries before the famous Victorian battles over the origin of species, failed to take his great insight into the enclosure reserved for the ghostly company of 'rational souls', 'persons', and 'thinking substances'.

Another source of the inability to see that questions may be asked about personal identity to which there can be no true or false answer (until and unless a new decision, which may be wise or unwise, is made about what is to be proper usage) lies in the familiar fact that people often know things about their pasts which they conceal from other people. We tend, being aware of this familiar truth, to assume that all questions about the identity of persons are always wholly factual, susceptible of straight true or false answers, long after we have realized that questions as to whether this is or is not the same thing may sometimes not be so straightforward. We feel that the person in question must himself always know (yes or no) whether he is the same person as the man who broke the bank at Monte Carlo. Even if we cannot discover the answer because he will not tell us or because we do not trust him, even if he protests that he does not know, still we assume that if he could (seem to himself to) remember that would settle the issue definitively.

We are not, obviously, inclined to think that the thing could tell us if it wanted to but we do tend to think that the person could, and, if he did, that would be that: "Wherever a man finds what he calls himself there, I think, another may say is the same person" (*Essay*, II, XXVII, 26). And "should the soul of a prince, carrying with it the consciousness of the prince's past life, enter and inform the body of a cobbler . . . everyone sees he would be the same person with the prince . . . ." (*Essay*, II, XXVII, 15). And so, confident that the subject must always know whether or not he is the same person, just as he always has the last word as to whether or not he is in pain, Locke proceeds to give his disastrous definition of personal identity; quite overlooking the facts of amnesia and paramnesia which show decisively that personal identity is in this respect not like pain. The honest testimony of the subject is not with personal identity as it is with pain the last word. But the fact that it is such very good evidence, combined with the fact that we are all all too familiar with human reticence and deceit misleads us into thinking that it is.

VII. AUTHOR'S POSTSCRIPT (1996)

In its earlier printings the above paper concluded with a summary paragraph. This claimed that it had shown Locke's account of personal identity to be irreparably erroneous, and had indicated five sources of his errors. The final sentence asserted that there had been no intention to tackle the problem itself. This, even if strictly true, was grossly misleading. For once it is appreciated that person words -- the personal pronouns, personal names, words for persons playing particular roles (such as 'official', 'spokesperson', 'president', and so on) -- are words referring to a very special species of creatures of flesh and blood, it surely becomes perfectly obvious what sort of evidence is needed to establish that the prisoner in the dock is the same person as did the deed. Certainly I myself always saw this paper as taking the first step on the road which was to lead to my Gifford Lectures in *The Logic of Mortality* in 1987.[12]

---

[12] Blackwell.

CHAPTER 6

PRIVATE IMAGES AND PUBLIC LANGUAGE
(1961)

Section II of Hume's *Inquiry Concerning Human Understanding* is a revised, smoother, and more persuasive version of the very first Section of the *Treatise*. These Sections contain the statements of what are often taken to be the fundamental principles of Hume's philosophizing. The method of challenge, which they are designed to explain and justify, is in fact applied here only to the idea of necessary connection; and that application both obscures his fundamental negative insight and distorts his investigation of the aetiology of the established error. On the other hand, it is to the presuppositions revealed, both in his formulation of the method and in the arguments presented in its support, that we must trace the sources of the two chief grounds for that all-corroding Pyrrhonian doubt which is always threatening to eat away the basis of the sort of world-outlook which Hume is most concerned to defend. Section II is therefore much more important than its brevity might suggest.

Hume is in effect restating in his own way what were at the time the commonplaces of Locke's new way of ideas, supplementing these with one or two precisifying amendments of his own. In the prefatory 'Epistle to the Reader' of the *Essay Concerning Human Understanding* Locke himself tells us how his master question arose. Deservedly it is an account almost as well known as Descartes' story of his meditations in the room with a stove. Locke was once one of a party of five or six friends "discoursing on a subject very remote from this" when they "found themselves quickly at a stand, by the difficulties that arose on every side. After we had awhile puzzled ourselves, without coming any nearer a resolution of these doubts that perplexed us, it came into my thoughts that we took a wrong course; and before we set

81

ourselves on enquiries of that nature, it was necessary to examine our own abilities, and see what objects our understandings were and were not fitted to deal with." The first move in the right direction is to appreciate that our understanding must be limited by the range of ideas available to us. Thus we cannot make progress in physics without acquiring some mathematical and physical concepts. We cannot gain a grasp of politics so long as we remain unfamiliar with such basic political notions as *coup d'etat, faction, election, taxation, institution,* or *state.* The next move is to argue that we are not born with any innate ideas: every human mind starts, as it were, "white paper, void of all characters, without any ideas." The third move is to enquire what sorts of ideas we do in fact have, and how these could be acquired from human experience; with the corollary that anyone who talks as if he had some idea which he could not have acquired from his experience must be using words without meaning.

By choosing for his book titles which echo that of Locke's *Essay* Hume suggests that he likewise will be concerned with the nature and limits of human understanding; though he also makes it very clear that he intends to give to his findings a more aggressive employment and a sharper cutting edge than would have appealed to Locke. Now in this second Section he presents his own amended version of Locke's new approach, protesting that really "it requires no nice discernment or metaphysical head" to grasp his meaning.

He, too, advances in three stages. First, "we may divide all the perceptions of the mind into two classes or species, which are distinguished by their different degrees of force and vivacity. The less forcible and lively are commonly denominated *thoughts* or *ideas.* The other species wants a name in our language . . ." For these Hume suggests the label *impressions.* "By the term *impression* . . . I mean all our more lively perceptions, when we hear, or see, or feel, or love, or hate, or desire, or will. And impressions are distinguished from ideas, which are the less lively perceptions of which we are conscious when we reflect on any of those sensations or movements . . ."

It might seem that "the thought of man, which not only escapes all human power and authority, but is not even restrained within the limits of nature and reality" is unbounded and unconfined. It might seem that: "What never was as thought or heard of may yet be conceived, nor is anything beyond the power of thought except what implies an absolute contradiction." But apparently there is in fact a further limitation; and with this we come to the second stage. For "though our thought seems to possess this unbounded liberty, we shall find upon a nearer examination that it is really confined within very narrow limits, and that this creative power of the mind amounts to no more than the faculty of compounding, transposing, augmenting, or diminishing the materials afforded us by the senses and experience." The analogy which Hume needs here is that of the kaleidoscope, which unfortunately was invented only in the following century. His point is that the imagination is kaleidoscopic, and not genuinely creative; "or, to express myself in philosophical language, all our ideas (or more feeble perceptions) are copies of our impressions (or more lively ones)."

The third stage consists in drawing a methodological moral: "All ideas, especially abstract ones, are naturally faint and obscure . . . they are apt to be confounded with other resembling ideas." Impressions "on the contrary . . . are strong and vivid . . . nor is it easy to fall into any error or mistake with regard to them. When we entertain, therefore, any suspicion that a philosophical term is employed without any meaning or idea . . . we need but enquire, 'From what impression is that supposed idea derived?'"

The first thing to appreciate is that in Hume's official view ideas always just are mental images. Furthermore, the meanings of words are ideas, ideas again being identified with mental images. From time to time, not surprisingly, he says things which are hard or impossible to square with this official position. Nevertheless, there is no doubt that this is his opinion when he is on guard. In the *Treatise* ideas are identified explicitly with mental images on page one: *impressions* are to include "all our sensations, passions, and emotions"; while *ideas* are "the faint images of these in thinking and reasoning." In the *Inquiry* he is never quite so explicit, but what he does say cannot bear any other interpretation. Thus, he begins this Section: "Everyone will allow that there is a considerable difference between the perceptions of the mind when a man feels the pain of excessive heat . . . and when he afterwards recalls to his memory this sensation, or anticipates it in his imagination. These faculties may mimic or copy the perceptions of the senses, but they can never entirely reach the force or vivacity of the original sentiment." This quotation comes from a discursive and introductory paragraph, and might therefore be discounted. But he insists on the same crucially significant word in his technical formulation: "in philosophical language, all our ideas (or more feeble perceptions) are copies of our impressions (or more lively ones)." "Feeble perceptions" which "mimic or copy" in this way can only be mental images. The identification of meanings with ideas, and hence with mental images, comes out most clearly in the pointing of the methodological moral: when Hume considers that if "we have often employed any term, though without any distinct meaning, we are apt to imagine that it has a determinate idea annexed to it"; or when he entertains the "suspicion that a philosophical term is employed without any meaning or idea."

The upshot is that Hume becomes committed to defending a psychological thesis about the limitations of the capacity to form mental imagery; and to mistaking this for a ground, both for a criterion of the meaningfulness of words, and for a method of clarifying their meanings. Given slight amendment, and considered only as a psychological hypothesis, the thesis is perhaps plausible enough in itself. Yet, as a mere generalization, logically contingent and without any theoretical backing, it could not have the strength to support a challenging criterion of the sort which Hume claims to have supplied. Much more important, such a psychological principle however well supported could have no essential connection with questions about the meanings of words. For the meanings of words are not mental images; the capacity to form mental images is neither a logically necessary nor a logically sufficient condition of understanding the meaning of a term; and to have acquired the concept of something is neither the same thing as, nor even a guarantee of, having learnt to summon up mental images of whatever it may be.

The issues here are as important as they are involved. Hume's position owes much of its appeal to the possibilities of confusing the distinction he was actually making, the proposition which he was in fact maintaining, and the conclusion which he himself wished to rest upon it, with various other distinctions, propositions, and conclusions. Indeed, in expounding his view, Hume employs some phrases and offers some reasons which both suggest and would be more appropriate to other distinctions and propositions. Some of these are not only plausible in themselves but also more suited to support the kind of conclusion he wants than are those to which he is officially committed.[1]

It is convenient to begin the work of disentangling some of these knotted issues, and of examining the fundamental mistake and some of its ramifications, by considering the case Hume presents for his proposition that all ideas originate from impressions. He offers two supporting arguments. "First, when we analyze our thoughts or ideas, however compounded or sublime, we always find that they resolve themselves into such simple ideas as were copied from a precedent feeling or sentiment." This is alleged to apply even in those cases which superficially might appear least amenable to such analysis: thus, "the idea of God, as meaning an infinitely intelligent wise and good Being, arises from reflecting on the operations of our own mind and augmenting, without limit, those qualities of goodness and wisdom."

The choice of this particular example, which is not that given in the *Treatise*, is interesting. The idea of God is one of the two which Descartes in the fourth Part of the *Discourse on Method* offers as falsifying counter examples against the maxim: "Nihil est in intellectu quod non prius fuit in

---

[1] [Editor's note: Some of the text in the original version of this work was omitted at the request of Professor Flew. His suggestions were intended to improve the flow of his text, particularly in places where it was redundant.]

sensu." This is the Scholastic ancestor of Hume's thesis that all our ideas are derived from impressions: "the philosophers of the Schools hold it as a maxim that there is nothing in the understanding which has not first of all been in the senses, in which there is certainly, however, no doubt that the ideas of God and of the soul have never been." By urging that this idea can in fact be derived from the internal operations of our minds Hume goes some part of the way to meet the objection that it cannot be constructed out of purely sensory experience. Descartes also concludes, at the end of the third of his *Meditations,* that "one certainly ought not to find it strange that God, in creating me, placed this idea within me to be like the mark of the workman imprinted on his work." Hume, by implication, disposes of Descartes' argument for this egregious conclusion when later he comes to urge that it is impossible to know a priori that anything either could not, or must necessarily, be the cause of anything else: "If we reason a priori, anything may appear able to produce anything."

In choosing the idea of God as his example to illustrate his first consideration Hume appears momentarily to have forgotten the precise character of the contention which these considerations are advanced to support. For it is peculiarly implausible to suggest that to have this particular concept, that of the God of the theists, is a matter of being able to form some sophisticated construction of mental imagery, however it may have been in the first instance derived. Coming to his second consideration, Hume recovers himself: "If it happen, from a defect of the organ, that a man is not susceptible of any species of sensation, we always find that he is as little susceptible of the correspondent idea. A blind man can form no notion of the colours, a deaf man of sounds. Restore either of them that sense in which he is deficient, by opening this new inlet for his sensations, you also open an inlet for the ideas, and he finds no difficulty in conceiving these objects." Similarly, we have to allow "that other beings may possess many senses of which we can have no conception, because the ideas of them have never been introduced to us in the only manner by which an idea can have access to the mind, to wit, by the actual feeling and sensation."

Now, as a piece of armchair psychology, this might, or might not, be all very well. If Hume had been proposing to leave it at that, it might also have been all very well to dig in, as he does, against all comers: "Those who would assert that this position is not universally true, nor without exception, have only one, and that an easy, method of refuting it; by producing that idea which in their opinion, is not derived from this source. It will then be incumbent on us, if we would maintain our doctrine, to produce the impression (or lively perception) which corresponds to it." This leaves the doctrine a contingent generalization, open to falsification by the production of a recalcitrant negative generalization, open to falsification by the production of a recalcitrant negative instance. But Hume wants also to base a method of challenge on precisely the same proposition, taking the absence of any appropriate antecedent impressions as a sufficient reason for saying of any supposed idea that there really is no such idea: "When we entertain . . . any suspicion that a philosophical term is employed without any meaning or idea . . . we need but enquire, 'From what impression is that supposed idea derived?' And if it be impossible to assign any, this will serve to confirm our suspicion."

This will not do. It is like announcing that all Jews are good business men, supporting this generalization with some more or less relevant evidence, and then dismissing any suggested falsifying counter example on the grounds that, no matter what the appearances to the contrary, the person in question cannot really be a Jew: because, notoriously, all Jews are good business men; which he is not.

This is an intellectual misdemeanour of a common type, for which it is salutary to have some easily remembered nickname. Essentially it consists in first presenting a generalization as a matter of universal but contingent fact, something which could without contradiction be denied (although of course the contention is that it happens to be true); and then refusing to accept as authentic any counter example suggested, and this on the sole ground that, as the original generalization is true, what is offered cannot possibly be a genuine case of whatever it is which would falsify it. Since to do this has the effect of changing what started as a contingent generalization into a pretentious tautology, true in virtue of the conventions for the (mis)use of the words employed in its expression, the move is sometimes spoken of very colloquially as going into a *Conventionalist Sulk.* These conventions of misuse really are arbitrary: something which, contrary to common assumption, is not the case with all conventions. Because the metamorphosis is often marked by the insertion of the words *true* or *real* to qualify the subject of the original assertion, the whole operation is also sometimes given various nicknames of the form, *The No-True-Briton (or what have you) Move.*

These labels apply to what Hume seems to be doing here. It amounts to making such sentences as "all our ideas . . . are copies of our impressions" ambiguous: most of the time they are taken to express a contingent generalization; but at some moments of crisis he apparently construes them as embodying a necessary proposition. Such manoeuvres have the effect of making it look as if the immunity to falsification of a necessary truth had been gloriously combined with the substantial assertiveness of a contingent generalization. But this, as Hume himself is going soon most clearly and unequivocally to insist, is impossible.

The ground which Hume tried to defend is thus manifestly untenable. Yet, to have appreciated that and why this is so is to have reached no more than the end of the beginning. Suppose that someone, ignoring the ill-starred attempt to transmute the original hypothesis into a criterion of meaning, wished simply to test it. Hume confidently announces: "If it happen, from a defect of the organ, that a man is not susceptible of any species of sensation, we always find that he is as little susceptible of the correspondent idea." There is no reason to suppose that he or anyone else in his day had ever conducted a serious investigation, and found that this is in fact so. Indeed the first real investigation to come near this question seems to have been that by Professor Jastrow of Princeton, published in 1888. Jastrow has the priority: unless we are to count Locke's "studious blind man who . . . bragged one day that he now understood what *scarlet* signified," and explained, "It was like the sound of a trumpet," or Hume's own questioning in later life of his friend the blind poet Blacklock. So it looks as if we have here one of those cases, still all too common in the psychological and social field, where a proposition which could be established only, if at all, by close empirical study is strongly held to stand to reason, and to be so obviously true that no systematic enquiry is called for: as when someone on the Clapham omnibus clearly and distinctly conceives that hanging and flogging must be the supremely effective deterrents to murder and to lesser crimes of violence, respectively.

So soon as we begin to consider practically the problems of testing the hypothesis that all our ideas are copies of our impressions a peculiar difficulty emerges. We get in touch with some people who have been totally blind or deaf from birth. We persuade them to visit our laboratory. If it was a matter of assessing the kind of capacity usually studied by experimental psychologists, we should have, or could develop, a suitable battery of tests. It is different with the capacity to form mental images. Hume challenges "those who would assert that this position is not universally true" to refute it "by producing that idea which in their opinion, is not derived from this source." This is radically misleading. It does not even make sense to speak of (literally) producing a mental image. Nothing which could be produced for inspection could count as a mental image. The whole point of calling these *mental* precisely is that they must be (logically) private and not public. In the only (and metaphorical) sense in which it might be possible to speak of producing a mental image for public scrutiny what is involved is the (literal) production not of the image itself but of some description or physical representation. So there would be nothing for it but to ask our subjects direct questions. Yet how could they understand our questions? No doubt we could explain to the man deaf, but not blind, from birth that auditory images are the auditory analogue of visual images, and that hearing bears the same relation to the ears as sight to the eyes. With the appropriate alterations the same could be done with the blind man. But even if, surprisingly, he did enjoy visual imagery, we surely could not hope for any answers to our questions about its colour. Presumably the only way in which he could ever come to give us what we want would be by first gaining the use of his eyes (by a corneal graft perhaps) and then learning in the usual way which colour words are used to refer to what colours. Then and only then might he be able to tell us that even before his operation he had had vivid green and scarlet imagery, and know what he was talking about when he said so.

This suggests that it may be possible to transpose Hume's psychological hypothesis into something which might possess the power to generate the sort of criterion he wants. Various things he says can be taken as hints. There is a sentence in the *Treatise* which finds no echo in the revised version: "To give a child an idea of scarlet or orange, of sweet or bitter, I present the objects, or, in other words, convey to him these impressions; but proceed not so absurdly as to endeavour to produce the impressions by exciting the ideas." The notion of teaching something to a child has since proved fruitful here; and surely it is just a little curious to be speaking of absurdity, as opposed to error plain and simple, if what is involved is purely a matter of contingent fact. Then, in the first paragraph of the present Section, there is another sentence: "All the colours of poetry, however splendid, can never paint natural objects in such a manner as to make the description be taken for a real landscape." This is incongruous. For in place of 'ideas (or more feeble perceptions)' Hume is now talking of something of an altogether different order, descriptions. While in place of impressions (our more lively perceptions) he refers to something else which again is of an altogether different order, a real landscape. For, in spite of his easy insinuation of synonymity, or, in other words, physical objects and real landscapes cannot be allocated to the same category as impressions. In the final Section he is able so far to forget his official view of the nature of ideas and of the correct procedure for their clarification as to remark that all difficulty in "those pretended syllogistical reasonings" which occur outside mathematics "proceeds entirely from the undeterminate meaning of words, which is corrected by juster definitions."

One sort of transposition that has been suggested would transform Hume's position, which, if a label is wanted, might be called a psychological imagist empiricism, into a species of logical empiricism. It then becomes the doctrine that the meaning of any word or symbol which we can understand must be explicable in terms of our experience. The crux ceases to be a matter of genetic psychology, of how we have come to have some idea. It becomes instead one of how the meaning of a word is to be understood and explained now. To this such questions as "How would you teach that word to a child?" or "How do we first learn the meaning of that sort of word?" are relevant only, but very importantly, insofar as they help to prise away our illusions. Hume's basic division runs between thinking, in a very broad sense, and feeling, again in a very broad sense. The substitute dichotomy is between language, including the non-verbal varieties, and experience, which amounts to pretty well what Hume meant by *feeling* when he claimed "that it is impossible for us to *think* of anything which we have not antecedently *felt* either by our external or internal senses."

The original uneasy distinction between simple and complex ideas is replaced by one between indefinable and definable terms. Hume says that complex ideas such as that of God "resolve themselves into such simple ideas as were copied from a precedent feeling or sentiment." The logical empiricist will say that words such as *God*, which are certainly not ostensively explicable (not, that is, explicable by any sort of pointing), are, or must be, definable by means of other words which are, or must be, themselves explicable in terms of actual or possible experience. If in any particular case this cannot be done, he will say that the word in question is one of those "employed without any meaning . . . (as is but too frequent)."

This suggestion we have called a transposition, not a translation, because, whereas the translator represents the original substance in the different words of another language, this replaces it by something substantially different, while nevertheless retaining a certain similarity of structure and theme.

Such a transposition has a great many advantages over its original. That started by trying to divide all the "perceptions of the mind" into two classes distinguishable purely by their intrinsic, as opposed to relational, qualities ("their different degrees of force and vivacity"). It proceeded inconsistently to allow that when "the mind be disordered by disease or madness" this may be impossible; while all the time assuming that the proposed division could still be made. It also assumed throughout that the division between ideas and impressions was either the same as or congruent with those between thought and experience, and between language and reality. The transposition avoids these inconsistencies, ambiguities, and false assumptions.

With the original, Hume found he had to admit as an authentic exception to his supposedly universal rule the possibility that someone might form an image of a particular variety within a species of sensation notwithstanding that he had never had actually that particular variety of the sensation. Not allowing this concession to put him off his stride, Hume went on brazenly to dismiss the fault as only a little one: "scarcely worth our observing . . . does not merit that for it alone we should alter our general maxim." The transposition allows us to say that Hume's intuition of irrelevance here was at bottom sound. For the missing shade required could be specified with the help of other colour words. This, after all, is exactly what Hume did when he explained the case he had in mind.

Here one must guard against the temptation to say that some form of logical empiricism was what Hume really meant. It is no compliment either to an author's ingenuousness or to his capacity for self-expression to suggest that he really meant something different from what he actually said. In this case, to follow the promptings of misguided charity would be to make an historical mistake too. The great merit of this transposition precisely is that it replaces by a philosophical thesis what in Hume certainly was, and was intended to be, a psychological proposition. Whatever its offsetting faults, this philosophical thesis is at least of the right kind to support a challenging method of semantic analysis such as he was proposing.

The changes, however, have still not gone far enough. The fundamental thing about mental images is not that they are faint or feeble, lacking in liveliness and vivacity: indeed to some, called *eidetic*, these epithets are inapplicable by definition. The real fundamental is that they are (necessarily) private to the person who has them and (logically) cannot be accessible to public observation in the way in which both material things and such other physical phenomena as flames and rainbows must in principle always be.

The next most fundamental fact is contingent: "It is in the field of imagery that some of the most extreme human individual differences are to be found." This was discovered by Francis Galton, who seems to have been the first person to undertake a genuine and systematic study of imagery. Some of his observations can be philosophically as well as psychologically instructive. To his own great surprise he learnt that "Men who declare themselves entirely deficient in the power of seeing mental pictures can nevertheless give lifelike descriptions of what they have seen, and can otherwise express themselves as if they were gifted with a vivid visual imagination. They can also become painters of the rank of Royal Academicians." Again: "To my astonishment I found that the great majority of men of science to whom I first applied protested that mental imagery was unknown to them, and they looked on me as fanciful and fantastic in supposing that the words *mental imagery* really expressed what I believed everyone supposed them to mean."

The consequences of these two basic propositions should give pause to any philosopher tempted to cast mental imagery for a star role in his analyses. If my having a mental image of a particular sort, or indeed of any sort at all, is to be a necessary condition of the applicability to me of a certain term, then no one else can ever possibly be in a position to know whether or not that term is applicable to me; until and unless, that is, I supply a remarkably uneager world with the supposedly crucial relevant information to which in the first instance I alone have access.

If there was only the necessary truth to take account of, an agile and resolute philosopher might try to escape this consequence by appealing to some presumption of uniformity; which might justify the confident use of the word under discussion, even when no particular enquiry had been made as to the occurrence of the mental imagery specified in his proposed analysis. But in the face of the ascertained brute fact rebutting any such presumption the implication cannot be denied. When the term so analyzed is one which people regularly and unhesitatingly apply to one another without having enquired after the imagery supposedly involved, this would amount to saying that all the positive attributions made were unwarranted, whether or not they happened in fact to be correct. This is surprising: but, since it could be taken as one more indication of deplorably low popular standards of evidence, the paradox might be positively attractive to some philosophers. Another implication, which, in view of the intellectual calibre of so many of those who have little or no image experience, might be felt as more burdensomely paradoxical, is that those who know nothing of mental imagery must all be systematically misusing all the terms to be analyzed in this way. In the face of Galton's discoveries, presumably we just have to accept that this is the case with the expression *mental image* itself, and perhaps one or two others. Neither of these implications alone constitutes a reason anything like sufficient to justify wholesale rejection of such analyses. But both are enough to encourage a cautious approach.

Hume here has comparatively little to say about memory and imagination. Nevertheless, what he does say makes it quite clear that he believed mental imagery to be essentially involved in both. Thus a man's impressions of immediate experience are contrasted with his ideas "when he afterwards recalls to his memory this sensation or anticipates it by his imagination." But suppose we ask how claims to remember may be denied. More light will usually be got from considering what we should have to do to deny an assertion than by wondering what we might say in answer to a request for elucidation.

Someone says: "I remember how that tune went"; or "I can remember the names of all the premiers of the French Fourth Republic"; or "I always remember what Senator McCarthy said about General Marshall." Any of these claims would be denied by insisting: either that the speaker was not in a position to remember any such thing, because he had never been in a position to learn it in the first place; or that he did not in fact know what he said he could remember, because all that he was able to offer in response to a challenge to produce the appropriate information was something less than adequate. Thus, the first claim could be denied either by saying that the speaker had never come across the tune or that he did not know how it went. Again, the second and third could not be maintained in the face of proof: either that the speaker had never been acquainted with the names of the premiers, or with the Senator's words; or that he did not now know those names or those words. It would, however, be entirely beside the point to object to any of the three claims on the ground that the speaker neither was having, nor was able to summon up, any mental imagery from which the information he was claiming to remember might be read off. Since to establish a claim to remember the names of all the premiers of the French Fourth Republic it is sufficient to show that the claimant has at some time in the past been acquainted with the list and that he now knows it, it cannot be the case that all remembering necessarily involves the occurrence of some mental imagery.

The same, perhaps more surprisingly, applies with imagination. There is at least one very common sense of *imagine* in which, usually in a past tense, it is a synonym for *think* (*probably mistakenly*): "I had imagined that they were relying on some secret guarantees"; or, to take an example from this very Section, "We are apt to imagine it has a determinate idea annexed to it." Closely connected with this are the uses of *imaginary* and *imagination* in such propositions as "The conspiracy was entirely imaginary"; or "The Doctors' Plot was a figment of Stalin's imagination." In any of these it would surely be preposterous to reject the assertions simply on the grounds that no mental imagery in fact had or could have occurred.

Then there are the uses of *imaginative* in which people and things are said to be imaginative or unimaginative. To decide which award is more suitable for a particular child it is not necessary first to discover, either directly or indirectly, the quantity and quality of its actual or potential private image life. To say that some piece of architectural design is unimaginative is to say something about the all too public deficiencies of the design, not something about the much more easily tolerated private inadequacies of the images and imaging powers of the architect. It would be a grotesque evasion for some complacent spokesman to pretend to meet the charge without any reference to the building, simply calling in evidence diaries recording the spectacular and varied quality of the logically private life of his protege.

A third sort of case, and one in which perhaps we come nearest to what philosophers and psychologists usually have in mind when they discuss imagination, is that in which imagining seems at least partly to overlap supposing and conceiving: "Imagine what it would have been like to live under a Nazi occupation, if they had succeeded in conquering Britain too." Yet even here it would surely meet the request in full simply to describe to oneself the consequences of such defeat. Provided your listener did this, and provided he did not seem too unmoved, it would be strange to insist that in addition he must supply himself with a series of grim mental illustrations of those consequences.

There may perhaps be slightly more reluctance to concede this last case. Did not Descartes in a memorable passage at the beginning of the sixth of the *Meditations* urge a distinction between imagining and conceiving? "I remark . . . the difference that exists between the imagination and conception. For example, when I imagine a triangle, I do not conceive it only as a figure comprehended by three lines, but I also apprehend these three lines as present by the power and inward vision of my mind, and this is what I call imagining. But if I desire to think of a chiliagon, I certainly conceive truly that it is a figure composed of a thousand sides, . . . but I cannot in any way imagine the thousand sides of a chiliagon . . ." This presumably is one of the passages from Descartes which Hume has in mind when he entertains, only to reject, the proposition: "What never was seen or heard of, may yet be conceived; nor is anything beyond the power of thought, except what implies an absolute contradiction."

There may also be a similar unwillingness to grant that the occurrence of imagery is not logically essential in some cases of remembering, particularly those in which the suggestion of a presently occurring phenomenon is strongest: "I can remember vividly even now how we watched from our bivouac on the main ridge of the Cuillin while the sun set behind the Western Isles"; or "When he saw the barbed wire all the horrors of Karaganda came back to him."

Nevertheless, the wisest moral to draw from the privacy of mental imagery and from the fact that image experience varies so widely from person to person is surely that we should insist that a reference to such experience is not a necessary part of the meaning of any term, except in those few cases where all or a large part of the point of employing the term lies in its reference to mental imagery. The criterion for whether or not all or a large part of the point lies there is simply whether this reference in fact enters into the actual use. The fact that the differences discovered by Galton lay for so long hidden is a powerful reason for believing that this criterion is rarely satisfied. For if questions about the occurrence of imagery entered into our life and language, as the questions whether he was there and whether the information he is offering is correct most certainly and continually do so enter, then there would be far more direct interrogation and far more unambiguous reporting about mental imagery than there is. In that event the variety of human image experience would surely have been a long and widely known fact. If you never try to make sure before applying a word whether or not imagery has occurred; if you never raise any question about its occurrence when challenging the application of that word by someone else: then the occurrence of mental imagery cannot be an essential part of what you mean by it. Though Descartes' use of *imagination* certainly satisfies our suggested criterion, this is not sufficient reason for saying that in our third case imaging is always even part of what is meant by *imagining*. On the contrary, it was only by specifying and studiously maintaining a distinction between conceiving and imagining that he made his requirement that imaging should occur as an essential working part of his use of the term *imagination*. Where this is not done, imaging is not a logically necessary condition of imagining, in the sense there being given to that word. It seems in fact to be done merely by a handful of philosophers, and by them only when on their very best behaviour. It is, therefore, clear that imaging is not involved necessarily in all memory and imagination. Applying a similar analysis now to understanding the meaning of a term, it becomes obvious immediately that to say that he understands the meaning of the word *oscillograph*, or that he knows as well as you do what is meant in this context by *election*, is not to make assertions about imagery; although, of course, the particular people concerned may well associate particular images with these words. For, to show that they do not know the meanings, it is enough to show that they do not know how the words are used: that, perhaps, the one thinks that *oscillograph* is a synonym for *orrery*; while the other is under the misapprehension that here to speak of an election is to imply that there will be rival candidates. Nor will it be even relevant to object that someone has no power to form imagery if once it is admitted that he cannot be faulted on his usage. No schoolmaster having satisfied himself that a class had mastered the use of the fresh words he had been teaching them would ever insist on a further examination into their powers of imaging before he was willing to concede that they really had learnt what the terms meant.

Hume's view that memory and imagination both necessarily involve mental imagery does not bear directly on any of the main arguments of this *Inquiry*. But his assumptions, neither argued nor fully expounded, that the meaning of a term is an image, and that understanding the meaning of a term is a matter of having or being able to have the appropriate imagery, are directly though not perhaps ostentatiously relevant. For instance, it is chiefly to them that we must trace the origin of those embarrassing and unresolved difficulties about infinite divisibility which are mentioned in the final Section as threats to the foundations of mathematics; though the branches of mathematics are the only studies with any really hopeful claim to be "sciences, properly so called." If this were all, we might treat each of these overestimations of the importance of mental imagery as a more or less isolated slip, to be noticed, corrected, and forgotten. But, in fact, they are all symptoms of an approach to language, and hence to philosophy, which is wholly inverted.

Unlike such of his classical predecessors as Plato or Hobbes or Locke or Berkeley, Hume seems himself to have had little interest in or respect for any questions which he thought of as semantic. Thus, in this *Inquiry*, he contemptuously presents the upshot of his "reconciling project with regard to the question of liberty and necessity" as a demonstration "that the whole dispute . . . has been hitherto merely verbal." The icebergs of his own assumptions about language therefore make little show above the surface. To appreciate their full enormity it is best to turn again to Locke, who was very much interested and who devoted the whole of the third Book of his *Essay* explicitly to the subject 'Of Words.' Hume is and always must be the supreme authority on Hume. Yet, precisely because Hume was not so much interested, it is Locke's statement which provides the sharper picture of the assumptions Hume inherited.

In the first two chapters of that Book, Locke outlines his view. God designed man to be a social creature, and therefore equipped him with the capacity "to frame articulate sounds, which we call words." But this was not enough: parrots could do the same. "It was further necessary that he should be able to use these sounds as signs of internal conceptions; and to make them stand as marks for the ideas within his own mind, whereby they might be made known to others, and the thoughts of men's minds be conveyed from one to the other." This notion of the primacy of the private is developed and underlined in the second chapter. "Man, though he have a great variety of thoughts, and such from which others as well as himself might receive profit and delight; yet they are all within his own breast, invisible and hidden from others, nor can of themselves be made to appear . . . it was necessary that man should find out some external sensible signs, whereof those invisible ideas, which his thoughts are made up of, might be made known to others . . . . The use, then, of words, is to be the sensible marks of ideas; and the ideas they stand for are their proper and immediate signification . . . . That then which words are the marks of are the ideas of the speaker: nor can anyone apply them as marks, immediately, to anything but the ideas that he himself hath . . . . But though words, as they are used by men, can properly and immediately signify nothing but the ideas that are in the mind of the speaker; yet in their thoughts they give them secret reference to other things." These other things are, first, "ideas in the minds also of other men" and, second, "the reality of things." (One has all the time to remember that Locke is not making a distinction between ideas and impressions.)

From the premises already stated it follows that these practices are strictly unwarranted. Far from trying to avoid this consequence, Locke, as if gluttonous to outrage common sense, insists upon it. "It is a perverting the use of words, and brings . . . obscurity and confusion into their signification, whenever we make them stand for anything but those ideas we have in our own minds." He remarks next how often words are in fact employed without any accompanying ideas. This he interprets as a lamentable indication of our human propensity to "set . . . thoughts more on words than things." For unless "there is a constant connexion between the sound and the idea, and a designation that the one stands for the other," we are uttering parrot talk: "so much insignificant noise." He even notices: "that no one hath the power to make others have the same ideas in their minds that he has, when they use the same words that he does"; although "common use, by a tacit consent, appropriates certain sounds to certain ideas in all languages," and "unless a man's words excite the same ideas in the hearer which he makes them stand for in speaking, he does not speak intelligibly." Nevertheless, "whatever be the consequence of any man's using of words differently . . . . this is certain, their signification, in his use of them is limited to his ideas, and they can be signs of nothing else."

It is worth quoting extensively. Locke's view epitomizes in the sharpest outline one of two very different approaches to language. These set out from opposite directions: the first begins with the logically private realm of one man's experience; the second starts from the common public world of physical things and events, the world of "the reality of things" and of transactions between people. Locke's service is to state quite clearly, emphatically, and unequivocally a position which usually is found operating only as an unnoticed and hence unformulated presupposition; or else, if expressed, is expressed only in a muffled and half-hearted fashion. In this statement he almost seems to go out of his way both to underline some of the paradoxical implications (which leave him unabashed) and to give several hints encouraging an entirely opposite approach.

The main implication is that language is essentially private. It is not, like the ciphers and shorthands in which the cautious Locke himself sometimes wrote, just something which happens to be private only until and unless someone contrives to break into the system. It is that all the words in my language are given their meaning exclusively in terms of my (essentially subjective) experience. Their proper use is always and only to refer to that experience and nothing else: "It is a perverting the use of words . . . whenever we make them stand for anything but those ideas we have in our own minds." Experiences, both as ideas and as impressions, are essentially private: "all within his own breast, invisible and hidden from others, nor can of themselves be made to appear." So far Locke is prepared to go himself, most emphatically.

But now, if this is where we have to start, how could it ever be possible by communicating with other people to escape nightmare solitude? If my whole language is applicable to my experience exclusively, and yours is confined equally exclusively to yours, then we can have no common vocabulary at all. No messages can pass between our private worlds. We are even deprived of the consolation of talking extravertedly to ourselves: for it is just a muddle for me to think I can say anything either about the experience of other people or about "the reality of things." At this point, Locke, understandably as well as characteristically, begins to weaken: "It is true, common use, by a tacit consent, appropriates certain sounds to certain ideas . . . which so far limits the signification of that sound that unless a man applies it to the same idea, he does not speak properly." Perhaps after all we can accept Locke's principles while still going on very much as before.

That is not so. For how on these principles could anyone ever be in a position to know that his interlocutor was in fact appropriating the same word to the same idea? Indeed, what sense could he possibly give to the suggestion that someone else had the same, or a different, idea from that which he himself had? If my language were really applicable only to my own experience, to my own ideas (in the Lockean sense), then clearly it must be nonsense for me to speak of the ideas of anyone else. And even if there were any room (which, on Lockean principles, there surely is not) for the concept of directly inspecting an object on display, still it is in the very nature of the case impossible to produce an idea for inspection. Locke expressly insists that there is nothing but an arbitrary connection between particular words and particular ideas: "Words . . . signify only men's peculiar ideas, and that *by a perfect arbitrary imposition* . . . no one hath the power to make others have the same ideas in their minds that he has when they use the same words that he does." Equally expressly he rebukes the assumption that the public use is in any way connected necessarily with the meaning of a word, with (as he would say) the idea it signifies. Regrettably, "men stand not usually to examine, whether the idea they and those they discourse with have in their minds be the same: but think it enough that they use the word, as they imagine, in the common acceptation . . . ."

If there is thus no necessary connection between either the form or the use of the word, the two things which are available to general scrutiny, and the ideas in your mind and in my mind, neither of which can possibly in any suitably literal sense be brought out for public view, then the question remains unanswered, and on Locke's principles unanswerable: "How could I ever know whether the idea I and those I discourse with have in our minds be the same?" There would be no possible way of telling whether your idea of a pineapple was the same as mine, and hence no sense to any distinction between my ideas and your ideas. On these principles, it could make no sense for me to talk of anything but my ideas; and, strictly speaking, it could make no sense even to call them mine.

Interestingly, elsewhere in the *Essay*, Locke shows himself aware of the lack of any possible criterion, though not of the corollary. For he considers, what he presumes to be a logical possibility, "that the same object should produce in several men's minds different ideas at the same time; e.g., if the idea that a violet produced in one man's mind by his eyes were the same that a marigold produced in another man's, and vice versa." It is important to appreciate that the supposition is not of any ordinary, or even extraordinary, form of colour blindness or speech disorder. We are not asked to contemplate: the case of a man who cannot make the colour discriminations which others can, a weakness which could be detected by putting him through the Ishihara test; nor yet that of a man whose usage of colour words is manifestly irregular or chaotic, which again is something which everyone could know about. Locke carefully so arranges the specification that there could be no possible way of determining whether his putative supposition was or was not ever realized. He nevertheless suggests that many reasons could be offered for thinking that in fact it is not. Unfortunately he excuses himself from offering even one; on the grounds that the question is not relevant to his present purposes and that anyway it is idle inasmuch as the answer could make no difference to anyone or anything.

This is a remarkable conclusion. On his principles, the possibility of communication depends absolutely on people using the same words for the same ideas in their several minds. Yet here he is arguing: both, exactly as we have done, that on these assumptions there is no way of knowing whether you associate the same ideas with the same words as I do; and, very much as we shall do, that none of this matters because really the crucial thing is the public use of the words. Nevertheless, he still takes it for granted that it makes sense to suggest that, even in circumstances where every conceivable test had been applied and had indicated the opposite conclusion, my idea might be different from your idea.

On Locke's principles, this obviously will not do. For if they were right, he could have no means of giving sense to any talk about other people and their ideas.

So much for the most outrageously paradoxical implications of Locke's approach. Like Hume, he provides also what can be taken as hints towards something entirely opposite. Instead of my trying to start from the essentially private, only to find that I must in consequence be held forever incommunicado in logically private solitary confinement, suppose I begin from the other end, from the public world of "the reality of things" and of transactions between people. In fact, language surely is in the first instance adapted to playing a part in social life. Only very secondarily is it applied to the description or the evocation of logically private worlds. Scarcely ever indeed do any man's imagings become a subject of conversation and of concern to other people.

This contention can be regarded as a weaker version of the extreme Wittgensteinian thesis of the impossibility of any essentially private language. In our perspective, Hume's emphasis on the importance of the Humean ideas of sense is bound to stand out as misplaced, and his whole account of our sensory vocabulary must appear inverted and tortuous. We have already touched on the case he mentions of men lacking the use of one of the standard senses. He also recognizes the possibility of other senses: "It is readily allowed that other beings may possess many senses of which we can have no conception, because the ideas of them have never been introduced to us in the only manner by which an idea can have access to the mind, to wit, by the actual feeling and sensation." The case is one which Locke had already considered. Certainly, it is perfectly conceivable that other beings might possess, or that human beings might acquire, senses that we do not have. But that does not imply that we can have no conception of such senses. If anything, it implies the contrary. It is perfectly possible to know what one of them might be, and to be in a position to test a man's claim to possess that particular possible sense.

Suppose someone claims to have the gift of *Roentgening*, defined as the exercise of a sense bearing to X-rays the same relation as hearing to sounds or smelling to smells. Then the very first thing to do is to experiment to find whether he can detect without apparatus the X-rays which we can only discover indirectly by means of fluorescent screens or Geiger counters or special photographic plates. If he fails this test, then the claim must fall. Even if he passes, there are still one or two more rivers to cross. To enquire exactly how many and what rivers would be interesting. But, for the present purposes, it is enough to add that presumably we should want also to make sure that the candidate sense was localized in some organ, and certainly we should have to satisfy ourselves that it provided a range of experience peculiar to itself and as different from any of the standard ones as olfactory is from visual or visual from auditory.

Now, insofar as Hume's psychological hypothesis is right, what we who lack the gift of Roentgening cannot do is to form any mental image of any quality from this fresh range. Only the man who has the sense can have the appropriate impressions: only the person who has had the impressions can form the ideas. This may very well be true. But it does not even begin to show that we can have no conception of such a new sense. We have in fact just described it. What we shall lack is the new sense. For all the discriminations which might be made by Roentgening we shall need laboriously to employ apparatus, while a whole range of possible sensory experience will be closed to us. This may be a lot to lack, as anyone can appreciate who considers for a moment what the loss of even a minor sense like smell would mean to him. But it should nevertheless be possible to build up a fairly rich Roentgen vocabulary, intelligible both to those who had and to those who lacked the gift of Roentgening.

Certainly there is no theoretical difficulty about giving meaning to words for whatever Roentgen qualities we are able to develop apparatus to discriminate. The fundamental principle is the same which applies to all (public) language the meaning of a word must be explicable by reference, direct or indirect, to the public world, to "the reality of things." The essence of the operation must be to produce some radiation having and some lacking the quality in question, and with the help of these examples to indicate the class of occasions on which the word is and the class on which it is not applicable. The only difference between pupils relevant in this exercise is that those unable to Roentgen will need apparatus if they are to learn from the examples, whereas those gifted with this sense will not. This one difference, so important perhaps for their lives even if not for their understanding of language, must nevertheless carry with it two linguistic corollaries.

Let us try as far as possible, but without prejudice, to express these in Humean terms. The gifted ones will be able to apply each word they learn to the appropriate variety of impression, and they will also be able to apply it to the corresponding variety of idea if they ever happen to have it. The Roentgen blind cannot apply that word to any impression because, presumably by definition, they cannot have any Roentgen impressions to which to apply it. While even if, incredibly, they did happen to have the corresponding idea, they could not possibly know that the word was applicable. Never having had the impression, they could never have learnt that this was the sort of impression to which the word was applicable, and hence they could have no standard by which to judge that it was also applicable to this idea. Thus it seems that to describe this part of the reality of things, X-rays, it is not necessary to have had any Roentgen impressions, nor yet to have any Roentgen ideas. The impressions are needed only, if at all, in order to enable the person who has had them to describe his ideas; while the ideas themselves are, for the purposes of communication, entirely idle and superfluous.

The question now arises of the function and status of impressions. Consider again a sentence quoted from the *Treatise* earlier: "To give a child an idea of scarlet or orange, of sweet or bitter, I present the objects, or, in other words, convey to him these impressions; but proceed not so absurdly as to endeavour to produce the impressions by exciting the ideas." In our new perspective, the notion of impression also is seen to be redundant. For to understand such words as *scarlet* or *orange*, *sweet* or *bitter*, and to apply them correctly to the appropriate physical phenomena, it is essential only to know to which things they can and to which things they cannot properly be applied. To be able to do this and to know this it is not theoretically necessary to possess the particular senses of sight and taste. In theory, it is enough to have instruments. To possess or to have possessed the particular sense which corresponds is theoretically indispensable merely in the practically trivial and derivative case of the application of the word to one's own mental imagery. Here, though the need to be able to understand the meaning of the word by reference to the public world is the same, instruments cannot substitute for the sense itself, simply because a mental image cannot be produced and presented to them.

Of course, it is perfectly conceivable that a man who had always been blind might not only enjoy visual imagery but might also be able to apply to it the correct colour words. But until and unless he acquired the sense of sight he could never properly claim to know that his private usage had been correct. For the standard of correct usage in any language in which two different people are both to be mutually intelligible and to know that they are, is and can only be a public standard. Terms in such a language may be applicable to (private) images, sensations, and what not. But they can only have and be known to have meaning in these private contexts insofar as that meaning can in one way or another be explained by reference to the public world. So even in this special off-centre case of employing words to describe mental imagery the crucial condition of understanding is not to have enjoyed any sort of necessarily private experience, but to have been able, or to be able, to inspect "the reality of things."

Now it will certainly be objected that this is completely beside the point: either on the ground that to talk of having an impression of "the relish of wine" is just Hume's technical way of describing the agreeable pastime of wine tasting; or on the ground that really impressions are the inescapable intermediaries between us and that reality. The first of these suggestions is both symptomatic of one view of the place of technical terms in philosophy and at the same time unflattering to Hume's achievement as a stylist. It is as an interpretation manifestly mistaken. *Impressions* are defined as constituting with ideas the class of "perceptions of the mind." While wine must be (logically) public, the impression of wine, like the idea of wine, must be (logically) private. Whereas the presence of wine tautologically guarantees the presence of wine, the occurrence of an impression of wine is by no means a sufficient condition of the presence of wine, because an impression of wine, but not, of course, real wine, may be hallucinatory. Impressions belong to the category of subjective experiences: wine is cellared in that of physical things.

Hume's own objection would undoubtedly have been urged on grounds of the second sort. Thus, in the *Treatise*, he wrote "It is universally allowed by philosophers, and is besides pretty obvious of itself, that nothing is ever really present to the mind but its perceptions, or impressions and ideas, and that external objects become known to us only by those perceptions they occasion." This conviction appears in our *Inquiry* as one of two main sources of that extreme Pyrrhonian scepticism which is always threatening to break out of control and "to introduce a universal doubt into all subjects of human knowledge and enquiry." "These are the obvious dictates of reason; and no man who reflects ever doubted that the existences which we consider when we say *this house* and *that tree* are nothing but perceptions in the mind and fleeting copies of other existences which remain uniform and independent."

In one version or another, this basic belief was common ground between Hume and all his major immediate predecessors and contemporaries. The same dogma remains still one of the most widespread metaphysical doctrines, cherished not only by philosophers but also by many others who would repudiate the charge of being in any serious sense metaphysicians. It seems to have an especial appeal for tough-minded working scientists. Nevertheless, however intricate and difficult the task of showing in particular detail what is wrong with even one version, and with all the various arguments which might be deployed in its support, it is surely certain that every variety must be wrong. For to express such doctrines at all presupposes the truth of propositions with which they are radically inconsistent.

The arguments developed already against Locke's account of language apply with equal force here too. Humean impressions and ideas are but the twin species of the genus Lockean idea. Working on Hume's own example: if it really were the case that the use of the material thing expressions *this house* and *this tree* is to refer to the perceptions of my mind, then before you could understand what I was talking about when I used the words *tree* and *house* I should have to be able to explain by reference to things to which we both have access what it was that I meant by them. To speak here as Hume does (and in this he is a thoroughly representative spokesman) in the first person plural instead of in the first person singular, or better still quite impersonally, is to the last degree prejudicial and misleading. It takes for granted that it is possible for different people to communicate, while at the same time denying a presupposition of any common language. To understand such a language, and to know that we understand it, we must have access, and know that we have access, to a common public world.

It is only by a systematic failure to launch and to press home a really determined attempt to state the position consistently that its fundamental impossibility is concealed. Consider, for instance, Hume's unblushing use in his account 'Of the Origin of Ideas' both of material thing terms and of other terms which quite obviously presuppose a knowledge of material things: "By the term *impression* . . . I mean all our more lively perceptions, when we hear or see." But to speak of hearing or seeing, as opposed to 'hearing' or 'seeing,' implies that there is something objective and physical there to be heard or seen. And later, in the treatment of the case of the man blind or deaf from birth, he writes: "The case is the same if the object proper for exciting any sensation has never been applied to the organ. A Laplander or (an African) has no notion of the relish of wine." This, no doubt, is all very well in itself. But it is entirely inconsistent with any view that the knowledge of (logically private) ideas and impressions is somehow prior to the knowledge of (necessarily public) material things. For it provides a convincing indication that it is impossible to explain what is meant either by *idea* and *impression,* or by the terms applied to characterize particular ideas and impressions, without immediately or ultimately presupposing both the existence and our knowledge of a public world of physical objects.

The objection which we have been deploying must be distinguished from a similar one often fielded against the same opponents. The other argument starts from the general principle that reality expressions must be logically prior to appearance expressions. *Reality expressions* and *appearance expressions* are simply our own improvised temporary labels for two ad hoc holding categories, each of which brings together an enormous variety of very different sorts of expression. These categories are constructed and these terms introduced solely in order to make one extremely general but nevertheless important point. To understand the meaning of any appearance expression you must already understand the meaning of the corresponding reality expression. To be in a position to say: "It looks to me as if it were a sloth," "Perhaps what the photographs showed were only dummy aircraft," or "They worshipped false Gods"; you must first know what a sloth or an aircraft is, or what a true God would have to be.

From this it is argued that talk about impressions or sense data must be logically secondary to talk about the reality of things. Therefore, all those who have urged that our own sense data, and our knowledge of these sense data, are more fundamental than this public reality, and our knowledge of the universe around us, must be wrong. This misconception is perennially seductive.

Philosophers first recognize that it is always conceivable that any material thing assertion may turn out to have been mistaken, and then hope to find in a self-denying confinement to some sort of appearance propositions a security against this endemic possibility of error. The temptation is to think that, since the way to be cautious and to minimize your assertive commitments in any one particular case is to confine yourself to appearance assertions, and to eschew all reckless statements as to what actually is, the whole terminology of appearance must therefore be somehow more basic and elementary than that of unhesitating and categorical commitment about reality. This is exactly the reverse of the truth.

The second objection, appealing to the priority of the category of reality over that of appearance, is in that respect similar to the first; which appeals to the priority of the necessarily public over the logically privates and which insists on the knowledge of a common world as a presupposition or mutual intelligibility. Its basis is certainly sound, although excessively difficult to formulate satisfactorily. For it surely is hopeless to try to analyze the meaning of a reality expression such as *That is a kipper* in terms only of appearance expressions: whether categorical, like *It looks to me like a kipper*; or merely hypothetical, like *It would look like a kipper to you if you were here.* This should occasion no surprise. A large part of the point of having these important sorts of appearance expression precisely is to enable us to make guarded statements, without thereby committing ourselves to asserting outright that things in themselves do actually stand thus and thus.

Nevertheless, the second objection, unlike the first, contains a fatal flaw. For it assumes a false equation between appearance talk and talk about the private impressions or sense data of the speaker. Unless this assumption is made the objection is not even relevant: for it is concerned with the priority of reality over appearance expressions: while the supposed opponent speaks only of his own impressions and sense data. But the equation is false. For talk about how things look and about what they appear to be is either forthright talk about the looks of things or else guarded talk about how things are. Whereas discourse about my private impressions and sense data would be wholly autobiographical, and not necessarily either superficial or guarded. If I claim that a figure looks square, then the appropriate verification procedure is either to look to see if it does or else to measure the sides and the angles to discover whether it really is. It would be entirely beside the point to ask me to introspect more carefully.

Our everyday vocabulary equips us richly to make a wide range of subtle different assertions, both forthright and guarded, about both things and the looks of things. (This is a fact which is inevitably concealed by our present use of the wholesale category *appearance expression.*) But it is only by a special effort that we can make clear what we are up to if for some reason we want to describe neither things as they are, nor yet the public appearances of things, but rather and exclusively our private impressions,

CHAPTER 7

WHAT IMPRESSIONS OF NECESSITY?
(1992)

My question is this: 'Why and how was it that Hume failed to find a kind of impression from which to legitimate the complementary ideas of physical necessity and physical impossibility?' We can best begin from his first published discussion of causation.

1. In *Treatise* 1.3.2, the section, 'Of probability; and of the idea of cause and effect', Hume asserts that, "The idea . . . of causation must be deriv'd from some *relation* among objects; and that relation we must now endeavour to discover."[1] His first efforts are directed to establishing that two causally related objects must be both spatio-temporally contiguous and temporally successive, the cause object preceding the effect object. But "[h]aving thus discover'd or suppos'd" this conclusion, Hume finds that he is "stopt short, and can proceed no farther in considering any single instance of cause and effect" (T 76). We might, therefore, have expected that his next move would have been to consider series of resembling cause objects and their relations to series of resembling effect objects. But such a consideration is in fact deferred from section 2 until section 14, 'Of the idea of necessary connection'; a section starting all of seventy-seven pages later. Instead, the immediately following paragraph reads:

---

[1] David Hume, *A Treatise of Human Nature*, ed. L. A. Selby-Bigge, 2d ed., rev., ed. P. H. Nidditch, Oxford, 1987, 75 (hereafter cited as "T"). [Editor's note: I have followed Flew's use of this abbreviation for this essay only, conforming to his usage in the original article.]

107

Shou'd any one leave this instance, and pretend to define a cause, by saying it is something productive of another, 'tis evident he wou'd say nothing. For what does he mean by *production*? Can he give any definition of it, that will not be the same with that of causation? If he can; I desire it may be produc'd. If he cannot; he here runs in a circle, and gives a synonimous term instead of a definition. (T 77)

The phrasing of that paragraph perhaps constitutes one of those infelicities in the *Treatise* which Hume was later to recognize and regret. For if and inasmuch as 'causation' and 'production' are synonyms, any adequate definition of either word must be equally adequate for both. Rashly assuming that his challenge to produce such a definition will not and cannot be met, Hume proceeds at once to ask and to answer his own consequential question:

Shall we then rest contented with these two relations of contiguity and succession, as affording a compleat idea of causation? By no means. An object may be contiguous and prior to another, without being consider'd as its cause. There is a NECESSARY CONNEXION to be taken into consideration; and that relation is of much greater importance, than any of the other two above-mention'd. (T 77)

2. But now, why 'necessary connexion' rather than either 'causal connexion' or 'connexion' without prefix or suffix? Suppose that you were the Adam of the *Abstract* "created in the full vigour of understanding," yet altogether "without experience" (T 650). And suppose that you had noticed some A's both spatio-temporally contiguous to and precedent to B's. Then, assuming that your understanding was not only vigorous but also equipped with all essential concepts, you might well ask yourself, or perhaps, if she was now available, your partner, whether there was any causal connection here at all; or, more specifically, whether these A's were causing these B's. You might even proceed to put the question to experimental test: either by producing further A's in hopes of consequentially producing further B's, or, *when A's occurred spontaneously, by trying to inhibit the subsequent occurrence of B*'s.

What such an Adam would surely not do (not unless he had developed proto-Humean desires): both to demonstrate the absence here of any logically necessary connections; and thus, hopefully, also to discredit the idea that any other kind of necessity might be involved) is to suggest that the third, crucial, and so far unidentified element in any adequate account of causation must be *necessary* connection; as opposed, that is, to either causal connection or just plain unqualified connection.

It is, of course, obvious that Hume himself is eager to get on, first to denying logically necessary connections, and then to the first business which he relates to this denial. For it is in the immediately following section 3, 'Why a cause is always necessary', that he presents his argument for the conclusion that, whereas "Every effect must have a cause" is, "Every event must have a cause" is not a logically necessary truth. The development of the fully comprehensive empirical contention that it is from experience alone that we can learn what particular things or sorts of things are or are not the causes of other particular things or sorts of things is deferred till section 14. Even there the formulation of this conclusion is less incisive and decisive than in the *Abstract*:

> The mind can always *conceive* any effect to follow from any cause, and indeed any event to follow upon another: whatever we *conceive* is possible, at least in a metaphysical sense: but wherever a demonstration takes place, the contrary is impossible, and implies a contradiction. There is no demonstration, therefore, for any conjunction of cause and effect. (T 650-51)

3. Way back in the antediluvian days of my own first readings of the *Treatise*, I was eager, like Hume, to hasten on to those famously exciting empiricist denials, and to Hume's positive account of causal efficacy as a sort of secondary quality. Since John Davis is a close contemporary I suspect that his background was similar, and that he, too, made no attempt during his first readings to meet Hume's challenge to produce, not a mere synonym or synonyms, but a properly explicative definition. If so, we were together, as we shall see, in abundant company; a company surely increased by the hazing effect of the infelicities of the peremptory paragraph putting the challenge.

But those days are long past. So why not now, for a start, say that causing is making something happen? In order to overcome the objection that this by itself is merely providing a synonym, we need to develop and apply a distinction elsewhere seminally suggested by Hume himself. In the essay, 'Of National Characters', he wrote: "By *moral* causes, I mean all circumstances, which are fitted to work on the mind as motives or reasons . . . . By *physical* causes I mean those qualities of the air and climate, which are supposed to work insensibly on the temper, by altering the tone and habit of the body."[2] The former can operate only upon agents and, in so doing (to borrow a famous phrase from Leibniz) they incline but do not necessitate. By conveying some splendid news to someone I provide them with good cause to celebrate. But I do not thereby compel them to celebrate, willy-nilly. Such moral causing is sometimes described as agent causation. This is, however, misleading, since it suggests: not, what is true, that it is only agents who can be moved by moral causes; but instead, what is false, that it is only agents who are able to cause in this way.[3]

Physical causes, on the other hand, do necessitate. A physical cause causes or produces its effects by making their occurrence physically necessary and their non-occurrence physically impossible. This notion of making things happen and the associated ideas of physical necessity and physical impossibility are the essentials missing from any and every Humean analysis of causation. It is because physical causes produce or bring about their effects that there is no room in logical space for any conception of backwards causation: if the putative past 'effect' has already happened, then its supposed later 'cause' must be redundant and hence ineffective; whereas, if it has not previously happened, then its postulated future 'cause' will need to make to have happened something which has not happened.[4] It is only and precisely because propositions asserting physical causation, like propositions asserting laws of nature, contain the two associated ideas of physical necessity and physical impossibility that they can license inferences to contrary-to-fact conditionals.[5]

---

[2] David Hume, *Essays Moral, Political and Literary*, E. F. Miller (ed.), Liberty Press, 1985, 198.

[3] For further discussion of this confusion compare Antony Flew and Godfrey Vesey, *Agency and Necessity*, Blackwell, 1987, passim.

[4] Significantly, in introducing the symposium on 'Can an Effect Precede its Cause', *Proceedings of the Aristotelian Society*, Supplement, Vol. 28, 1954, Michael Dummett took as his premise the claim: "On the ordinary Humean view of cause, a cause is simply a sufficient condition: it is merely that we have observed that whenever *A* happens *B* follows . . . however we elaborate on the notions of sufficient and necessary conditions, the relation can hold as well between a later event and an earlier as between an earlier and a later." But this confident claim fails to distinguish: logically necessary and sufficient conditions; necessary and sufficient conditions defined extensionally in terms of material implication; and causally necessary and sufficient conditions. The latter must, it should go without saying, either precede or be simultaneous with whatever they condition.

[5] It is noteworthy, and it is nowadays commonly noted, that Hume in the first *Enquiry* makes just such an unlicensed inference, and makes it with panache: "Suitably to this experience, therefore, we may define a cause to be *an object, followed by another, and where all the objects similar to*

It is also only and precisely because Hume refuses to admit either the notion of making things happen or the associated ideas of physical necessity and physical impossibility that his "reconciling project", attempted in the first *Enquiry*, can at least seem to go through at the trot (E 95). For "this reasoning", as he had explained in the *Abstract*, "puts the whole controversy in a new light, by giving a new definition of necessity" (T 661). New it certainly is, although it constitutes a dissolution rather than a definition. For what is thus presented as "a new definition of necessity" is in truth an account of nothing but a sort of regular sequence, which deliberately precludes any kind of necessity.[6]

4. In the present context, Locke's great chapter, 'Of Power',[7] must be the most appropriate starting point of a search for the sorts of impressions from which the essential ideas omitted from Hume's account of causation could be derived, and by reference to which they may be legitimated. For it is to this chapter and its author that Hume makes reference in his treatments, 'Of the idea of necessary connexion' in both the *Treatise* (T 157) and the first *Enquiry* (E 64). In order to reap the maximum profit we will approach the sorts of impressions sought indirectly; by way of the idea, or rather the ideas, of power.

The chief reason why Hume failed to recognize any of those described in this chapter as being suitable is that his constant and overriding objective was to banish logical necessities. It was always these which he was targeting. Thus in the better, later treatment, he speaks for Locke: "It may be said, that we are every moment conscious of internal power; while we feel, that, by the simple command of our will, we can move the organs of our body, or direct the faculties of our mind" (E 64). The nub of Hume's objection to this is put in the single sentence:

---

the first are followed by objects similar to the second. Or in other words *where, if the first object had not been, the second never had existed."* David Hume, *Enquiries Concerning Human Understanding and Concerning the Principles of Morals*, L. A. Selby-Bigge (ed.), 3d ed., rev., P. H. Nidditch (ed.), Oxford, 1975, 76 (hereafter cited as "E"). [Editor's note: Again, I have followed Flew's abbreviations for this essay only.]

[6]   Compare the statement of a Neo-Humean Compatibilism first published in book form in the same antediluvian year as the materials mentioned in note 111, above. In A. J. Ayer, 'Freedom and Necessity', in *Philosophical Essays*, London, 1954, we read: "But, I repeat, the fact is simply that when an event of one type occurs, an event of another type occurs also, in a certain temporal or spatio-temporal relation to the first. The rest is only metaphor" (p. 283).

[7]   John Locke, *An Essay Concerning Human Understanding*, P.H. Nidditch (ed.), Oxford, 1975, bk. 2, chap. 21. All subsequent citations in this essay are to this edition.

This influence, we may observe, is a fact, which, like all other natural events, can be known only by experience, and can never be foreseen from any apparent energy or power in the cause, which connects it with the effect, and renders the one an infallible consequence of the other. (E 64-65)

Perfectly true, we may in our turn observe; and altogether irrelevant. To Hume, all this appears germane only because seemingly it never enters his head to assess Locke's suggestion as a suggestion: first about the origin of concepts incorporating another notion of necessity; and then about the sort of warrant we may have for believing propositions involving such concepts. Thus it is, though quite correct, entirely beside the point to insist that we can learn only through experience, and not from any insight into logical necessities, what is and is not subject to our wills. The facts, too, about what, if any, physical (or contingent) necessities obtain, and where, are of course contingent facts, not logically necessary truths. Nor is there any question but that, if we are to know any facts of this kind, our knowledge has to be grounded in experience. But once we allow ourselves to admit, besides the logical, another idea of necessary connection, everything here will be seen to be exactly as it should be, and as constituting no threat whatsoever to Hume's master insight: "If we reason *a priori*, anything may appear able to produce anything. The falling of a pebble may, for aught we know, extinguish the sun; or the wish of man control the planets in their orbits" (E 164).

Although neither Locke nor Hume explicitly distinguished two senses of 'power', Locke was in fact concerned with power solely in the sense in which it can be predicated only of people, or of such putative, quasi-personal beings as the theist God, the Olympian gods, archangels, angels, devils, and other assorted disembodied or ever-bodiless spirits. Let us, therefore, attach to power in the first sense the label 'power (personal)'. It was, presumably, power of this personal sort which Hume was darkly denying when he repudiated "[t]he distinction, which we often make betwixt *power* and the *exercise* of it" (T 171).

In the other sense, which is the only sense in which the word can be applied to inanimate objects and to most of animate nature, a power simply is a disposition to behave in such and such a way, given that such and such preconditions are satisfied. Thus we might say that the nuclear device dropped at Nagasaki possessed an explosive power equivalent to that of so many tons of TNT, or that full-weight nylon climbing rope has a breaking strain (of a power to hold up to) 4,500 pounds. Let us label this second sort of power 'power (physical)'. A power (personal) is an ability at will either to do or to abstain from doing whatever it may be. Thus we might say that in his heyday

J. V. Stalin had the power of life and death over all subjects of the Soviet Empire.

5. In three characteristically vivid passages Locke not only explains both what we have distinguished as the idea of power (personal) and the contrasting concepts of physical necessity and physical impossibility, but also demonstrates that there can be no question at all but that all these ideas have abundant application. It is to be regretted that in the third Locke mistakes it that he is explaining what is meant: not, generally, by 'an agent'; but rather, particularly, by 'a free agent'. The first reads:

This at least I think evident, that we find in ourselves a Power to begin or forbear, continue or end several actions of our minds, and motions of our Bodies . . . . This Power . . . thus to order the consideration of any idea, or the forbearing to consider it; or to prefer the motion of any part of the body to its rest, and *vice versa* in any particular instance, is that which we call the Will. (Locke, 236)

The second reads:

Everyone, I think, finds in himself a Power to begin or forbear, continue to put an end to several Actions in himself. From the consideration of the extent of this power of the mind over the actions of the Man, which everyone finds in himself, arise the Ideas of Liberty and Necessity. (Locke, 237)

The third passage, in which the Latin translates as St. Vitus' dance, reads:

We have instances enough, and often more than enough, in our own bodies. A Man's Heart beats, the Blood circulates, which t'is not in his Power . . . to stop; and therefore in respect of these Motions, where rest depends not on his choice . . . he is not a free agent. Convulsive Motions agitate his legs, so that though he will it never so much, he cannot . . . stop their motion (as in that odd disease called *chorea Sancti Viti*), but he is perpetually dancing: he is . . . under as much Necessity of moving as a Stone that falls or a Tennis-ball struck with a Racket. (Locke, 239)

With the reminders of these three passages before us we become equipped to develop ostensive definitions of two kinds of bodily movements. Going deliberately with, rather than against the grain of modern English usage, let those which can be either initiated or quashed at will be labelled 'movings', and those which cannot 'motions'. Certainly it is obvious that there are plenty of marginal cases. Nevertheless, so long as there are (as there are) far, far more which fall unequivocally upon one side or the other, we must resolutely and stubbornly refuse to be prevented from labouring this absolutely fundamental and decisive distinction by any such diversionary appeals to the existence of marginal cases.

Contemplation of these and similar passages in Locke should be sufficient to remind us that we all have the most direct, and the most inexpugnably certain experience: not only both of physical (as opposed to logical) necessity and of physical (as opposed to logical) impossibility; but also both, on some occasions, of being able to do other than we do do and, on other occasions, of being unable to behave in any other way than that in which we are behaving.

So it is in terms of our fundamental distinction between movings and motions that we can go on to establish and explicate the even more fundamental concept of action. An agent is a creature who, precisely and only in so far as he or she is an agent, can and cannot but make choices: choices between alternative courses of action both or all of which are open; real choices, notwithstanding both that sometimes by choosing one or even any of these open alternatives the agent will incur formidable costs. If, for instance, as in *The Godfather*, instructions were given that you were to be one of those who was to receive "an offer which he cannot refuse", you could nevertheless refuse; but only at the presumably unacceptable cost of it being your brains rather than your signature on the document signing away your property to the Mafia.

Agents, too, qua agents (it is the price of privilege) inescapably must choose, and can in no way avoid choosing, one of the two or more options which on particular occasions are open and available. The nerve of the distinction between the movements involved in an action, and those which constitute no more than items or partial components of necessitated behaviour, just is that such behaviour is necessitated, whereas the senses of actions not merely are not, but necessarily cannot be.

Once we are seized of these insights, we should be ready to recognize that there is no way in which creatures neither enjoying nor suffering experiences of both these two contrasting kinds could either acquire for themselves, or explicate to others, any of the crucial and indispensable notions: the notions, that is to say, of physical necessity and of physical impossibility, of making something happen and of being able or not able to do other than we do, and so on. The experiences in question, to repeat, are: on the one hand those of confronting physical necessities and physical impossibilities wholly beyond our control; and, the other hand, those of agents able and having to choose between acting in one way or another and not being necessitated to act in this way rather than that.

Those who are still, in spite of everything, reluctant to accept these contentions face a challenge, the challenge to excogitate their own alternative accounts of how all these key notions, including the not so far mentioned notion of counterfactual conditionality, might be acquired, explained, and understood by creatures who were (are) not agents and who did (do) not have such experiences. Maybe this challenge can, after all, be met; maybe. But, until and unless it is met, and met convincingly, the prudent philosopher is bound to adopt the archetypical attitude of the man from Missouri. Notoriously, if his reluctance to believe is to be overcome, he has to be shown.

CHAPTER 8

RESPONDING TO PLATO'S THRASYMACHUS
(1995)

> Listen then, he said, for I say that justice is nothing else but the advantage of the stronger. Plato: *The Republic*, 338C.

It is with this bitter intervention from Thrasymachus, occurring halfway through the first of its ten Books, that that work begins to come urgently alive. For the remainder of Book I the Socrates of the Dialogue asks questions and raises objections, while Thrasymachus keeps urging that in fact the just become through their very justice the victims of exploitation -- the suckers!

The arguments which Socrates deploys against Thrasymachus duly silence him, but do not, or at any rate should not, satisfy anyone. Immediately at the beginning of Book II Glaucon distinguishes three kinds of good, pressing Socrates to say to which being just belongs. The second of these kinds is that of those "which we value both for themselves and for their consequences, such as, for example, thought and sight and health" (357C). It is, of course, here that Socrates wants to put being just, "among those things which he who would be blessed must love both for their own sake and for their consequences" (358A).

The remainder of *The Republic* is presented as an attempt by Socrates (here presumably no more than Plato's mouthpiece) to meet Glaucon's challenge to show that their justice is indeed always advantageous to the just themselves and not exclusively to others. In response, Plato unfolds his design for a city ruled by an elite order of Guardians; the notorious Philosopher Kings whose knowledge of the Ideal Forms (the abstract essences of things) enables them to prescribe to the uninitiated vulgar the true, eternal and authoritative 2

117

standards. And it is through this vision of a Dorian city stately as a Dorian temple that Plato expounds his own answer to what is the official master question of the entire dialogue, namely, "What is justice?"

I

In *The Republic* the nearest approach to a satisfactory descriptive definition is the initial suggestion of Polemarchus, briskly dismissed by Socrates,[1] "That it is just . . . to render to each his due" (331E). Here we have a Greek anticipation of the Latin *suum cuique tribuere*, the key phrase in the classic definitions by Roman lawyers.[2] One vitiating fault, running right through *The Republic,* is the failure fully to appreciate and to come to terms with the fundamental distinction between what is the case and what ought to be. Thus, Thrasymachus appeals to his own excessively hard-bitten view of how things actually are, whereas Socrates rests a large part of his case upon claims which are more or less explicitly about what ought to be. No one seems to say or to see that this difference is crucial. Yet suppose we were to allow that Plato was right about what would be true in the supposedly ideal world of his visionary *Republic.* Still that must be and is enormously different from this world, which is the world in and about which Thrasymachus launched his original challenge.

I do not however want, in the present paper, to expatiate upon the actual treatment of the challenges of either Thrasymachus or Glaucon in *The Republic.* Instead I propose to consider the former directly and on my own account.

1. The angrily impatient intervention of Thrasymachus -- "that justice is nothing else but the advantage of the stronger"[3] -- is offered as if it were a knock-down decisive contribution to the search for a definition of the word 'justice'.

But when Socrates points out that this commits Thrasymachus to "maintaining . . . that Polydamas the athlete is stronger than we are, and that if oxmeat is advantageous for his body, this food will be advantageous and just . . ." (338C-D), Thrasymachus explains that what he actually wants to say is:

---

[1] For a dismissal of that dismissal, see my *Equality in Liberty and Justice,* Routledge, 1989, pp. 128-9.

[2] *Ibid.,* p.20.

[3] F. M. Cornford's translation goes so far as to render this passage: "listen then . . . What I say is that 'just'. . . means nothing but what is to the interest of the stronger party." He makes it clear that this is to be read unequivocally as a definition by putting the word 'just' between inverted commas, a refinement for which, of course, the Greek provides no warrant.

that some states are ruled by dictators, others are democracies, and others are aristocracies . . . . And each form of government lays down laws for its own advantage, a democracy laws for the benefit of the populace, a dictatorship laws for the benefit of the dictator, and the others likewise. By legislating in this way they make it plain that their advantage is justice for their subjects, and they punish anyone who gets out of line with this as a lawbreaker and an unjust man. So this is what I mean, you splendid fellow, that justice is in all states the same, and it is the advantage of the established government. For this, you agree, is strong; so that if you work it out correctly justice is everywhere the same -- the advantage of the stronger (338E-339A).

(i)   As a descriptive definition, "Justice is . . . the advantage of the stronger" will not do at all: the expression 'the advantage of the stronger' is manifestly not equivalent to the word supposedly being defined. The mistake which Thrasymachus is here assumed to be making is, however, no dull and lumpish gaffe. It deserves better than the incredulous references to Polydamas the athlete with which Socrates would dismiss it. For what on the present interpretation Thrasymachus is saying is not just wrong, period. To define the word 'justice' in such a way is not to say something which merely happens to be boringly mistaken. It is to make a move which is radically, spectacularly, diametrically, and hence most illuminatingly wrong.

It is of the essence of justice that appeals to justice are appeals to standards and principles logically independent of all particular individual and group interests. Only and precisely in so far as the standards and principles of justice are thus independent of all particular interests can it be in principle possible to assess any and every claim of any such interest by reference to these standards and principles. The point is elegantly put by Hume in one of his rather less frequently quoted paragraphs:

When a man denominates another his *enemy*, his *rival*, his *antagonist*, his *adversary*, he is understood to speak the language of self-love and to express sentiments peculiar to himself and arising from his particular circumstances and situation. But when he bestows on any man the epithets of *vicious* or *odious* or *depraved*, he then speaks another language and expresses sentiments in which he expects all his audience are to concur with him. He must here, therefore, depart from his private and particular situation and must choose a point of view common to him with others;   he must move some universal principle of the human frame and touch a string to which all mankind have an accord and symphony.[4]

(ii) Next we come to the equally fundamental but now all too familiar objection that a commendatory word cannot be adequately defined in terms only of neutral expressions. This now hackneyed though none-the-less vital point is one which it would be a little tricky to drive home with Thrasymachus, since he wants to remove or even to reverse the commendatory and prescriptive force of the terms 'justice' and 'injustice' (348C ff.). It is, surely, unnecessary to quote yet again the famous passage in which Hume insists upon a categorical distinction between ought and is?[5] Nevertheless it has to be said that some of our colleagues have on occasion failed to appreciate Hume's irony, and have mistaken it that he was asserting (perversely and falsely) that, although the distinction always is clearly made, it was left to the young Hume to notice it and to bring out its significance.

(iii) A third different yet again related consideration is best developed by reference to a famous passage in the *Euthyphro*. Plato's Socrates presses the question, in the particular case of holiness (or piety): "Is the holy loved by the gods because it is holy, or is it holy, because it is loved by the gods?"[6] If 'justice' were to be defined in terms of the interests or prescriptions of any power group, whether temporary or permanent, then those interests and prescriptions could not be criticized by reference to the idea and ideal of justice. Since they would by that token be just necessarily and as it were by definition rather than contingently and a matter of fortunate and meritorious fact, they could not sensibly be commended for possessing that characteristic.[7] At the human level it is obvious that, if in so far as 'justice' is taken to mean whatever some particular system of laws prescribes, then there can be no question but that these prescriptions really are just. But, by the same token, there can be no

---

[4] *An Enquiry Concerning the Principles or Morals*, L. A. Selby-Bigge (ed.), with revisions by P. H. Nidditch, Clarendon, 1975, IX (i), 272.

[5] *A Treatise of Human Nature*, L. A. Selby-Bigge (ed.), with revisions by P. H. Nidditch, Clarendon, 1974, III (i) 1, 469.

[6] 9E ff. We are bound to note that this basic distinction is being developed in the course of an argument intended to discredit Euthyphro, who was proposing to prosecute his own Father for being responsible for the death of a man who was nothing but a farm laborer. But it is perhaps permissible to hope that the historical Socrates did not share the callous indifference to lower class life seemingly shown by Plato's Socrates and even Plato himself.

[7] For some discussion of the application of these ideas to the God of Mosaic theism, compare my *Introduction to Western Philosophy*, Revised Edition, Thames and Hudson, 1989, 26-33.

possibility of commending or criticizing them for being as a matter of fact more or less just than any proposed alternative.

2. The present Part I, considering the first intervention of Thrasymachus as the suggestion of a descriptive definition of 'justice', can be elegantly concluded by referring to the Melian Dialogue[8] and comparing it with the 1968 exchanges between representatives of the U.S.S.R. and Czechoslovakia in a railway siding at Cierna nad Tisou. The former is a dramatic confrontation between the representatives of a great power (Athens) and those of a tiny island state (Melos). The Athenians wished to subjugate with as little fuss as possible this neutralist state, which fell unambiguously within their traditional sphere of influence. In fact they did, when the dialogue was over, 'normalize' the situation by an exercise of overwhelming military force.[9]

Now it is often and with reason suggested that Thrasymachus and Cleitophon in *The Republic*, and similar characters in other Platonic dialogues, are spokesmen for ideas which were already part of the contemporary intellectual scene, and, in particular that these ideas were put forward by the Athenians in the Melian Dialogue.[10] But when we actually examine the text we find that they began by indicating the very different framework which they thought appropriate to discussion between insiders:

We on our side will not offer a lengthy speech which no one would believe, with a lot of fine talk about how it is our right to have an empire because we defeated the Persians, or that we are coming against you now because we have been wronged; and we do not expect you to think to persuade us that the reason why you did not joint our camp was that you are kith and kin of the Spartans who originally settled Melos, or that you have done us no injury.

After this 400's B.C. equivalent of dismissing appeals to services rendered in the Great Anti-Fascist War, and of eschewing calls for the promotion of "socialism with a human face," the Athenians continue:

---

[8] Thucydides, *History of the Peloponnesian War*, Book V, Chapter 89.

[9] 'Normalization' was in fact the word favored by the U.S.S.R. as a description of the counter-revolution effected in Czechoslovakia after its reoccupation, with token support from some other Warsaw Pact members, by the Red Army.

[10] See, for example, Lord Lindsay's introduction to the Everyman translation of *The Republic of Plato*, Dent and Dutton, 1935, pp. xix-xxi.

Rather we expect you to try to do what is possible on the basis of the true thoughts of both parties, since you know and we know that it is part of the human condition to choose justice only when the balance of power is even, and those who have the advantage do what they have the power to do while the weak acquiesce.

The Melians accept that they cannot here appeal to justice as such:

Well we consider it expedient that you should not destroy something which is for the general good. (The word has to be 'expedient' since you have in this way laid down that we must speak of advantage rather than justice.)

II

Part I deployed decisive objections against any attempt to define the word 'justice' in terms of the interests or prescriptions of any particular power or power group. We are now ready to notice and neutralize two misleading idioms. In both a form of words is used which suggests that an account of meaning is being given. But in both it is essential to our understanding of what is being said that these semantic suggestions should be seen to be false.

1. In the first an epigram is presented as if it were a definition. If someone says, boringly, that the word 'uncle' means 'parents' brother' or 'brother-in-law', then they really are offering a definition of the word 'uncle'; and a correct definition at that. But when, in a perhaps rather smug way, you give us your favorite definition of the Roman genius as an infinite capacity for making drains, or of tanks as being armored and mechanized fire-power, then you are really making remarks about the Roman genius and about tanks, and quite good ones too. You certainly are not explicating the meanings of the expression 'the Roman genius' or of the word 'tank', for your remarks could not be understood by anyone who did not already know who the Romans were and what the words 'genius' and 'tank' mean. Nor could they be relished as good remarks by someone who mistakenly believed them to be tautological.

The second and most important of these two idioms is a favorite with debunkers. For instance: someone says, with a suitably angry sneer, that "when those Third World dictators ask for aid to raise the living standards of their wretched peoples, what they really mean is money both to continue themselves in power and to swell their own numbered Swiss bank accounts." Statements made in this idiom have point only and precisely in so far as what their subjects are said really to mean is not the meaning of what they are said to be saying. For, if it were, then the debunker's occupation would be gone. There would be no mask of hypocrisy to tear off.

These same hermeneutic ideas can, with appropriate alterations, be profitably applied to the famous claim that, "when you pronounce any action or character to be vicious, you mean nothing, but that from the constitution of your nature you have a feeling or sentiment of blame from the contemplation of it."[11] Those who see Hume as here suggesting a definition of 'vicious' mistake him to be producing not A Treatise of Human Nature but (two centuries before its foundation) a contribution to the journal Analysis.[12] His actual intentions are elucidated by the two subsequent sentences:

Vice and virtue, therefore, may be compared to sounds, colors, heat and cold, which according to modern philosophy, are not qualities in objects, but perceptions in the mind. And this discovery in morals, like that other in physics, is to be regarded as a considerable advancement of speculative sciences, tho', like that too, it has little or no influence on practice.

2. Anyone writing A New Republic for contemporary English speaking readers would have his Thrasymachus breaking in to say that his definition of justice (not 'justice') is the advantage of the stronger and/or that when those in power talk about justice what they really mean is their own advantage. What Plato actually scripted Thrasymachus to say should, I suggest, be construed with an eye to the correct interpretation of these modern English idioms.

For, as we saw in Part I, immediately after saying in best debunker's style "that justice is nothing else but the advantage of the stronger", Thrasymachus goes on to urge an empirical rather than a conceptual thesis: that "each form of government lays down laws for its own advantage, a democracy laws for the benefit of the populace, a dictatorship laws for the benefit of the dictator, and the others likewise."

As he continues, Thrasymachus finds himself employing give-away phrases which suggest that (whatever the truth of his empirical claims) the word 'justice' simply cannot be defined in terms of the advantage of the stronger: "By legislating in this way they make it plain that their advantage is justice for their subjects, and they punish anyone who gets out of line with this as a

---

[11] Treatise, III (i) 1, p. 469.

[12] For references see my contributions to V. C. Chappell (ed.) Hume, Doubleday, and Macmillan, 1966, and 1968.

lawbreaker and an unjust man." For if the mere fiat of the rulers were sufficient to make something just there would, surely, be no call for him to add "for their subjects", while his "they punish anyone who gets out of line with this as an . . . unjust man" at least hints at a suppressed "as if he were."

Nevertheless, it would be entirely wrong to suggest that any of this is clear to Thrasymachus himself. The development of the ensuing discussion shows that neither Thrasymachus nor Socrates within the dialogue nor, presumably, Plato outside composing it, is a thorough master of the distinction between contentions about the meanings of words and these about supposed matters of fact and real existence. For, after Thrasymachus has explained himself by saying things which suggest that he wants to maintain a thesis about the actual behavior of men in power, Socrates responds, not by appealing to counter-examples, which would show that the true political picture is not in fact as unrelievedly black as that painted by Thrasymachus, but by objecting that rulers may by mistake command what happens in fact not to be in their interests.

To this Thrasymachus replies, not by accepting the modest amendment proposed by Cleitophon (to say that those in power command not what is but what they believe to be in their own interests) but by going into what used to be nicknamed a 'Conventionalist Sulk'. He thus insists on so redefining 'ruler' that people are really and truly rulers only in so far as they make no mistakes about what is or would be in their own interests. This in turn encourages Socrates, who has shown no signs of needing much encouragement, to go on about how (true) rulers are definitionally concerned only with the good of their subjects. And so on.

The lesson for us to draw is one which *The Republic* is not ready to teach. It is that the sort of debunking thesis urged by Thrasymachus should not be construed as offering an ingenuous analysis of the ideas to be debunked. Instead it claims to reveal what actually is going on behind the fine talk; and this, if the whole is to be an exercise in debunking, must necessarily be something very different.

III

It is not, however, the account of justice provided by Thrasymachus which most immediately concerns Socrates, and, presumably, Plato. It is the consequence which Thrasymachus wants to derive from that and other similar accounts: "that the life of the unjust man is superior to that of the just man". This conclusion Thrasymachus founds upon the contention that to be just involves sacrificing one's own interests to those of other people, a contention which is in turn taken to warrant the further inference that the man who chooses to be just must be a fool:

> You must see, my most simple Socrates, that the just man always comes off worse than the unjust. Consider first commercial dealings, when a just and unjust man are partners. You will not find at the dissolution of the partnership that the just man ever has more than the unjust, but less. Then again in dealings with the state, when there are taxes to pay out of equal incomes the just man pays more, the unjust less. And, when it is a matter of taking, the one gains nothing, the other plenty (334D-E).

Thrasymachus states and overstates his case with cynical ferocity. He presses home the immoral moral that justice is, therefore, "a right noble simplicity", while injustice, if not perhaps exactly a virtue, certainly, is "good policy" (348C-D). This is the challenge which shocked Plato's Socrates, and which has gone on shocking generations of readers. Yet any satisfactory response to Thrasymachus must begin by stating emphatically and categorically that on his basic point he is right. For, as was surely brought out in Part I, it is of the essence of morality in general and of justice in particular that, in anything short of some humanly unrealizable Utopia, these must, from time to time, require sacrifices.

That this is indeed the case is precisely one mark which distinguishes this, our world, as not ideal. So one direction in which efforts are made to make it somewhat less not-ideal is by establishing penal and other institutions, part of the function of which is to supply artificial incentives through which some conduct which would otherwise be virtuous but not prudent may become prudent as well as virtuous. Only given the perfect enforcement of a system in which penalties were perfectly adjusted to both offenses and offenders would it be true that crime never pays. Even then, as any liberal reader must insist, there would be many offenses which remained immoral but not criminal. So, at best, some of these would still give rise to the questions why the wicked should so often prosper and why the sacrifices of the virtuous remain so often unrequited.

It is, therefore, radically misguided for Plato's Socrates to attempt to deny the Thrasymachean claim that in fact in this actual world morality often does demand sacrifices; and it is also, of course, unsound in method to try to meet his point about the actual world by appealing to what perhaps would be the case in another possible world. It is equally, but more interestingly misguided in method to inquire into the nature of justice by examining it first, writ large as it were, in a just collective: "So, if you agree, let us investigate its nature first in states, and only after look at it in the individual too, searching for the likeness of the greater in the form of the less" (369A).

This insidiously persuasive suggestion is, once again, diametrically wrong. For Thrasymachus has not disputed, or at any rate he has no need to dispute, that justice makes for the common good, that an observance by everybody of its dictates is in the collective interest. What and all a cautious Thrasymachus would be concerned to underline is that what is in the collective interest is not always and necessarily in the individual interests of members of that collective; and this is true. The truth (and it is a truth which the whole method of Plato's Socrates seems calculated to conceal) is that morality often does demand sacrifices, and when it does, then it is not profitable to oneself but, at best, to others. It would be preposterous to try to pretend that, for instance, if I can get away with not paying my fair share of some general levy, this evasion, which quite certainly harms the collective, cannot be to my individual advantage.

It is what should be an obvious consequence of what was said in Part I about the impossibility of defining the word 'justice' in terms of any particular interest, that there can be no necessary coincidence between my individual duty and my individual advantage. In so far as there is such a coincidence between the dictates of a purely self-interested prudence and the demands of decency and morality, this is a matter not of logically necessary connection but only of fortunate contingent fact. Had there been, either in fact or necessarily, a perfect congruence between the two it is hard to see how we could have come to employ (and so often to contrast) the notions both of prudence and of morality. The two could have been equated or identified as one within a dream system so perfect that no one would have needed to be good. What, finally, do we all think of the hypocritical wretches who upon absolutely every occasion discover a convenient congruence between their own self interests and their imperative duties?

IV

The main would-be factual contention of Thrasymachus has, therefore, simply to be accepted, although there certainly is need to moderate and to qualify the cynical extremism of his presentation. But there is another and more philosophical task still to be started. We have to challenge the assumption that the main thesis, that morality often calls for sacrifices, carries the implications: first, that anyone who knowingly makes such sacrifices must be a fool: and, second, "that the life of the unjust man is superior to that of the just man."

The reason why it does not follow, from the fact that some course of action would involve self-sacrifice, that it must be irrational knowingly to choose that course and to make that sacrifice, is, as we ought to have learnt from Hume,[13] that no particular desire and no choice of particular ends can as such be either rational or irrational. To choose this end rather than that may be usual or unusual, to be encouraged or to be discouraged. But it is itself no more either rational or irrational than it is rational or irrational to like or dislike kippers or to prefer daughters to sons or sons to daughters.

It is often assumed, both by those who see themselves as men of the world and by the world-rejecting authors of textbooks of moral theology, that it is paradigmatically rational for people single-mindedly to pursue each their own individual long-term self-interest.[14] Yet the falsity of this common assumption constitutes (at least in the relevant sense of 'rational') a rather rarely recognized corollary of Hume's perhaps over-dramatically expressed conclusions that "Reason is . . . the slave of the passions, and can never pretend to any other office than to serve and obey them."?[15] It is, therefore, no more necessarily rational to be single-mindedly devoted to the pursuit of one's own individual self-interest than it is necessarily irrational to choose, quite deliberately, to sacrifice possible but unfair gains. To be scrupulous is not, as such, to be a fool.

Again, since the claim "that the life of an unjust man is superior to that of the just man" is presumably a commendation, it cannot be derived directly and exclusively from the factual contention that the latter may involve sacrifices not required by the former. And, unless this factual contention is part of the meaning of that claim, it must be possible consistently to reject the claim, and to commend instead the life of the just man, while nevertheless accepting the neutral and purely factual as opposed to the partisan and commendatory elements in the case presented by Thrasymachus.

Many things may and of course need to be said about and against the standpoint of Thrasymachus. We might for instance, quote Robert Browning's Orwellian "there is a decency required," adding perhaps that justice tends to the common good. It is, however, obvious that all such consideration will leave Thrasymachus altogether unmoved, or, rather, will only increase his exasperation. But then what is he, and what are we looking for? We cannot

---

[13] *Treatise*, II (iii) pp. 3, 413-7.

[14] See, for instance, P. T. Geach, *God and the Soul*, Routledge and Kegan Paul, 1969, Chapter IX.

[15] *Treatise*, II (iii) pp. 3, 414.

show him that he is wrong in insisting that the dictates of morality often contradict the indications of prudence. For, in fact they do. So if in every such conflict he systematically prefers the latter, and has no general concern about morality as such, or indeed about anything but his own particular interests, then he will not be interested in whatever we may say about things which, though no doubt good in themselves, are certainly not always and necessarily good for him.

CHAPTER 9

COMMUNISM: THE PHILOSOPHICAL FOUNDATIONS
(1991)

I. A GERMAN PHILOSOPHER

"Karl Marx was a German philosopher." It is with this seminal sentence that Leszek Kolakowski begins his great work on *The Main Currents of Marxism: Its Rise, Growth and Dissolution.*[1] Both the two terms in the predicate expression are crucial. It is most illuminating to think of Marx as originally a philosopher, even though nothing in his vastly voluminous works makes any significant contribution to philosophy in any academic understanding of that term.[2] It is also essential to recognize that for both Marx and Engels philosophy was always primarily, indeed almost exclusively, what they and their successors called classical German philosophy. This was a tradition seen as achieving its climactic fulfillment in the work of Hegel, and one which they themselves identified as a main stimulus to their own thinking. Thus Engels, in *Ludwig Feuerbach and the End of Classical German Philosophy*, claimed that

---

[1] Clarendon, 1978.

[2] The fact that a joint composition by Marx and Engels first published only decades after their deaths, *The German Ideology*, was adopted a few years ago as a set-book for certain British school examinations in Philosophy has to be seen realistically: not as a belated admission of the authors' stature as philosophers comparable with the authors of the other works prescribed (Descartes, Hume and Mill); but instead as one more example of that servile fawning upon power to which George Orwell saw intellectuals as occupationally inclined.

129

"The German working-class movement is the inheritor of German classical philosophy."[3]

So we have to presume that neither Marx nor Engels ever studied Locke's *Essay Concerning Human Understanding* or the philosophical works of Hume. Certainly, even if the Founding Fathers of Marxism were in any way acquainted with these books, they never realized that they needed to come to terms with challenges contained therein. For both men were to all appearance totally innocent of Hume's fundamental distinction between propositions stating, or purporting to state, only "the relations of ideas," and propositions stating, or purporting to state, "matters of fact and real existence."[4]

Never having addressed themselves to Locke's naturalistic account of the origins and development of our conceptual equipment, and never having been subjected to probings by what among English-speaking philosophers is now nicknamed 'Hume's Fork', Marx and Engels were at no time forced to appreciate that substantial discoveries of "matters of fact and real existence" cannot be made by studying only particular ideas and "the relations of ideas." Nor, it seems, did they ever make the crucial distinction between logical and physical necessity. The former belongs to the world of language and discourse, the world of the relations of ideas and of propositions, whereas the latter is a matter of fact and real existence in the Universe around us. Much of the prophetic writing of Marx and Engels must in consequence fall under the ban imposed by Part III of the concluding Section XII in Hume's *Enquiry Concerning Human Understanding.*[5]

Apologists have attempted to brush Kolakowski's insightful contention aside. Thus Ralph Miliband wrote in a Critical Notice: "Marx was not, in fact, a 'German philosopher'. . . . No 'philosopher' of the kind Kolakowski has in mind could have written *Capital,* or would have felt any need to write it."[6] Again, in a slighter review, Tony Benn claimed that "unlike many other

---

[3] *Selected Works of Karl Marx and Friedrich Engels,* Moscow, Foreign Languages Publishing House, 1951, Vol. II, p. 361. In 'Three Sources and Three Component Parts of Marxism' Lenin wrote similarly: "The doctrine of Marx . . . is the legitimate successor of the best that was created by humanity in the nineteenth century . . . German philosophy, English political economy and French socialism."

[4] Compare my 'Prophecy or Philosophy? Historicism or History?', in R. Duncan and C. Wilson (eds.), *Marx Refuted,* Ashgrove, 1987, pp. 68-88.

[5] The final paragraph begins: "When we run over libraries, persuaded of these principles, what havoc must we make?" Then, referring to the sort of work to which the embargo applies, it concludes: "Commit it then to the flames, for it can contain nothing but sophistry and illusion."

[6] *Political Studies,* Vol. XXIX, No. 1, 1981, p. 117.

philosophers . . . Marx began by a deep study of the real world itself -- in order to understand how it worked and why, and then drew his own conclusions."[7]

But there is abundant evidence to show that Benn's biographical claim is false. It is indeed the direct reverse of the truth. For all the social and political doctrines peculiarly associated with Marx, all those so enormously influential doctrines which were presented most dramatically in 1848 in the *Communist Manifesto* (the doctrines, that is to say, of an inexorable yet always conflict-torn historical development, a development which is bound in the not impossibly remote future to find its blessed consummation in the revolutionary triumph of the class to end all classes) all these conclusions were originally derived, by what Marx himself described as a philosophical analysis, not from "a deep study of the real world itself," but from a priori manoeuvres with various abstract concepts.

These seminal, revolutionary ideas, and all the massively important would-be factual contentions in which they are embodied, were therefore not the final product of long years of labour poring over bluebooks in the Reading Room of the British Museum, but instead themselves provided the original incentive to embark upon those political and economic studies which eventually, in 1867, resulted in the publication of the first volume of *Capital*, this being as much of his long promised *magnum opus* as Marx himself could ever be brought to complete. Not only were all the major Marxist contentions presented in the *Communist Manifesto*, years before Marx first applied for his Reader's Card, but they are also to be found in his even earlier books and manuscripts.

In fact it was in 1845, before he had even thought of moving to London, that Marx signed a contract to compose the great book which was supposed to be going to provide empirical confirmation for revelatory conclusions already drawn by a priori analysis. Characteristically Marx proceeded forthwith to spend the remarkably (authors might say enviably) generous advance. But no book was produced under that contract, and the wretched publisher got nothing for his money. The whole revealing story of how long and how persistently Engels had to labour to induce Marx actually to produce that confirmatory book is best told in the most salutary and least devout of all the now numerous biographies.[8]

---

[7] *New Society* (London) for 3 November 1983.

[8] Leopold Schwartzschild, *The Red Prussian,* Pickwick, Second Edition, 1986.

II. DIALECTICAL MATERIALISM AND DIALECTICAL LOGIC

In the nineteen thirties and forties what was meant by the expression 'Marxist philosophy' (in the narrower, academic understanding of the word 'philosophy') was dialectical materialism.[9] The authoritative primary text, to which all Communist Parties in communion with Moscow used to refer, was J. V. Stalin's *Dialectical and Historical Materialism*. In the British Isles this was often supplemented by David Guest, *Dialectical Materialism* (London: Lawrence and Wishart, 1939), a work published only after the author was killed in action during the Spanish Civil War. Much later, following Khrushchev's secret speech to the Twentieth Congress, some 'New Left' fellow-travellers, labouring to escape the now abusive epithet 'Stalinist' began to contend that the *Economic and Philosophical Manuscripts of 1844* were the true foundation documents of Marxist philosophy; and, hence, that its key word was not 'dialectics' but 'alienation'.

In that now remote earlier period, before the Twentieth Congress, standard expositions typically started by contrasting dialectical materialism with the mechanical materialism of the seventeenth and eighteenth centuries. That, it was alleged, did not recognize development in the Universe whereas dialectical materialism put heavy emphasis upon development; thus, supposedly, providing a kind of justification for transforming capitalist into socialist and, ultimately, communist societies. Here it was *de rigueur* to quote Stalin: "Contrary to metaphysics, dialectics holds that nature is not a state of rest and immobility, stagnation and immutability, but a state of continuous movement and change . . . where something is always arising and developing, and something always disintegrating and dying away."

At this point well-girded unbelievers ought to raise and to press awkward questions: Who were these mechanical materialists of the seventeenth and eighteenth centuries, who somehow contrived not to "recognize development in the Universe?"; Who are the twentieth century metaphysicians who, in the spirit of the pre-Socratic Parmenides of Elea, allegedly assert that there is no such thing as change or motion?; and Why is a general emphasis upon development (as something which is in fact always occurring) thought somehow

---

[9] The outstanding critical study, unlikely ever to be superseded as a treatment of the period which it covers, is the Jesuit Father Gustav Wetter's *Dialectical Materialism: A Historical and Systematic Survey of Philosophy in the Soviet Union*, Praeger, 1958.

to justify the particular change from capitalism to communism as one which actually will and/or *ought* to occur?[10]

To emphasize "development in the universe," even with the specific purpose of justifying the changing of capitalist society into a communist one, could scarcely constitute an appropriate or sufficient principle of division between dialectical materialism and materialism without prefix or suffix. Nor should we carry things much further forward if we, like Engels in *Anti-Duhring*,[11] were to add to the emphasis upon change and development an insistence upon universal connectedness -- "the altogetherness of everything."

There is, of course, more to it than this; if little better. For the Marxist dialectic maintains that development is somehow realized by the unity and struggle of opposites. In the oft-quoted words of Lenin: "The unity (coincidence, identity, equal action) of opposites is conditional, temporary, transitory, relative. The struggle of mutually exclusive opposites is absolute, just as development and motion are absolute."

Some light is perhaps thrown on these dark sayings when later we are told: first, that, according to Marx, material development itself follows the process of thesis-antithesis-synthesis; and, hence, that whereas Hegel's dialectics were idealistic, those of Marx were materialistic. One supposed consequence is that Marxists are supposed to have developed what is called 'Dialectical Logic'. This maintains that the principle of contradiction is in error, since the change and development characteristic of all things implies that they somehow contain and embrace contradiction.

To all this stuff the most fundamental and overwhelming objection is one which has perhaps never been put better than it was by Herr Eugen Duhring, in the very *Course of Philosophy* against which Engels directed that most famous polemic, *Anti-Duhring*: "Contradiction is a category which can only appertain to a combination of thoughts, but not to reality. There are no contradictions in things, or, to put it in another way, contradiction applied to reality is itself the apex of absurdity."

Engels quotes these two sentences in the first paragraph of the first of the two chapters specifically devoted to this subject. He then complains: "This is

---

[10] Compare David McLellan, *Marx before Marxism*, Penguin, Revised Edition 1972, p. 67: "It was precisely this gap between what is and what ought to be that Marx considered to have been bridged by the Hegelian philosophy." Those wishing to learn the truth about this controverted topic should study W. D. Hudson (ed.), *The Is/Ought Question*, Macmillan, 1969.

[11] Friedrich Engels, *Herr Eugen Duhring's Revolution in Science (Anti-Duhring)*, translated by Emile Burns, Lawrence and Wishart, 1934.

practically all we are told about dialectics in the *Course of Philosophy*" (p. 134). Yet, though no doubt a very short way with dissent, it surely is at any rate for the non-specialist sufficient? For Duhring was absolutely right to insist that it is radically and irredeemably wrongheaded thus to collapse the fundamental distinction between, on the one hand, (verbal) contradictions, which can obtain only between propositions asserted, and, on the other hand, (physical) conflicts and tensions, which can occur only between animals or inanimate objects or other phenomena of the non-linguistic world. A little more, however, should perhaps be said: not about 'dialectical logic' but about dialectical materialism as supposedly somehow scientific. There can be no question but that Engels himself approached dialectical materialism through the natural sciences. Thus, in the unfinished manuscript eventually published as *The Dialectics of Nature*, he maintained that, whereas "the laws of dialectics" were by Hegel developed "as mere laws of thought," his own concern was to show that they "are really laws of development of nature, and therefore are valid also for theoretical natural sciences."[12]

Three of these putative dialectical laws of nature are listed in the first paragraph of Chapter II 'Dialectics'; (a) "The law of the transformation of quantity into quality and *vice versa*"; (b) "The law of the interpenetration of opposites"; and (c) "The law of the negation of the negation." After this Engels proceeded to list what he saw as some of "the most striking individual illustrations from nature" of the operation of these putative laws. For wherever Engels looked he found such illustrations, some perhaps more impressively persuasive than others, but all always serving as further perceived confirmations for his theories.

To anyone who has ever been to school with Popper this itself provides sufficient reason for suspicion.[13] For the semantic content of these 'dialectical laws' is so elusive and so indeterminate that prejudiced ingenuity will have little

---

[12] Friedrich Engels, *The Dialectics of Nature*, translated by Clemens Dutt, International, 1940, pp. 26-7. This edition contains a Preface and Notes by J. B. S. Haldane, who was at the time both Britain's leading geneticist and a member of the National Executive of the local Communist Party. He suggested that Einstein's low opinion of the work should be disregarded on the ground that Einstein probably saw only the admittedly worthless essay on electricity. So compare the Appendix to Sidney Hook's *Dialectical Materialism and Scientific Method*, Committee on Science and Freedom, 1955, which prints a letter from Einstein saying that Edward Bernstein showed him the entire manuscript.

[13] See, for instance, K. R. Popper, *Conjectures and Refutations: The Growth of Scientific Knowledge*, Routledge and Kegan Paul, 1963, especially Chapter 1.

difficulty in interpreting anything whatever which is found actually to happen as constituting the $n+1$th confirming instance.

To possess the logical form of a law of nature a proposition must imply that, under conditions of such and such a sort, it is physically necessary that conceivable events of one kind must occur, and physically impossible that conceivable events of another kind could occur. And, since every proposition is equivalent to the negation of its own negation, the extent and content of what is asserted by asserting any proposition is precisely proportionate to the extent and content of what is denied by denying that proposition. We have, therefore, to conclude: first, that until and unless our dialecticians can specify some sorts of conceivable phenomena which their 'dialectical laws' preclude as physically impossible, those 'laws' will remain perfectly vacuous; and that, second, if and when such sorts of conceivable but practically precluded phenomena have been specified, the substance and importance of the resulting laws must be precisely proportionate to the extent and nature of what is thereby precluded.

Communists make much of the necessities and impossibilities involved in laws of nature, and especially of the (in Popper's sense[14]) historicist laws of historical development which they believe were discovered by the Founding Fathers of their faith. Since, as we shall be seeing in Part III, its revelation of the alleged inevitabilities supposedly guaranteed by those historicist laws has been and remains the chief attraction of their system, that is scarcely surprising.

III. THE FAULTY PHILOSOPHICAL FOUNDATIONS

As was pointed out in Part I, it is a straightforward matter of established biographical fact that all the distinctive essentials of Marxism were originally derived, not from "a deep study of the real world itself," but from a priori manoeuvres with various abstract concepts; manoeuvres which appear to have been completed in 1844. This might not have mattered much: if only the resulting system of ideas had happened to correspond fairly closely to the realities; or if only Marx himself had been prepared openmindedly to investigate how far, or even whether, it truly did. But neither of these alternative protases comes anywhere near the truth. Here we are concerned solely with the second. Perhaps the most significant indication that, about all the issues which they perceived as fundamental, the minds of Marx and Engels were from then on

---

[14]   See K. R. Popper *The Poverty of Historicism*, Routledge and Kegan Paul, 1957; and compare my 'Popper and Historicist Necessities', in *Philosophy*, 1990, pp. 53-64.

entirely closed is that no one seems to be able to point to any passage in all the voluminous collected works in which either of them recognizes anything as constituting a serious difficulty for what in their correspondence they always described as "our view" or "our theory."

There were, I suggest, two main reasons for this closure of their minds. First: all the most personally meaningful activities and associations of both Marx and Engels were based upon the intellectual system (not first but) most vividly and most compellingly proclaimed in the *Communist Manifesto*. So both of them found it all too easy to yield to temptations to suppress or to distort any apparently irreconcilable facts. Consider, for instance, what Marx wrote to Engels in a letter dated 15 August 1857; a letter which has for us a double interest, in that it also reveals that for Marx himself dialectics was in large part a tactic of obfuscation:

> I took the risk of prognosticating in this way, as I was compelled to substitute for you as correspondent at the *Tribune* . . . . It is possible I may be discredited. But in that case it will still be possible to pull through with the help of a bit of dialectics. It goes without saying that I phrased my forecasts in such a way that I would prove to be right also in the opposite case.[15]

The second reason for the closure of minds was that Marx was a German philosopher; or, in deference to such giants of earlier generations as Leibniz and Albertus Magnus, perhaps we should say that he was a young, post-Hegelian, German philosopher. As such Marx never learnt the lessons which Locke and Hume had to teach. Above all Marx seems always to have taken it absolutely for granted that the main line of future historical development can be discovered by analysing concepts, that such abstract analysis can yield some knowledge of necessary and therefore inexorable historicist laws of historical development. Certainly much of the appeal of Marxism always has been, and still remains, that it is believed to provide (not a philosophical but) scientific proof that (as crude Comrade Khrushchev used to say) "Communism is at the end of all the roads in the world: we shall bury you!"[16]

---

[15] Can we, should we, refrain from repeating the concluding sentence of the obituary tribute Engels paid to Marx: "*So war dieser Mann der Wissenschaft?*"

[16] In my *Darwinian Evolution*, Granada Paladin, 1984, III 3, I argued at some length that it was because Engels was so right in the first claim made in that tribute (that Marx was always, before all else, the revolutionary) that he was so wrong in the second (that the achievement of Marx as a social scientist was on all fours with that of Darwin in biology). For, as I show there, Marx

In the *Economic and Philosophical Manuscripts of 1844,* Marx complains that the classical economists fail to bring out how "apparently accidental circumstances" are nothing but "the expression of a necessary development." The climactic end of that "necessary development" is proclaimed in the final sentences of the first section of the *Communist Manifesto*:   "What the bourgeoisie, therefore, produces, above all, is its own gravediggers. Its fall and the victory of the proletariat are equally inevitable." Six years later, in an article on 'The English Middle Class' for the *New York Daily Tribune* for August 1, 1854, Marx allowed that "though temporary defeat may await the working classes, great social and economical laws are in operation which must eventually ensure their triumph."[17]

In 1867, in the original German preface to the first volume of *Capital*, the book so long awaited as the philosopher prophet's promised proof, Marx explains "why England is used as the chief illustration in the development of my theoretical ideas."   Everything discovered here will eventually be just as applicable elsewhere: "Intrinsically, it is not a question of the higher or lower degree of development of the social antagonisms that result from the natural laws of capitalist production. It is a question of these laws themselves, of these tendencies working with iron necessity towards inevitable results. The country that is more developed industrially only shows, to the less developed, the image of its own future."[18] The only accounts of the Last Days which Marx himself was prepared to provide were studiously sketchy and abstract. Yet, surely, they should still be sufficient to make his prophecies altogether incredible? It was in their day all very well for the Saints and for the Fathers to develop a Christian historicism: beginning with the creation of the Universe itself and of Adam, the man made in God's image; continuing to the predestined and foreseen Fall; on to the Incarnation; and culminating in the final establishment of God's Kingdom upon Earth. For in that scheme the particular species of our species-being was from the beginning created by the Almighty with an all-seeing eye to its eventual and truly human destiny. We were created, in the splendid words of the old Scottish *Prayer Book*, "to glorify God and to enjoy him forever." In that scheme the inexpugnable guarantee that the Kingdom will

---

repeatedly, shamefully, and shamelessly preferred revolutionary rhetoric to scientific truth.

[17] On the appeal of this promise to the first Russian disciples see, for instance, R. G. Wesson, *Why Marxism?*, Temple Smith, 1976, p. 46.

[18] In *Early Writings*, translated by R. Livingstone and G. Berton, introduced by L. Colletti, Penguin, 1975, p. 323.

indeed come, never thereafter to be undermined or overthrown, lay in the absolute power and promise of Omnipotence.

How different it is with the secular substitute, the true People's Democratic Republic of Marx. Here the existence of God and his Providence have been contemptuously denied. Supposedly we are all atheists now, altogether rejecting religion as an obsolete illusion. It is, in the words of the *Manifesto*, nothing but "the cry of the hard-pressed creature, the heart of the heartless world, the soul of soulless circumstance, the laudanum of the masses."

How then can we fail to see the massive implausibility of this Marxist eschatology, indeed its internal incoherence? The whole continuing human life-process has perhaps never before been presented in so harsh a light. For instance, the *Communist Manifesto* proper begins: "The history of all hitherto existing society is the history of class struggles," and "law, morality, religion," along with everything else once thought to stand between humanity and the abyss, are nothing but feeble fig leaves miserably failing to conceal unlovely class interests. Yet this long succession of savage struggles is, we are assured, bound to end (and to end pretty soon too) in the annihilating victory of a class to end all classes; a victory to be followed without fail, again in pretty short order, by the establishment of a conflict-free utopia; an utopia in which, harried by no class or other group conflicts, "the free development of each will be a condition of the free development of all."

So how, we should now ask, does the atheist Marx come by his secular revelation? It was, to borrow what should be the famous and revealing words of Engels, by "the philosophic path." Moses Hess was the first to reach Communism by that path, and a year or two later Marx made his own way along the same route.[19] This framework of the philosophical ideas of Hegel and his immediate successors is of the greatest importance. For, although the historicism of his historical materialism always has been and is by aficionados presented as scientific socialism, the laborious empirical researches of Marx were in fact undertaken in order to illustrate, to confirm, and to fill out what he considered had been in all essentials already provided by a kind of philosophical argument. It is in this light that we may best hope to understand certain besetting errors and deficiencies of the Marxist system.

Three features of this long-neglected background are especially relevant. The first is the hardest to characterize. Feuerbach was pointing to it when he said that all speculative philosophers are priests in disguise, and that all the

---

[19] See, for instance, McClellan *op. cit., passim.* In his *Karl Marx: His Life and Thought,* Granada Paladin, 1976, McClellan cites a remark supposedly made by Louis Philippe in 1845: "We must purge Paris of German philosophers" (p. 135).

classical German creations (Hegel's Idea, Fichte's Ego, and Schelling's Absolute) were simply substitutes for the Deity reduced to a more abstract form. The whole climate of opinion was suffused with a profound, providential, Christian or post-Christian conviction that in the end all manner of things will be well: a usually unstated and therefore never examined or abandoned assumption that ultimately, the Universe is not indifferent to human concerns. The two further features are inseparably connected. There was, second, equally profound and equally unexamined assumption that a priori reasoning can discover necessary truths about both the structure of the Universe and our true and proper life within it. Third, such rational reasoning (reasoning which is rationalist in the technical philosopher's sense, in contrast to empiricist) is typically all-the-balls-in-the-air juggling with terms referring to abstract and indeterminate collectivities.

To indicate the atmosphere it is best to begin by quoting here one or two sentences from Hegel's Inaugural Lecture at Heidelberg, noting that in a passing moment of infidel insight Marx himself spoke of the drunken speculations of this master wizard: "We shall see . . . that in other European countries . . . Philosophy, excepting in name, has sunk even from memory, and that it is in the German nation that it has been retained as a peculiar possession. We have received the higher call of Nature to preserve this holy flame, just as the Eumolpidae in Athens had the conservation of the Eleusinian mysteries, the inhabitants of the island of Samothrace the preservation of a higher divine service . . . ."

There is now no escaping what, for anyone raised in the English speaking philosophical world, is bound to be an excruciating experience. Perhaps this exercise can best be seen as a sort of intellectual inoculation: an injection of a small shot of the virus or the bacillus in order to build up antibodies, lest worse befall. What we have to do now is briefly to immerse ourselves into those intoxicated verbalizings which the Founding Fathers presented and accepted as proving the principles of their new 'scientific socialism.' To parody a later and funnier Marx, "These arguments may appear to possess no force at all. Yet don't be misled. For they do not possess any force at all."

In the Introduction to his unfinished *Critique of Hegel's Philosophy of Law* Marx characteristically conjures up the barely embryonic German proletariat in order to provide an answer to his question: "So where is positive possibility of German emancipation?" The answer, he asserts, lies:

> . . . in the formation of a class with *radical* chains, a class which is the dissolution of all classes, a sphere which has a universal character because of its universal suffering and which lays claim to no

particular right because the wrong it suffers is not a *particular wrong*
but *wrong in general*; a sphere of society which can no longer lay
claim to *a historical* title, but merely to a *human* one, which does not
stand in one-sided opposition to the consequences but in all-sided
opposition to the premises of the German political system; and finally
a sphere which cannot emancipate itself without emancipating itself
from -- and thereby emancipating -- all the other spheres of society,
which is, in a word, the total loss of humanity and which can
therefore redeem itself only through the *total redemption of humanity.*
This dissolution of society as a particular class is the proletariat.[20]

So now, no doubt, we know. And, as if that outburst of drunken
pontification was not already too much, here from the *Economic and
Philosophical Manuscripts of 1844* is something even more abstract, more
arbitrary, more technical and (if that is possible) even less concrete and down
to earth:

Communism is the *positive* suppression of *private property* as *human
self-estrangement,* and hence the true *appropriation* of the *human*
essence through and for man; it is the complete restoration of man to
himself as a *social,* i.e. *human,* being, a restoration which has become
conscious and which takes place within the entire wealth of previous
states of development.   This communism, as fully developed
naturalism, equals humanism, and as fully developed humanism
equals naturalism; it is the *genuine* resolution of the conflict between
man and nature, and between man and man, the true resolution of the
conflict between existence and being, between objectification and
self-affirmation, between freedom and necessity, between individual
and species. It is the solution of the riddle of history and knows itself
to be the solution. The entire movement of history is therefore both
the *actual* act of creation of communism -- the birth of its empirical
existence -- and, for its thinking consciousness, the *comprehended*
and *known* movement of its *becoming* . . . .[21]

To achieve as much or as little understanding of such passages as is in fact
possible, it would be necessary to make an enormous investment of time and

---

[20]   *Early Writings, op. cit.,* p. 256, original emphasis.

[21]   *Ibid.,* p. 348, original emphasis.

study in Hegel and in other immediate predecessors and contemporaries of Marx, and in the predecessors of those predecessors.[22] The first four chapters of the first volume of Kolakowski's three-decker treatise would serve only as a compressed introduction to some of the main primary sources. Fortunately it is sufficient to realize what no amount of background study ever would or could discover.

It would not and could not in any of these writings discover any distinction of physical from logical necessity. Nor would it discover any instructions on how the key terms are to be empirically cashed. For instance: no amount of immersion in the intellectual milieu of the Young Marx would leave us any better able than we are now to set about constructing sociologically viable indices either of German emancipation or of human self-estrangement.

The thinking of Marx is here so remote from the concrete, the particular and the individual that we may be accused of idle frivolity or of a deficiency of historical imagination for pressing questions on how we are supposed to determine how far any of these putative processes have or have not progressed. Still, braving these charges, what observable characteristics will distinguish the blessedly dealienated from those still afflicted with that exotic metaphysical disease, self-estrangement -- a disease everywhere endemic before and until the wholesale nationalization of "all the means of production, distribution, and exchange"? And what instructions are to be given to the field workers if our research is to determine whether, in this or that actual society of flesh and blood human beings, the conflicts "between existence and being . . . between objectification and self-affirmation, between freedom and necessity, between individual and species" have been or are being *genuinely* resolved?

The fact that no answer to such questions is provided by and within the theory both makes that theory, because in principle unfalsifiable, unscientific, and at the same time makes it endlessly attractive to those who are or aspire to become members of some despotic Leninist elite.[23] Of course it would be entirely possible to give a clear, precise and scientifically useful sense to 'alienation' or to any of the other key terms. So the fact that this seems never to have been done by any of our Marxist or Marxisant sociologists shows how far they are from actually being the truth-concerned and critical social scientists which they pretend to be.

We could, for instance, suggest that the alienation is perhaps a condition

---

[22] Anyone insisting upon such explorations will find the best guide in S. Hook, *From Hegel to Marx*, Michigan University Press, New Edition, 1962.

[23] See, for instance, M. Voslensky, *Nomenklatura: Anatomy of the Soviet Ruling Class*, The Bodley Head, 1984.

afflicting some or all assembly line workers in (privately owned) mass production industries (the condition displayed in Charles Chaplin's film *Modern Times* or in Rene Clair's *A Nous la Liberté*). Given this it would not be impossibly hard to assemble measures which would together constitute an Alienation Index. But, of course, committed Marxists are not going to do this. For they cannot fail to fear that, in any understanding which allows their claims about alienation to be in principle falsifiable, it might become possible to demonstrate that these claims are in fact false.

It is, for instance, said that Fiat have built in the U.S.S.R. a motor plant physically identical with one owned and operated by the same firm in Italy. Suppose this is the case, and suppose that some Marxist sociologists were unexpectedly to show their scientific good faith by constructing a viable Alienation Index. Then we might, if ever *glasnost* went so far as to permit such independent and external study of Soviet realities, once and for all settle the long disputed question whether the full implementation of the old original Clause IV of the Constitution of the British Labour Party (demanding the public ownership of "all the means of production, distribution and exchange") really would be, if not a panacea for all the ills to which the flesh is heir, then at any rate a cure for this particular and particularly elusive and intractable condition of alienation. But, of course, this sustained reluctance either to require or to permit the claim that total socialism constitutes the Sovereign remedy for alienation to be first precisely and unambiguously formulated and then put to decisive experimental test should itself be recognized as revealing. For it shows that what we have here is not now, and perhaps never has been, a truth-concerned conjecture. Instead alienation, even if it was not always, has certainly become an indefinite description of an indeterminate condition; a condition postulated to serve as the elusive yet all-pervasive disease for which socialism (its original promise to provide both emancipation and abundance so visibly and so catastrophically unfulfilled) may still continue to be promoted as the sole and sovereign remedy.

CHAPTER 10

RUSSELL'S JUDGMENT ON BOLSHEVISM
(1979)

(1) In 1920 Bertrand Russell visited the USSR in the company, although not strictly as a member, of a British Labour Party delegation. In the same year he published *The Practice and Theory of Bolshevism*, his assessment of the regime established by what was later to take the name of the Communist Party of the Soviet Union (Bolsheviks). In his Prefatory Note for the 2nd edition, written in October 1948, Russell was able to say: "If I were writing now, some things would be differently said, but in all major respects I adhere to the view of Russian Communism which I took in 1920, and its subsequent development has been not unlike what I expected."[1]

The gist of Russell's assessment can be given in a few sentences: "Regarded as a splendid attempt . . . Bolshevism deserves the gratitude and admiration of all the progressive part of mankind . . . if Bolshevism falls, it will have contributed a legend and a heroic attempt without which ultimate success might never have come."[2] But:

---

[1] My references to *The Practice and Theory of Bolshevism* (hereafter *TPTB*) will all be to this Second Edition, George Allen & Unwin, 1949. The text differs from that of the 1st edition in only two respects, according to Russell: On the one hand, I have omitted a chapter of which I was not the author; on the other hand, I have found it necessary, in order to conform to modern usage, to alter the word 'Communism' to 'Socialism' in many places. In 1920, there was not yet the sharp distinction between the two words that now exists, and a wrong impression would be made but for this change. (p. 5).

[2] *TPTB*, pp. 7-9.

Western Socialists who have visited Russia have seen fit to suppress the harsher features of the present regime . . . . Even those Socialists who are not Bolsheviks for their own country have mostly done very little to help men in appraising the merits or demerits of Bolshevik methods. By this lack of courage they have exposed Western Socialism to the danger of becoming Bolshevik through ignorance of the price that has to be paid and of the uncertainty as to whether the desired goal will be reached in the end. I believe that the West is capable of adopting less painful and more certain methods of reaching Socialism than those which have seemed necessary in Russia. And I believe that while some forms of Socialism are immeasurably better than capitalism, others are even worse. Among those that are worse I reckon the form which is being achieved in Russia, not only in itself, but as a more insuperable barrier to further progress.[3]

When, still later, he looked back upon the reception given to his own exercise in courage, and in dissenting integrity, Russell wrote:

The end of the war was not the end of my isolation, but, on the contrary, the prelude to an even more complete isolation (except from close personal friends) which was due to my failure to applaud the new revolutionary government of Russia. When the Russian Revolution first broke out I welcomed it as did almost everybody else, including the British Embassy in Petrograd (as it then was) . . . . But in 1920 I went to Russia . . . . I thought the regime already hateful and certain to become more so. I found the source of evil in a contempt for liberty and democracy which was a natural outcome of fanaticism. It was thought by Radicals in those days that one ought to support the Russian Revolution whatever it might be doing, since it was opposed by reactionaries, and criticism of it played into their hands. I felt the force of this argument . . . . But in the end I decided in favour of what seemed to me to be the truth. I stated publicly that I thought the Bolshevik regime abominable, and I have never seen any reason to change this opinion . . . . Most people still hated me

---

[3] *Ibid.*, pp. 20-1.

for having opposed the war, and the minority, who did not hate me on this ground, denounced me for not praising the Bolsheviks.[4]

Russell must, I think, have penned this retrospect without refreshing his memories of what he published in 1920. For here in *Portraits from Memory* he goes on:

> My visit to Russia in 1920 was a turning-point in my life. During the time that I was there I felt a gradually increasing horror which became an almost intolerable oppression. The country seemed to me one vast prison in which the jailers were cruel bigots. When I found my friends applauding these men as liberators and regarding the regime that they were creating as a paradise, I wondered in a bewildered manner whether it was my friends or I that were mad.[5]

Whereas Russell earlier had been prepared to match for the Bolsheviks of 1917, the tribute paid by Marx to the Communards of 1871, who 'stormed heaven', Russell now is no longer reflecting that "if Bolshevism falls, it will have contributed a legend and a heroic attempt without which ultimate success might never have come."

Again, the Russell of 1956 is harsher than the Russell of 1920 in his appreciation of the Bolshevik leaders. Thus, to the more Chomsky Russell of 1920, characteristically:

> It seems evident, from the attitude of the capitalist world to Soviet Russia, of the Entente to the Central Empires, and of England to Ireland and India, that there is no depth of cruelty, perfidy or brutality from which the present holders of power will shrink when they feel themselves threatened . . . . The present holders of power are evil men, and the present manner of life is doomed.[6]

It is, on the other hand, "essential . . . that melodrama should no longer determine our views of the Bolsheviks: they are neither angels to be worshipped

---

[4] *Portraits from Memory,* George Allen & Unwin, 1956, p. 13 (hereafter *PFM*). For reasons of the same sort as those given by Russell for altering the word 'Communism' to 'Socialism', I have promoted his original 'radicals' to 'Radicals'.

[5] *PFM*, pp. 13-14.

[6] *TPTB*, p. 10.

nor devils to be exterminated, but merely bold and able men attempting with great skill an almost impossible task."[7]

When in 1920 Russell reports his personal contacts with some of these Bolshevik leaders, they are not dismissed in the wholesale fashion (Ought we not to say 'melodramatic'?) deemed proper with the damned 'present holders of power' at points further West. Of Trotsky Russell said:

> I thought, perhaps wrongly, that his vanity was even greater than his love of power . . . . But I had no means of estimating the strength of his Communist conviction, which may be very sincere and profound.[8]

Nor was Lenin then presented as a monster of wickedness:

> He laughs a great deal; at first his laugh seems merely friendly and jolly, but gradually I came to feel it rather grim. He is dictatorial, calm, incapable of fear, extraordinarily devoid of self-seeking, an embodied theory.[9]

The nearest the 1920 book comes to saying that Lenin was not only bigoted but also cruel is the statement that he "laughed over the exchange the peasant is compelled to make, of food for paper . . . ." And whereas, presumably, Lenin was, in fact, amused that peasants were being in this sophisticated and collectivist way robbed, Russell added as his own explanation then: "the worthlessness of Russian paper struck him as comic."[10] It was, so far as I know, only in 1950 that Russell published in book form his second specimen of Lenin's Bolshevik humour:

> My most vivid impressions were of bigotry and Mongolian cruelty . . . . He explained with glee how he had incited the poorer peasants against the richer ones "and they soon hanged them from the nearest tree -- ha ha ha!" His guffaw at the thought of those massacred made my blood run cold.[11]

---

[7] *Ibid.*, p. 76.

[8] *Ibid.*, p. 38.

[9] *Ibid.*, p. 33.

[10] *Ibid.*, p. 35.

[11] *Unpopular Essays*, George Allen & Unwin, 1950, p. 219 (hereafter *UE*).

These differences between what actually was said in the book of 1920, and what books of 1950 or 1956 say or suggest was said, are, however, relatively unimportant. Certainly nothing which, in fact, was said in the former is either inconsistent with, or should lead us to be surprised by, such drastic and quite un-Chomsky later remarks as: "I have no doubt that the Soviet government is even worse than Hitler's, and it will be a misfortune if it survives";[12] and "For a long time after the Russian Revolution, it was customary to say, 'No doubt the new regime has its faults, but at any rate it is better than that which it has superseded'. This was a complete delusion."[13]

The first of these remarks was made in 1941. It could, by anyone prepared to be condemned for 'professional anti-communism,' or dismissed as a 'Cold War warrior,'[14] be provided with some precision and backing by appealing to comparisons between the proportions of the peoples concerned who have been deliberately exiled, imprisoned, dispossessed, executed or starved to death.[15]

---

[12]   In a letter to Gilbert Murray, dated 18 January 1941, printed in *The Autobiography of Bertrand Russell*, Vol. II, George Allen & Unwin, 1968, pp. 248-9.

[13]   *PFM*, pp. 203-4. Anyone surprised or distressed either here or elsewhere by my hostile references to Noam Chomsky ought to look again, in a perhaps cooler hour, at his *American Power and the New Mandarins*, Pantheon and Vintage, hardcover and paperback, respectively, 1969; maybe with the help of my 'New Left Isolationism', *Humanist* (Buffalo), September-October 1971, pp. 38-40).

Chomsky is, for instance, capable of writing, in a throwaway aside on p. 12: "the people of Vietnam (the Communists, that is)." Chomsky, thus, by implication dismisses all Vietnamese anti-communists (including many hundreds of thousands of Roman Catholic refugees from communist religious persecution) as not really people, nor deserving of consideration as such. Irrespective of our assessments of American involvement in Vietnam, we ought to be able to see that this is (despite all professions to the contrary, both from Chomsky and from his fans) an expression of a concern which is motivated more by political venom than by impartial morality.

Its pretensions to be humanist are equally to be rejected. We humanists (if not, apparently, these new Radicals) recognise even our religious and political opponents as human beings. It is a sad index of the disarray into which the Vietnam war threw so much American liberal opinion that Chomsky's political outbursts used, I am told, to get standing ovations from university audiences.

[14]   I have myself met these two phrases most recently on the back cover of H. E. Salisbury's edition of A. D. Sakharov, *Progress, Coexistence and Intellectual Freedom*, Penguin, 1969, and in Kai Nielsen, 'In Defence of Radicalism', in *Question 7*, Pemberton, 1974, respectively. Their attraction to those who use them (whether committed Radicals or mere trendies) lies precisely in the imprecision of the offence. No one thus sneeringly dismissed can know against what charge he has to try to defend himself, other than that of membership in a despised, detested and untrendy out-group.

[15]   For some data on the less well publicized side of such comparisons see, for instance, Robert Conquest, *The Great Terror*, Macmillan, 1968, especially pp. 19-26 and pp. 525-35. Compare also the same author's *The Nation Killers*, Macmillan, 1970.

Russell himself supports the second remark by pointing to material in the lives of Trotsky and other revolutionaries. This "reveals a degree of political and intellectual freedom to which there is nothing comparable in present-day Russia."[16]

What ought both to surprise and to distress us, and what are hard if not impossible to reconcile with any of Russell's earlier verdicts on Bolshevism, are some of the statements and actions of his latest years. Certainly Russell remained to the end eager to act on behalf of individual victims of persecution, irrespective of whether their victimization was or was not approved by the local Communist parties. Certainly (like a few of those parties themselves), he condemned the 1968 reconquest of Czechoslovakia, and (like rather fewer of them) he never backslid from his condemnation. Nevertheless Russell's pronouncements upon the Cuban missile crisis, or the Vietnam war, or many other issues of the period, can scarcely be said to have been formed or informed by any of the insights acquired from that first visit to the USSR.

It is, for instance, one thing to maintain that the USA was misguided, or even that it was morally at fault, to intervene militarily on behalf of the governments of South Vietnam, first against the local Vietcong, and then later also against the invaders from the north. But it was, surely, quite another to send to Hanoi, as Russell did on 11 June 1966, a message which concluded:

> I extend my warm regards and full solidarity for President Ho Chi Minh and for the people of Vietnam. I convey my great wish that the day may not be far off when a united and liberated Vietnam will celebrate its victory in a free Saigon.[17]

Happily the present chapter is not immediately or primarily concerned with such questions; neither with questions of consistency or inconsistency throughout a very long lifetime; nor with questions of the relative or absolute badness of different regimes. I want instead to consider some matters of what might be called, in a rather broad sense, political theory. These still (perhaps increasingly) urgent issues arise from things either said, or significantly not said, by Russell in *The Practice and Theory of Bolshevism.*   Even where I

---

[16] *PFM,* p. 204. For some quantitative material see, for instance, Robert Conquest, *Lenin,* Fontana, 1972, pp. 126-9.

[17] For plenty more of this sort of stuff on Cuba and the USSR, see his *Unarmed Victory,* Penguin, 1963, and, on Vietnam, see his *War Crimes in Vietnam,* George Allen & Unwin, 1967.

disagree with Russell's conclusions, or otherwise fault him, everything I say springs from the same fundamental shared conviction:

I think there are lessons to be learnt which must be learnt if the world is ever to achieve what is desired by those in the West who have sympathy with the original aims of the Bolsheviks. I do not think these lessons can be learnt except by facing frankly and fully whatever elements of failure there are in Russia. I think these elements of failure are . . . attributable . . . to an impatient philosophy, which aims at creating a new world without sufficient preparation in the opinions and feelings of ordinary men and women.[18]

(2) Although Russell does say here that the main trouble is a bad philosophy, the word 'philosophy' seems to be being employed only in the sort of sense in which a playboy might employ it to proclaim: "My philosophy is, the more sex the better." Certainly, there is nothing in the whole book to falsify S. N. Hampshire's contention: "Unlike his predecessors and peers in public philosophy -- Plato, Aristotle, Spinoza, Locke, Hume, Hegel -- Russell did not apply to politics the analytical methods which he called for in the theory of knowledge."[19]

Such philosophical alertness and acumen could have been most usefully directed to the key idea, or key ideas, of socialism. It is not. Russell begins: "By far the most important aspect of the Russian Revolution is as an attempt to realize Socialism. I believe that Socialism is necessary to the world . . ."[20] On the following page he tells us two things. First, "the method by which Moscow aims at establishing Socialism is a pioneer method, rough and dangerous, too heroic to count the cost of the opposition it arouses," and "I do not believe that by this method a stable or desirable form of Socialism can be established." Second, "although I do not believe that Socialism can be realized immediately by the spread of Bolshevism, I do believe that, if Bolshevism falls,

---

[18] *TPTB*, p. 8.

[19] In 'Russell, Radicalism, and Reason', a review of the third volume of the Autobiography for *The New York Review of Books*, reprinted in V. Held, K. Nielsen, and C. Parsons (eds.), *Philosophy and Political Action*, Oxford University Press, 1972, p. 262.

[20] *TPTB*, p. 7.

it will have contributed a legend and a heroic attempt without which ultimate success might never have come."[21]

(a) Although these two claims are not, exactly as they stand, contradictory, it does nevertheless appear that Russell wants to maintain: both, at the top of the page, that Bolshevik methods can produce socialism, albeit not a stable or desirable variety; and, at the bottom of the page, that they cannot produce any kind of socialism at all whether stable or unstable, desirable or undesirable. Clearly, what we need is some distinction between two senses of 'socialism'. In one the realisation of socialism must necessarily involve the realisation of (at least a large part of) Russell's ideals. In the other Russell could consistently say (as we have already seen that he elsewhere does say), "that while some forms of Socialism are immeasurably better than capitalism, others are even worse."

Once this first need is appreciated, it becomes, to any politically literate Englishman, obvious that we must start, even if we do not finish, by specifying both senses of 'socialism' partly or wholly in terms of some version of clause IV of the Constitution of the British Labour Party. This is the clause by which that party has since 1918 been committed as its ultimate aim to transferring into some form of public or communal ownership all the means of production, distribution and exchange. It is this clause, now slightly, but only slightly, revised, which has for as long as I can remember been printed as the only statement of aims on every membership card. (It was there when I joined in 1946; still there when I resigned in the early 1950s; and, in its revised form, still there when at long last in 1973 my wife too resigned!)

That something like this clause IV must be at least part of the essence of socialism may not seem equally obvious to citizens of the USA. For there it is usual (especially among those opposed to them) to describe publicly financed welfare measures, which are by no means necessarily connected with any public ownership of the economy, as socialistic (or even as rank socialism). Yet the difference which is thus obscured may be believed to be (and I myself believe is) extremely important. In Britain, for instance, a Conservative so totally opposed to nationalisation, and so dedicated to economic liberalism, as Mr. Enoch Powell, does not feel bound for that reason to oppose in principle a publicly financed National Health Service. On the contrary: Mr. Powell himself was, and remains, proud to have served as a Minister of Health, in very active charge of the development of that service. Once we appreciate the distinction just made, it becomes clear that his position is not in this respect inconsistent.

The usage common in the USA is, therefore, unfortunate. Failure to

---

[21] *Ibid.*, p. 8.

appreciate the difference which it obscures must have played at least some small part in strengthening opposition to Medicare programmes: programmes which surely are (if a non-citizen may be permitted to express an opinion upon a purely domestic matter) in some form or other that country's most urgent welfare need. This failure tends to associate such programmes with Britain's notoriously abysmal economic performance. It is, however, though perhaps surprising, true that many British Conservatives would argue that the main reason why the once famous British 'Welfare State' has recently in many respects fallen behind its opposite numbers in North-West Europe is that the social democratic parties there have nothing like the same hostility to private enterprise, to profits and to free markets as is shown by the more doctrinaire British Labour Party. Both in and out of office, but through the trade unions always in power, that corrosive hostility tends, we maintain, to choke the goose which might have laid so many more of the golden eggs of welfare.

Be all that as it may. What, tendentiously, we have asserted to be obvious to any politically literate Englishman, is what is relevant to present purposes. Russell was always incorrigibly English, and he had by 1920 been for several years a member of the Labour Party. For the Bolsheviks, too, clause IV is logically essential to socialism. Lenin and his colleagues displayed their commitment to this total socialism immediately after completing their coup in October. They proceeded forthwith to decree nationalisation, without compensation, for all industrial plant, banks and railways.

The first sense which Russell needs (and by no means only Russell) is one in which the realisation of socialism must involve both the full implementation of some version of clause IV and something else (perhaps a lot else) as well. The second sense which Russell needs (and, for the foreseeable future, everyone else too) is one in which that implementation must by itself constitute the consummation wished by some so persistently, if not perhaps devoutly. In the former, enriched, sense there might reasonably be dispute as to whether the Bolsheviks already had in 1920 achieved socialism, or in due course would; although a precondition of its reasonableness is to stipulate what the something else is to be.

In the latter, the basic clause IV sense, the only room for disagreement is about agriculture. For by 1920 the Bolsheviks had only redistributed that small proportion of the land which was not by 1917 already in the hands of the peasants.[22] Russell asked Lenin, "what to reply to critics who say that in the country" the Bolsheviks have "merely created peasant proprietorship, not Communism: he replied that that is not quite the truth, but he did not say what the truth is."[23] There is no indication that this was even part of Russell's reason for doubting whether they had established, or could hope to establish, socialism. But the point certainly was pressed with that aim by the doyen of orthodox Marxism, Karl Kautsky, in a work written in the August of 1918.[24]

(b) It is common nowadays (much too common) to find people dedicated to basic socialism (clause IV) who try to dismiss embarrassing evidence about conditions in countries which are in this sense undeniably socialist as irrelevant: "that is not truly socialism, or true socialism," they say; but only, perhaps, 'state capitalism'. Provided that some appropriate usage is stipulated, both for the term 'socialism' in the second sense suggested (*true* socialism), and for the paradoxical expression 'state capitalism'; and provided that that usage is in fact followed, with scrupulous consistency: then maybe no harm is done, except that others may still be confused through failing to grasp exactly what is going on.

These seemingly modest provisos are, however, much less easy to meet than one might in innocence have hoped; and much less often met. I have, for instance, twice in the last few months seen in the British quality press reports, one about Egypt and the other about Iraq, in which arrangements which are in the basic sense unquestionably socialist were described, with no explanation given, not as socialist but as 'state capitalist'.[25] Russell himself in discussing the Russian Bolsheviks speaks not of state capitalism, but of 'state socialism'. He too fails to make explicit what other and contrasting sort of socialism it is supposed that there might be, and which he cherishes as his own ideal: ". . . the successors of Peter the Great . . . are preparing to develop the natural resources

---

[22]   In a parenthetic comment upon the agrarian policies of Prime Minister Stolypin under Nicholas II, Conquest writes: "(And in fact by 1917 the peasants already owned more than three-quarters of the land. The gain in arable land to the peasantry of all the confiscations and reforms of the Revolution was about 16 percent)." *Lenin*, pp. 61-2.

[23]   *TPTB*, p. 36.

[24]   This is available in English as *The Dictatorship of the Proletariat*, J. H. Kautsky (ed.), Michigan University Press, 1964; see ch. IX (a), 'Agriculture'. As a glimpse of the world we have lost, notice that it simply does not occur to Kautsky that the peasants might be forced into collective farms, as at the end of a decade they were. Karl Kautsky, as we shall be seeing later, insisted that democracy was essential to traditional Marxist social democracy, as it quite certainly is, for instance, to the non-Marxist and largely non-socialist (clause IV) contemporary social democracy of German Chancellor Willi Brandt.

[25]   The first, reprinted from the *Guardian*, I saw in the *Calgary Herald*, 27 March 1973, while the second was in the *Financial Times*, 24 July 1973.

of their country by the methods of State Socialism, for which, in Russia, there is much to be said."[26]

Although Russell is, as we have seen, here confused in his treatment of socialism, he does both here and elsewhere give useful clues as to how he would have wanted to enrich the basic idea. The first, and more manifest, way is by somehow building into the enriched concept some stipulation about equality in distribution. The second way, which is in this book much less manifest, is by inserting a similar demand for democracy as a third essential.

(i) The concern for equality is revealed first in a rather oblique fashion. Russell, who was surely one of those who believe that justice requires levelling, wrote in the original Preface: "If a more just economic system were only attainable by closing men's minds against free inquiry, and plunging them back into the intellectual prison of the middle ages, I should consider the price too high."[27] Later the same concern for justice as levelling comes out in his characteristic and lamentably neglected emphases upon the importance, both of the desire for power, and of making its distribution more even. Thus, Russell estimates what is "likely to happen in Russia: the establishment of a bureaucratic aristocracy, concentrating authority in its own hands."[28] He then glosses this estimate:

Marxians never sufficiently recognize that the love of power is quite as strong a motive, and quite as great a source of injustice, as love of money; yet this must be obvious to any unbiased student of politics. It is also obvious that the method of violent revolution leading to a minority dictatorship is one peculiarly calculated to create habits of despotism which would survive the crisis by which they were generated.[29]

---

[26] *TPTB*, p. 69.

[27] *Ibid.*, p. 9.

[28] *Ibid.*, p. 92. It is a pity but again, I am afraid, characteristic that the final clause of the sentence reads: "and creating a regime just as oppressive and cruel as that of capitalism." To anyone who has really taken the measure of what Russell was later to call "the vast horror of Russian Communism" (*PFM*, p. 11), such a comparison between its evils and all the relatively minor evils of the advanced capitalist countries must now sound silly, and (to borrow a favourite boo-word of our Leninising student militants) hysterical. But, since anything I say on such matters will, in the quarters where it needs to be said, be dismissed as the unfashionable carping of an avowed enemy of socialism, I appeal for support to a well-known media figure, who has fought elections for the Labour Party, and intends to continue without repentance in the same course. So see Bryan Magee, *The New Radicalism*, Secker & Warburg, 1962, pp. 102-10, 142-3 and passim.

[29] *TPTB*, pp. 92-3.

Later there is a set-piece statement:

What are the chief evils of the present system? I do not think that mere inequality of wealth, in itself, is a very grave evil. If everybody had enough, the fact that some have more than enough would be unimportant. With a very moderate improvement in methods of production, it would be easy to ensure that everybody should have enough, even under capitalism . . . . The graver evils of the capitalist system all arise from its uneven distribution of power.[30]

It is tempting to digress into a consideration of the implications of the essential relativity of the notion of poverty. But our next business is to call in evidence one further passage, this time from a much later work:

Only democracy and free publicity prevent the holders of power from establishing a servile state, with luxury for the few and overworked poverty for the many. That is what is being done by the Soviet government wherever it is in secure control.[31]

Now, what can we develop from these hints? The answer is that we can develop, but here only sketch, a double-barrelled argument for a practically important conclusion. The conclusion is that for anyone for whom even in part "Socialism is about equality," a commitment to socialism must also be a commitment to democracy. The first, and philosophically uninteresting, reason is suggested by the last of the passages from Russell just quoted. This reason is empirical but general. Systems in which power is concentrated, and in which criticism of the high and the mighty is drastically inhibited, have, as compared with systems in which power is more diffused, and in which criticism is more free, a much greater inherent tendency towards the erection and retention of inordinate privilege. For (as Marxists must be the first to agree) those who are excluded from privileges are those most likely to attack the system which sanctions such privileges; while these same unprivileged persons can and will make their opposition effective only and precisely in so far as they are able to know what is going on, and have some power to alter things. Systems in which power derives (not from the barrel of a gun but) from electorates possess a

---

[30] *Ibid.*, p. 109.
[31] *UE*, p. 59.

built-in bias towards fiercely progressive taxation and other widely popular forms of levelling.

This is not the place to deploy at length, with abundant supporting illustrations, a case for what are anyway obvious, empirical truths. Suffice it merely to draw attention to the nature and importance of this argument; and to notice that in 1920 Russell "talked to an obviously hungry working man in Moscow, who pointed to the Kremlin and remarked: 'In there they have enough to eat'."[32] This incident will remind those who lived through the Second World War of the far crueller contrasts reported then by Western representatives attending the state banquets inside.[33] The carnal details were not, of course, printed in the Soviet press or described on the Soviet radio. But it would in any case have been in the last degree imprudent, as well as futile, for the successors of Russell's working man to have demanded the imposition of more "equality of sacrifice."

The second and theoretically interesting reason why, if socialism is to be even in part about equality, a commitment to socialism must also be a commitment to democracy, is of a different kind. While the first depends on an appeal to fundamental contingent facts, about how the universe actually is (but conceivably might not have been); the second involves an analysis of concepts, and urges that one part of this possible ideal of socialism (enriched) appears to require the other also. This is not, surely, an instance of entailment. At least at the present level of abstraction, our notions of egalitarianism, and of democracy, are too polymorphous and too indeterminate for that. It is, rather, a matter of what can and cannot be maintained without an intolerable degree of arbitrariness.

It is scarcely possible to formulate a substantial egalitarian principle which is both presentably general and yet narrow enough to exclude politics. But if

---

[32] *TPTB*, p. 117.

[33] They may also remember the surprise and shock of those British and American servicemen who met high-ranking Soviet officers in 1945, and discovered that the factors by which pay of a Soviet marshal differed from the pay of a Soviet private were significantly greater that the comparable factors in their own services. They also discovered that, of course, Soviet income taxes are much less punitively progressive than those sustained by the electorates of democratic countries.

I cannot now put my hand on a suitably authoritative source in the case of the USSR. But many may be even more startled to learn that much the same applied in China. Edgar Snow's *Red China Today*, Pelican, 1970, a source very sympathetic indeed to the regime, says that in that country in 1962 (giving rough equivalents in US dollars) "privates started at $2.50 monthly; corporals got $4 . . . marshals of the army, $360-$400" (p. 285). Incidentally, Snow is another who employs, without explanation of how its referent is supposed to differ from socialism, the expression 'state capitalism' (pp. 194-5).

that egalitarian principle does require one man, or, better, one person one vote, then it must by the same token also require that the casting of these votes has some relevance and significance. This condition is not met if there are no alternatives for the elector to make a choice between; or if, in whatever sense the choice is made, that choice in fact determines nothing. Suppose that the elector is presented with a single official list and no other. Or suppose that, although there are alternatives on offer, it will nevertheless make no difference at all to anything whoever wins the election. Then there is a vast gulf, an enormous and flagrant inequality: between any and all of the ordinary run-of-the-mill electors and those fortunate and privileged few who make the actual decisions. Such elitist and authoritarian offences, offences against both egalitarianism and democracy, are in the world today so common as to constitute the *de facto* norm, both within the 'socialist bloc,' and outside.[34] But for us here one in particular is the pre-eminently appropriate illustration. Immediately after the October coup the elections for a Constituent Assembly were held, more or less as previously arranged by the provisional government:

> According to Lenin's own figures, the Bolsheviks got just over 9 million votes, the Socialist Revolutionaries nearly 21 million, and liberal groups over 4 1/2 million. When that Constituent Assembly, for which all Russia's revolutionaries and liberals had worked for nearly a century, met in January 1918, it was simply dissolved by force.[35]

The inequality between any and all of the vast mass of ordinary electors and the decisive handful on Lenin's Central Committee is here immeasurably more flagrant than the most extreme inequalities of mere wealth or income, without political power.

(ii) The concern for democracy appears in the present book as a concern about the best or only means rather than as a concern for one constitutive element in an (enriched) socialist ideal. Thus, as we saw in the second paragraph of our section (1), Russell writes in the original Preface: "I believe

---

[34] Those who are sincerely devoted to either or both of these ideals may obtain some trifle of consolation from recognising that the shams themselves constitute good evidence of the popularity of the real thing. They are the hypocritical tribute which elitist and authoritarian vice pays to egalitarian and democratic virtue. There would be no point in staging the shams if no one had any desire for the genuine article. See 'What Socrates should have said to Thrasymachus', in C. L. Carter (ed.), *Skepticism and Moral Principles*, New University Press, 1973.

[35] R. Conquest, *Lenin*, p. 92.

that the West is capable of adopting less painful and more certain methods of reaching Socialism than those which have seemed necessary in Russia." Later he once or twice notices that methods first adopted and justified as means must have their effects upon the agents themselves, and will consequently in part determine the actual outcome. He observes, for instance:

> The Bolshevik theory is that a small minority are to seize power, and are to hold it until Communism is accepted practically universally . . . . But power is sweet, and few men surrender it voluntarily. It is especially sweet to those who have the habit of it, and the habit becomes most ingrained in those who have governed by bayonets.[36]

Again, in contending that "Self-government in industry is . . . the road by which England can best approach Socialism," Russell remarks "that the practice of self-government is the only effective method of political education."[37]

In all this it is accepted that the disagreements between communist parties and social democratic parties of the old pre-Leninist type are disagreements only about possible or most desirable routes for reaching exactly the same desired destination, socialism. But this frame of reference fits only in so far as the word 'socialism' is construed in its most basic sense (clause IV). It is quite another story when such basic socialism becomes either itself a means to some different end or only one element in an enriched socialist ideal. In this changed perspective a common commitment only to the implementation of clause IV should no longer be seen as a natural or even as a possible basis for a political alliance. For differences between the ends to which basic socialism is desired as a means, or differences over the further ends encapsulated in the new and enriched concept of socialism, may quite reasonably render the individuals or the parties sharing the clause IV commitment still practically irreconcilable. When (as today in France and Chile) Communist parties press for a united or popular front to be supported by all socialists, it is wise to ponder the Chinese proverb: "Those who are going in opposite directions do not make plans together."

With the passing years the inappropriateness of the framework accepted by Russell in 1920, and by so many others since, ought to have become increasingly obvious. It has, indeed, also become progressively more inappropriate. For those processes of self-change through action and inaction,

---

[36] *TPTB*, p. 106.
[37] *Ibid.*, pp. 127 and 129.

which at the end of the previous paragraph we noticed Russell noticing, have of course continued to operate on all the people and all the organisations concerned. The man who created "a party of a new type," used it to seize power in a coup, then retained and extended that power by chicanery and terror, must thereby have transformed himself. That party too must have been, and was, at the same time both wittingly and otherwise transforming itself similarly. The actually operative ideals both of persons and of institutions may be, and almost always are, changed both by their circumstances and by their own practice. What were once our means or our ends thus change places, or cease to be either.[38]

Allow that the young Lenin did share the ideals, though not the opinions, of the Russell of 1920. Still it must be in the last degree unlikely that, after living the life he did live, the operative ideals of the Lenin of 1920 were substantially those of the Lenin of, say, 1905. The same must apply even more, with appropriate alterations, to institutions. For, with the effluxion of time, a continuing institution will be manned by successors. And the people who devote themselves to outlaw parties without for the foreseeable future any prospects of power, will be of another sort from the people who join when there can be more or less immediate hopes of place and privilege.

It is the opinion of the Russell of 1920 that democracy is the only, or the best, means to the end of socialism, or of a desirable form of socialism. In earlier works there are strong hints of some more than contingent connection between the two. Thus a quarter of a century before, in his study of *German Social Democracy*, he had picked out as "two essential items," objectives which he believed that "the Party could not abandon without political suicide . . . . *Political Democracy and Economic Collectivism.*"[39] Although he went on in the following sentence to speak of "carrying the ideals of political democracy into the economic sphere," his point then was institutional rather than

---

[38] A most sinister and relevant example is provided by some sentences from a document, 'The Falsifiers of Scientific Communism', issued early in 1972 by the Institute of Marxism-Leninism in Moscow. These sentences suggest that, whereas Lenin first created his 'party of a new type' as an instrument to bring about socialism, the present central directors of such parties are now more inclined to see socialism (clause IV) as itself the means to secure irremovable and absolute dominion for their parties: "Having once acquired political power, the working class implements the liquidation of the private ownership of the means of production . . . . As a result, under Socialism, there remains no ground for the existence of any opposition parties counterbalancing the Communist Party." The whole document was published originally in the Moscow journal *Kommunist*, no. 3, 1972, pp. 101-15. But this crucial passage is most easily found in *The Economist*, 17 June 1972, p. 23.

[39] George Allen & Unwin, 1896, p. 165, emphasis his.

conceptual. But there is in *Roads to Freedom* a definite suggestion of a strictly conceptual link:

> I think we shall come nearest to the essence of Socialism by defining it as the advocacy of the communal ownership of land and capital. Communal ownership may mean ownership by a democratic state, but cannot be held to include ownership by any state which is not democratic.[40]

The conceptual point which needs to be developed and underlined most emphatically is this. Someone can significantly be said to share in the ownership of something only and precisely in so far as that person has, even if he or she chooses not to use, a right to a part-share in the disposition of those assets of which he or she is being described as being the part-owner. Most of what is, in fact, called public ownership, or even common ownership, would, therefore, be more correctly characterised as state ownership. People may of course benefit, just as they may suffer, as a result of the exploitation of such state-owned assets. But being in this way a beneficiary no more makes you in any non-Pickwickian sense an owner than being, correspondingly, a victim makes you an owner. Ownership is about rights to control.

To say that something is state-owned is not to say that all the citizens of the state in question must, simply in virtue of their citizenship, possess some rights to share, however indirectly, in the disposition of that state-owned asset. It is to say only that the state itself possesses all such rights. Assets may, therefore, be state-owned in some country which no one at all would wish to call democratic; and where, consequently, these assets, precisely because they are owned by the state, are in no way subject to the control of the citizens as such. On the other hand, following Russell, I stipulatively so define 'communal ownership' that every member of the community in question must as such have a right to a share in the disposition of any assets so owned. Given this stipulative definition of 'communal ownership', something may be: either state-owned, but not communally owned; or communally owned, but not state-owned; or both state-owned and communally owned.

Now suppose that the word 'socialism' is itself defined in terms not of state-ownership but of communal ownership. Then it will follow that whatever is to be said to be thus owned must be subject to the control of those who are to be asserted to be its communal owners. It is from this that it surely follows,

---

[40] George Allen & Unwin, 1918, p. 23.

in turn, that socialism, construed as a commitment to communal ownership, necessarily involves a measure of democracy; I claim that Russell grasped this, if only momentarily, in *Roads to Freedom.*

Please recognise both how much, and how little, this involves. Since the premise is vague, the conclusion has to be equally vague. For example: in this interpretation, the socialist is as such committed to democracy only in the operation of socialist enterprises. We have to describe as socialist any set-up in which all or most economic undertakings are communally owned. We should have to say this just the same even in a case where the state machinery was not subject to any democratic control. On the other hand, once we have given the word 'socialist' this meaning, it becomes false and scandalous for us to characterise as socialist a country in which clause IV is law, and all the means of production, distribution and exchange are owned by the state; but where the state machinery is in the hands of an electorally irremovable Leninist elite, ensuring that every legal organisation acts as a 'transmission belt' implementing whatever policies the central directorate may from time to time privately determine. In the real world Yugoslavia appears to approach most nearly to the first of these two extremes; while the second possibility is as near as makes little matter fully realised in all the official card-carrying members of the 'socialist bloc,' and perhaps now in some few other countries as well.

(c) It would be a great gain for clear thinking, and indirectly for the beleaguered cause of liberal democracy also, if this distinction between state ownership and communal ownership were everywhere understood, and if everyone always employed a vocabulary which brought out the issues clearly and correctly. We have already, at the beginning of the previous sub-subsection (2) (b) (ii), looked at one potentially catastrophic confusion encouraged by the fact that the basic clause IV sense of 'socialism' is indeterminate in respect of this distinction. Another such confusion can be approached by meditating upon a passage quoted once before:

> And I believe that while some forms of Socialism are immeasurably better than capitalism, others are even worse. Among those that are worse I reckon the form which is being achieved in Russia, not only in itself, but as a more insuperable barrier to further progress.[41]

Concentrate upon that final clause; and, in terms of our distinction between basic and enriched senses of the ambiguous word 'socialism', think of what

---

[41] *TPTB*, p. 21.

Russell is saying. Following but improving on Russell, we may hold that the point is that it would be far more difficult, and it would take far longer, to establish enriched socialism in the USSR than it would in many countries where very little of the economy is as yet basically socialist. Indeed (though now myself no socialist in either sense) I would be prepared, given a suitable occasion, to argue that the prospects for such an enriched socialism were in Russia generally better before the October Revolution than they have since become. But the point which I have to make here is of another kind altogether. This point is (whether or not even the more modest Russellian thesis is true) that it must be unsound in principle to infer from the premise that basic socialism is a theoretically necessary condition of enriched socialism, the conclusion that to achieve basic socialism is necessarily to take a step, even a giant step, towards enriched socialism.

This unsound inference is enormously tempting. It is, nevertheless, unsound. It is unsound because it equivocates between two totally different interpretations of the key expression 'necessary condition'. In the premise this is construed as being equivalent to 'logically necessary condition'. In this interpretation, the premise is certainly true. It is certainly true because basic socialism (clause IV), which is indeterminate as between state ownership and communal ownership, is part of what is meant by the word 'socialism', taken in any enriched sense. But the proposed conclusion of the argument is not in this way merely verbal. It is rather that any country where clause IV is law is in practice farther along the road to socialism, in some enriched and essentially democratic construction of that word. The argument is, therefore, as invalid as its conclusion is, in Russell's view and mine, false.

I labour the point about the invalidity of this and other arguments to that false conclusion, because these arguments and this conclusion still possess continuing baleful appeal, despite all the experience of Bolshevism accumulated since 1917. Never a day passes but we have forced upon our attention instances of their influence upon the hearts and minds and conduct of many who claim, and think themselves sincere in claiming, to be socialists in some enriched sense essentially involving democracy and civil liberties. For example, in the week during which I was actually writing the present chapter, Prime Minister Whitlam of Australia committed his country to supporting (among other things) any United Nations move to oust "colonialist Portugal" from her African territories. Suppose, perhaps too charitably, we allow this to be neither a politically disingenuous gesture (designed to enable rich, white, Australia to pass as a country of "the Third World") nor yet the expression of ignorance of the colonialist realities of "the Second World", ignorance which would disgrace the chairman of a rural district council. Then how else are we to explain

Premier Whitlam's failure to include in his robust repudiation of all colonial subjection the case of reconquered Tibet, or those of any of the non-Russian peoples within the empire of what the new mandarins now so aptly call 'the new Tsars'? How else, save as an expression of the indulgence thought to be due to those whom the premier still cannot help seeing as his fellow socialists?[42]

(3) At the beginning of section (2), I quoted Hampshire: "Russell did not apply to politics the analytical methods which he called for in the theory of knowledge." The whole section then displayed both the need, and Russell's failure, to apply such methods to the crucial concept, or concepts, of socialism. His treatment of Bolshevism as a religion constitutes another, and more subtle, example of the same thing. Again it is one which continues to be relevant to the problems of our later generation.

Decades before the Kremlin found it convenient to become the Protector of the Arabs, Russell discerned the similarities between Bolshevism and Islam: "Bolshevism combines the characteristics of the French Revolution with those of the rise of Islam"[43] and "Marx has taught that Communism is fatally predestined to come about; this . . . produces a state of mind not unlike that of the early successors of Mahomet."[44] So Russell concludes: "Mahommedanism and Bolshevism are practical, social, unspiritual, concerned to win the empire of this world . . . . What Mahommedanism did for the Arabs, Bolshevism may do for the Russians."[45]

From this religious aspect of Bolshevism Russell, as we should expect, differs fundamentally:

> This habit, of militant certainty about objectively doubtful matters, is one from which, since the Renaissance, the world has been gradually emerging, into that temper of constructive and fruitful scepticism

---

[42] See the files of any good newspaper for the week beginning 13 August 1973. Magee gives many examples of similar thinking in the British Labour Party (op. cit.: e.g., 11-12, 89-90, 99-100, and 107-8). There is perhaps an element of speculation in my interpretation of the distant mental processes of Mr. Whitlam. The same could not be said of the case of the position of my former colleague Kai Nielsen, examined in my 'In Defence of Reformism', *Question* 7, Pemberton, 1974.

Notice too, Jean-Francois Revel's *Without Marx or Jesus*, Paladin, 1972. The author of this admirably non-conformist work needs all the distinctions developed in the present section (2), yet appears to be unable himself to make any of them. See, if you doubt it, my review in the *New Humanist* for August 1973.

[43] *TPTB*, p. 7.

[44] *Ibid.*, p. 27.

[45] *Ibid.*, p. 74.

which constitutes the scientific outlook. I believe the scientific outlook to be immeasurably important to the human race.[46]

It is immediately after this, and as his reason, that Russell expresses a judgment quoted earlier: "If a more just economic system were only attainable by closing men's minds against free inquiry, and plunging them back into the intellectual prison of the middle ages, I should consider the price too high." Certainly I do not wish to dissent from anything quoted in the previous two paragraphs, so far as it goes. But what we have to notice is that Russell is conspicuously not relating his academic to his social values. There is here no Popperian suggestion that the exploratory and undogmatic approach which is required in the investigation of nature, is even more urgently needed in the development and vindication of social policies: "A policy is a hypothesis which has to be tested against reality and corrected in the light of experience."[47] Because the subject matter of social policies is people; because what happens to people matters more than anything else; and because every social policy is bound to have at least some unintended consequences: the protagonists of such policies ought always to be willing to learn from experience, and to revise or to withdraw such policies in the light of that experience.

It is not necessary to develop here what should now be the familiar Popperian argument: "Rationality, logic, and a scientific approach all point to a society which is 'open' and pluralistic, within which incompatible views are expressed and conflicting aims pursued . . . and above all a society in which the government's policies are changed in the light of criticism."[48] But it is worth indicating that and how questions about willingness not merely to permit but to encourage independent investigation of the actual effects of policies, and to take account of criticism based upon such investigation, are connected with questions about the nature and sincerity of the aims professed by protagonists of these policies.

The crux, and it is a crux with innumerable and important practical implications, is this. Suppose that you propose a certain policy. Suppose, too, that you offer as your reasons for wanting this policy to be implemented, that

---

[46] *Ibid.*, p. 9.

[47] Bryan Magee, *Popper*, Fontana, 1973, p. 75. This excellent short work perhaps provides a better introduction than any of Popper's own more elaborate books to Popper's social ideas, especially to the connections between these social ideas, on the one hand, and the Popperian rationale for science, on the other. Russell himself had come much closer to this kind of integration of the practical-political with the theoretical-scientific by 1950 (cf. *UE*, pp. 27-32).

[48] *Ibid.*, p. 79.

it will have such and such effects; which effects you hold to be good. And suppose next that you are uninterested in the question what effects it actually does have; that you even attempt to inhibit free inquiry in this area; or that you resolutely refuse to adapt the favoured policy to take account of the results of whatever investigations may in fact be made. Then the moral which we have to draw must surely be that you either always were, or have since become, indifferent to the objectives to which you originally referred. The policy now appeals to you, it seems, or perhaps really it always has appealed to you: either as something in itself desirable, rather than as a means to further ends; or else, though still as a means, as a means to ends different from those proclaimed when the policy was first proposed.

Let us make the case a little more concrete. If, and in so far as, for you the implementation of socialism (clause IV) is a means to various other supposed or actual goods; then, and to that extent, you will be concerned to monitor the actual operation of whatever socialist policies are adopted. You will be so concerned (or you will be so concerned in so far as you are rational) both in order to know how far your ends are in fact being achieved, and still more to ensure that the policies adopted as means to these ends shall be revised or abandoned in so far as they prove to be ineffective or counterproductive. This just is what it is to be a rational man treating something as a means to some end outside itself.

Now, by way of contrast, suppose someone equally rational, who also maintains that socialism (clause IV) is for him not an end in itself but the means to the same putative goods. But suppose that this other person is uninterested in the findings of inquiry; or even tries to prevent any such inquiry; and when relevant results are available still resolutely refuses to think of revising his socialist policies, much less abandoning them. Then, surely, we have no option but to infer that, for him, either the true ends lie elsewhere, or else the policies themselves are the ends. (Or, of course, and as always, a bit of both. But to specify such complications every time would make the arguments, for no sufficient reason, unreadably complex.)

The application of all this to our understanding of the actual aims and commitments of contemporary Bolshevism is, or ought to be, obvious.[49] So let us conclude the present section with a quotation from the much-abused but

---

[49]   See, however, note 38 above, and consider the maybe false assumption which seems to have guided the leadership of the countries participating in the 1968 invasion of Czechoslovakia. They and their spokesmen throughout the world insisted, and still do insist, that the liberal reforms initiated by Alexander Dubcek and his associates were as near as makes no matter certain to result in the overthrow of socialism, unless checked in the nick of time by the tanks of normalisation!

little-read Karl Kautsky. He makes it clear, both that for him socialism (clause IV) is a means, and that he appreciates what this involves:

If . . . we place the Socialist way of production as the goal, it is because in the technical and economic conditions which prevail today Socialistic production appears to be the sole means of attaining our object. Should it be proved to us that we are wrong in so doing, and that somehow the emancipation of the proletariat and of mankind could be achieved solely on the basis of private property . . . then we would throw Socialism overboard, without in the least giving up our object, and even in the interests of this object.[50]

(4) At only one point in *The Practice and Theory of Bolshevism* is the reader reminded that the author was at the time of writing the most distinguished living British philosopher. This is when Russell says: "Far closer than any actual historical parallel is the parallel of Plato's Republic."[51] But even here Russell does not proceed to make any kind of philosophical comparison. He says only: "The Communist Party corresponds to the guardians; the soldiers have about the same status in both; there is in Russia an attempt to deal with family life more or less as Plato suggested."   What is missing is any review of the differences and similarities between the doctrines offered in justification, as well as a thorough comparison of actual Bolshevik institutions with those proposed by Plato.[52]

For us the most relevant comparison is between the foundations of authority in the two cases. Where Plato urged the necessity of discovering and breeding golden natures, which must then also be appropriately trained; the

---

[50] Kautsky, *The Dictatorship of the Proletariat, op. cit.*, p. 5. Of course, I am not suggesting that Kautsky was any sort of premature Popperian. For one thing, and it is only one thing, any sort of commitment to total socialism (clause IV) would presumably be seen by Popper as involving at least a hankering after 'Utopian social engineering'. Magee, wishing for his own reasons to make out that the Labour Party is not in this sense socialist, notwithstanding that as of now it quite obviously is, generates a gratuitous problem of understanding why Popper, who admittedly "is no longer a socialist," fails, as Magee puts it, "to accept in matters of practical politics, the radical consequences of his own ideas" (*Popper*, p. 84).

[51] *TPTB*, pp. 28-9.

[52] For an essay on these lines, see R. H. S. Crossman's *Plato Today*, George Allen & Unwin, rev. 2nd edn., 1959, ch. VIII. This is the same Crossman who was a leading Labour Party politician. The first edition was published in 1937, while Crossman was still a philosophy don at Oxford. It was a landmark in Platonic studies, treating "the founder of the Academy not as the first academic but as a politician manque" (p. 7).

Communist parties put all their emphasis upon the environment and the possibilities of environmental manipulation. (Stalin's support for Lysenko's onslaught on genetics and geneticists was no ephemeral fluke, any more than is the recent neo-Lysenkoist hostility to the notion of IQ and the practice of IQ testing.) Again, where communist ideology is, in Marxist terms, materialist, Plato's account of the nature and status of the Forms is, in terms of the same Marxist antithesis, a paradigm case of idealism. What the guardian order and the Communist parties have in common is a claim to absolute power and authority, based upon their peculiar knowledge of the true ideology.

Through their knowledge of the Forms, the guardians become uniquely qualified to prescribe for everyone what is good, and hence what ought to be. It is precisely and only on the grounds that they and they alone possess this knowledge that the Socrates of *The Republic* contends that philosophers -- true philosophers -- should be kings. The guardians are, by both vocation and training, truly philosophers. For the word 'philosopher' is persuasively defined as 'one who knows the Forms'. So all manner of things will be well if, but only if, all power is rendered up to these true philosophers. Communists are, in the first instance, concerned only for the proletariat. It is through and only through their own Marxist-Leninist understanding and leadership that the interests of the proletariat can and will triumph. And ultimately, by this triumph, a society will be produced which satisfies the interests and fulfils the needs of all.

Notice now how this shared claim to absolute authority is one which refers, and must refer, to needs or interests, rather than to actual wants. For while there may be room for an expert to tell me what is in my interests, or what it is that I need for some purpose, or even what I ought to do; there can be no room at all for experts knowing better than I do myself what it is that I actually and consciously want. This is why Plato is forever using (and most grossly abusing)[53] -- medical analogies. My doctor can tell me, thanks to his professional knowledge, what treatment I need if I am to satisfy my want to get well. But the doctor has no such special competence (nor is any required) to determine whether or not I do, in fact, want to get well. There can be occasions when in fact I do not; and then (in so far as the doctor is serving me as my professional adviser) he will leave me alone.

Much more to the present purpose, this is why the contemporary communist concept of democracy stresses interests and needs rather than wants. A free election might reveal that most of them want us communists out. But, even supposing that we were in some unguarded moment to concede that this

---

[53] See my *Crime or Disease?*, Macmillan and Barnes and Noble, 1973, pt. 1.

is in fact so, still we could quite consistently maintain (and would) that our power serves their interests, and meets their needs. Thus, it was in just such a moment of truth that Janos Kadar, addressing the Hungarian National Assembly on 11 May 1957, the year after the friendly neighbourhood Soviet tanks had installed him in office, said:

> The task of the leaders is not to put into effect the wishes and will of the masses . . . . The task of the leaders is to accomplish the interests of the masses. Why do I differentiate between the will and the interests of the masses? In the recent past we have encountered the phenomenon of certain categories of workers acting against their interests.[54]

This point about the contemporary communist concept of democracy is the more worth making, since it is so often obscured by various politically motivated attempts to make out that the communist regimes and the communist parties are democratic in quite a different sense. It is sometimes suggested that the word 'democracy' is beyond redemption. I once heard the late Professor J. L. Austin say as much in a lecture.[55] But this is far too defeatist. All that is required to give the word a harmless and necessary life (or lives) is that we should first make, and always thereafter insist upon, certain distinctions.

Suppose we put on one side as irrelevant that established sense in which it refers to social equality and equality of opportunity. It is in this sense that people talk of the need to democratise the British Foreign Service; meaning that its officials should be drawn from a wider range of schools, and that missions abroad should have more comprehensive and less socially exclusive contacts.

Then there is one fundamental distinction to make. This is the distinction, already suggested: between a sense which refers to the people's needs or interests, and a sense which refers to their actual wishes. In the latter sense a

---

[54] Reported in *East Europe*, July 1957, p. 56. I owe this reference to Sidney Hook's *Political Power and Personal Freedom*, Collier, 1962, p. 147. It would be mean not to share my own favourite, from a speech by the late Abdul Kharume, first Vice President of Tanzania: "Our Government is democratic because it makes its decisions in the interests of and for the benefit of the people. I wonder why men who are unemployed are surprised and resentful at the Government . . . sending them back to the land for their own advantage." This was reported in the Dar-es-Salaam press on 8 July 1967. Mr. Kharume, who has since been assassinated, was, as his Afro-Shirazi Party in Zanzibar still is, strongly influenced by advisers from the self-styled German Democratic Republic.

[55] 'There are, however, a few notoriously useless words -- "democracy", for instance'. J. L. Austin, *Sense and Sensibilia*, Clarendon, 1962, p. 127.

set-up is democratic precisely and only to the extent that those above can be voted out by those below. Whether the wishes thus expressed happen to coincide with their interests or their needs is, as far as the question of democracy is concerned, neither here nor there. Given these two basic senses of the word 'democracy' (which we will have to call 'Eastern' and 'Western', respectively, until someone invents a better pair of labels) then we may if we wish proceed to introduce or to distinguish further, enriched, senses.

What we must not do, once we have allowed that there are these two fundamentally different senses of the word 'democracy', is to think of these as two different forms of democracy. There may indeed be, and surely are, different forms of both democracy (Western) and democracy (Eastern). But, exactly in so far as the word 'democracy' is indeed ambiguous, the different forms of the former and the different forms of the latter cannot constitute all varieties within one and the same univocal species, democracy. So Soviet democracy is not a kind of democracy (Western). Yet, I recently heard an able and active philosopher employ this shameful sophism. He thus hoped to reconcile his claim to be a socialist, in a sense which he says essentially involves (Western) democracy, with his practice of describing (and systematically favouring) the countries of the "socialist bloc" as socialist.)

Earlier in the present section I allowed that "there may be room for an expert to tell me what is in my interests, or what it is that I need for some purpose, or even what I ought to do." I now conclude the section by quoting from a leading Radical philosopher a few sentences referring to the third of these possible kinds of expertise. He is referring to "the claim that fundamental value judgments are not truth-claims but have a non-cognitive logical status." Having elsewhere contended that this claim is false:

> . . . I want to argue that such an account of normative or value judgments indirectly supports and reinforces pluralism and bourgeois individualism . . . . If someone accepts and takes this conception of valuation to heart, he is very likely to accept democratic pluralism as the most adequate political model . . . .   What is reasonable to do . . . is simply, where possible, to give people whatever it is they want, when doing that is compatible with others having their wants treated in the same way . . . . On such an account, it is thought to be a kind of cultural imperialism . . . to tell people what they should

want or to say that certain wants are irrational.[56]

Cognitivism about value is, thus, commended as the basis for telling people what they should want, and working to ensure that willy-nilly that, and only that, is what they shall have.

(5) At the beginning of the previous section, I noticed that *The Practice and Theory of Bolshevism* does almost nothing to remind the reader "that the author must have been at the time of writing the most distinguished living British philosopher." Perhaps even more remarkable, the nearest we get to a hint that he was also the author of *German Social Democracy* is his comment that in the USSR "The police play, altogether, a much greater part in daily life than they do in other countries -- much greater than they did, for example, in Prussia twenty-five years ago, when there was a vigorous campaign against Socialism."[57]

It was most unfortunate that Russell thus made no attempt to relate his Russian experience to what he had learnt a quarter of a century earlier, both about German social democracy as an institution, and about Marx's materialist conception of history as then interpreted. Such knowledge was then even rarer among British observers than it is now. Had Russell used it, he could have achieved deeper perspective and richer understanding. As it is, he compounds this first neglect by failing (like so many others since) to distinguish the February revolution against the Tsarist autocracy,   from the Bolshevik coup

---

[56] Kai Nielsen, 'Is Empiricism an Ideology?', *Metaphilosophy*, October 1972, pp. 269-271. Since Nielsen proceeds to appeal to Marcuse, it is both fair and relevant to say that Marcuse makes it about as plain as he ever makes anything that his revolution requires "the dictatorship of an elite over the people." It is, indeed, for Marcuse a main grievance against the 'late capitalist' order that the despised majority not merely does not want, but has no interest in, the Marcusian revolution:

By the same token, those minorities which strive for a change in the whole itself will . . . be left free to deliberate and discuss, to speak and to assemble . . . and will be left harmless and helpless in the face of the overwhelming majority . . . . The majority is firmly grounded in the increasing satisfaction of needs, and technological and mental co-ordination, which testify to the general helplessness of radical groups in a well-functioning social system. (H. Marcuse, B. Moore and R. Wolff, *A Critique of Pure Tolerance*, Cape, 1969, pp. 107-8, 134, emphasis added).

For an examination of the appeal of Marxist ideas to impatient and authoritarian intellectuals, see L. S. Feuer, *Marx and the Intellectuals*, Doubleday Anchor, 1969.

[57] *TPTB*, p. 58.

against the provisional government of Kerensky in October. He speaks indiscriminately of "the Russian Revolution" and of "the October Revolution."

Even much later, in *Portraits from Memory*, he is capable of writing, as we saw earlier: "When the Russian Revolution first broke out I welcomed it as did almost everyone else, including the British Embassy."[58] Although he is talking about the Bolsheviks, he does not notice that even a British Embassy could scarcely have welcomed a coup by a party committed to abandoning, among others, its British allies. Russell thus did his bit to encourage, even if he did not himself actually share, one deplorable (and deplorably common) popular misconception: that the Bolsheviks executed a revolution against the Tsarist government; and that what they did may be justified by reference to the, always grotesquely exaggerated, demerits of that regime.

A good way to see what Russell might have seen, had he deployed all the resources available to him, is to look at Karl Kautsky's *The Dictatorship of the Proletariat*. This was written, and first published, in German in the summer of 1918. Kautsky in his youth had known both Marx and Engels. He virtually founded, and for thirty-five years edited, *Die Neue Zeit*, the main theoretical organ of German social democracy. So he had been the almost universally recognised doyen of Marxist orthodoxy. Up till the outbreak of the First World War Lenin himself always spoke of him with great respect, trying to show that his own position squared with Marxism as interpreted by Kautsky. In particular Lenin had approved of Kautsky's stand against the revisionism of Bernstein. Both Kautsky and Bernstein, it must be emphasised, stood for the realisation of socialism through democracy. Kautsky's anti-revisionism consisted in his suggestion that in face of the resistance of the German ruling classes neither democracy nor socialism could be attained peacefully.

The gist of what Kautsky said in 1918 was, in effect, that 'Marxism-Leninism' is a self-contradictory expression: first, because democracy was essential to the ideals and practice of traditional German social democracy; and, second, because a successful proletarian revolution in the Russia of 1917 must constitute a decisive falsification of that very conception of history in the name of which it was made. It is significant that Lenin's counterblast, *The Proletarian Revolution and the Renegade Kautsky*, was, even by Lenin's standards, egregiously vituperative.[59]

---

[58] *PFM*, p. 13.

[59] There are many editions in many languages; mine is Volume 21 in the *Little Lenin Library*, International Publishers, 1934. Trotsky's *Terrorism and Communism* was a contribution to the same controversy. This, too, is available in English edited by M. Shachtman, University of Michigan Press, 1961. Kautsky returned to the charge, several times.

(a) In presenting the first count of his indictment Kautsky appeals both to the traditions of social democracy as an institution and to the writings of Marx. The appeals to Marx will strike those who have also read Lenin as agreeably scholarly, with none of that religious temper which so distressed Russell. Kautsky said of Marx:

The dictatorship of the proletariat was for him a condition which necessarily arose in a real democracy, because of the overwhelming numbers of the proletariat. Marx must not, therefore, be cited by those who support dictatorship in preference to democracy. Of course, this does not prove it to be wrong.[60]

But Kautsky's main, substantive point comes immediately after the sentences quoted already at the end of section (3), above. It surely is, if 'liberation' is to be the name of the game, a knockout:

Socialism and democracy are therefore not distinguished by the one being a means and the other the end. Both are means to the same end. The distinction between them must be sought elsewhere. Socialism as a means to the emancipation of the proletariat, without democracy, is unthinkable.[61]

It is at this point that we ought to recall: first, when Lenin first put forward his proposals for a party of a new type; second, how he then justified these proposals; and, third, against what sort of regime the October revolution was made. These proposals (what later came to be known, half-truly, as the principles of democratic centralism) were first put forward in such pamphlets as *What is to be Done?* (1902), *A Letter to a Comrade on our Organization Tasks* (1902) and *One Step Forward, Two Steps Back* (1904).[62] They were at that time justified as necessary for effective struggle in the conditions of Tsarist repression; and Lenin himself contrasted these conspiratorial necessities with the openness and democracy enviably possible in the happier conditions of German

---

[60] Kautsky, *Dictatorship of the Proletariat*, p. 45.

[61] *Ibid.*, p. 5.

[62] The relevant volumes of Lenin's *Collected Works* are V-VII, Moscow, Foreign Languages Publishing House, 1961. My references to *What is to be Done?* are to the edition by S. V. Utechin, Panther, 1970.

social democracy.[63] Yet Lenin in 1917 used the instrument forged in and for
the struggle against Tsarism in order to execute a coup against a regime which
was moving towards representative democracy. And he used it in conditions in
which openness and free assembly were in Russia possible as never before, or
since.

It was, therefore, wrong for Russell, while rightly deploring "that truly
terrible degree of centralization which now exists in Russia," to add, charitably,
that "The Russians have been forced to centralize."[64] Lenin and the Bolsheviks
were not forced by intolerable oppression to revolt in October. Lenin saw an
opportunity to seize power, and he took it. Nor was he compelled to refuse to
share that power with other parties; or to dissolve the Constituent Assembly by
force; and so on; and on and on. He was compelled, that is, only in so far as
the desire to have and to hold such absolute power is itself allowed to be the
compulsion.

In part, Russell dissents from those "apologists of Bolshevism" who
"excuse its harshness on the ground that it has been produced by the necessity
of fighting the Entente and its mercenaries." He then says: "A great part of the
despotism which characterizes the Bolsheviks belongs to the essence of their
social philosophy."[65] Yet he also lapses into the typically British illusion that
foreigners are only what we make them: "If we continue to antagonize the
Bolsheviks, I do not see what force exists that can prevent them from acquiring
the whole of Asia within ten years."[66] What Russell never discerns is how the
despotic social philosophy is rooted in the Leninist party.

For this insight we have to go not to Russell, nor to Kautsky, but to Rosa
Luxemburg. In a pamphlet first published in 1904, she said of *One Step
Forward, Two Steps Back*:

> The viewpoint presented with incomparable vigour and logic in this
> book, is that of pitiless centralism . . . . Lenin's thesis is that the
> party Central Committee should have the privilege of naming all the
> local committees of the party . . . . It should have the right to rule
> without appeal on such questions as the dissolution and reconstitution

---

[63]   *What is to be Done?*, pp. 163 ff., on the justification, and pp. 185-6, on the happier
conditions.   Notice that at this stage Lenin was not, apparently, inclined to claim that such
conspiratorial organisation is democratic; but rather that democratic organization, however desirable,
was not in the unfortunate conditions of Tsarist Russia practically possible.

[64]   *TPTB*, p. 128.

[65]   *Ibid.*, p. 22.

[66]   *Ibid.*, p. 70.

of local organizations. This way the Central Committee could determine, to suit itself, the composition of the highest party organs as well as the party congress.[67]

She concluded: "What is today only a phantom haunting Lenin's imagination may become reality tomorrow."[68] To understand Bolshevism it is essential to come to terms with this reality.

(b) Kautsky's second point was about neither ideals nor institutions, but Marxist theory. The Russia of 1917 did not satisfy the conditions for a successful proletarian revolution: capitalism, and consequently the proletariat, were insufficiently developed. This was the universal Marxist, and Bolshevik, assessment until Lenin returned to Russia on 3 April 1917; and, to everyone's astonishment, presented his April theses. Then and later Lenin's own achievements in turning the course of history themselves constitute a further decisive falsification of Marxism. For neither Marxism, nor indeed any other similar theory, can possibly allow so enormous a role to such an accidental factor as the presence or absence and particular qualities of one individual. But this is not Kautsky's thesis.[69] His point was simply that the materialist conception of history could not compass a proletarian revolution at that time and in that place.

Kautsky quoted Marx: ". . . even when a society has got on the right track for the discovery of the natural laws of its movement -- it can neither clear by bold leaps, nor remove by legal enactments, the obstacles offered by the successive phases of its normal development."[70] The expropriators cannot be expropriated, before they have produced their own despoilers. Capitalism cannot be buried, before it has given birth to its grave-diggers.

---

[67] *Leninism or Marxism?*, edited by B. D. Wolfe, bound up in one volume with *The Russian Revolution*, University of Michigan Press, 1961, pp. 84-5.

[68] *Ibid.*, p. 102.

[69] It is, however, persuasively developed by Sidney Hook in ch. X of *The Hero in History*, Humanities Press, 1943.

[70] Preface to the 1st edition of *Capital*, quoted by Kautsky, *The Dictatorship of the Proletariat*, p. 98.

CHAPTER 11

STEPHEN HAWKING AND THE MIND OF GOD
(1996)

Stephen Hawking's *A Brief History of Time*[1] has been a record-breaking best seller. A note in his later collection, *Black Holes and Baby Universes*,[2] reveals that *A Brief History* remained on the best-seller list of *The New York Times* for fifty-three weeks, that as of February 1993 it had been on *The Sunday Times* best-seller list for 205 weeks, and that translations into 33 languages other than English had already been published (p. 29). Also in that later collection, Hawking remarks parenthetically: "In the proof stage I nearly cut the last sentence in the book . . . Had I done so, the sales might have been halved."[3] To appreciate that sentence it is necessary to read the whole paragraph with which the earlier book concludes:

However, if we discover a complete theory, it should in time be understandable by everyone, not just by a few scientists. Then we shall all, philosophers, scientists and just ordinary people, be able to take part in the discussion of the question of why it is that we and the universe exist. If we find the answer to that, it would be the ultimate triumph of human reason -- for then we should know the mind of God. (p. 193)

---

[1] Bantam, 1988.

[2] Bantam, 1993.

[3] *Ibid.*, p. 33.

Since this *Brief History* has achieved such an enormous circulation, and since the author believes that this has in large part been due to the book's actual or supposed theological implications, these surely deserve some critical examination. But the fact that he came so close to deleting that final sentence suggests that he himself was not very interested in such possible implications. Certainly he fails to make any of the distinctions needed for their fruitful discussion.

For instance: if there is a true answer to "the question of why it is that we and the universe exist" it can only be because, as a matter of fact, the universe was and/or is caused to exist by something outside itself. Even if that is indeed the case it still does not necessarily follow -- as is too often and too easily assumed[4] -- that such a cause must be a personal God capable of harbouring purposes in creating and sustaining us and the universe which we inhabit.

Many of the greatest scientists of earlier centuries -- Michael Faraday, for instance -- believed that all natural laws, and not only the yet to be discovered most fundamental, provide insights into the mind of God. For these natural laws were and are, in their view, the principles upon which God designs and controls His universe.

For them, and presumably for most of Hawking's readers, the word 'God' refers to an hypothesized omnipotent, omniscient, incorporeal yet personal Creator; the traditional Mosaic God of Judaism, Christianity and Islam. This conception of God needs to be, but here is not, sharply distinguished from that of Einstein; which, I suspect, is for at least part of the time that of Hawking. Einstein was once asked -- to settle an argument -- whether he believed in God. He replied that he believed in Spinoza's God.[5] Since for Spinoza the words 'God' and 'Nature' were synonymous Einstein was, in the eyes of Judaism, Christianity and Islam, unequivocally an atheist.[6] It was in this Spinozistic understanding of the word 'God' that Einstein protested against quantum theory "The Lord God does not play dice." And it is in a similar way that we have to interpret his statement, now inscribed over a fireplace in Fine Hall in Princeton

---

[4] "Perhaps the simplest and most psychologically satisfying explanation of any observed phenomenon is that it happened that way because someone wanted it to happen that way." Thomas Sowell, *Knowledge and Decisions*, Basic Books, 1980, p. 97.

[5] A. Sommerfeld, 'To Albert Einstein's Seventieth Birthday', in P. A. Schilpp (ed.), *Albert Einstein: Philosopher Scientist*, Harper Torchbooks, Vol. I, 1959, p. 103.

[6] For a statement of his reasons for this atheism, see his *Out of My Later Years*, Thames & Hudson, 1950, pp. 26-27. For most of those later years Einstein was an Honorary Associate of the Rationalist Press Association.

University: "God who creates and is nature is very difficult to understand, but he is not arbitrary or malicious."

I. WAS THERE A BIG BANG BEGINNING?

Suppose now that having made this distinction we proceed to ask what if any evidencing reason Hawking has provided for believing that the universe was and/or is caused to exist and to have the characteristics which it is observed to have by a God in the first and more traditional and popular of the two understandings distinguished. Despite that concluding sentence in his first book the answer in that book appears to be "None at all." It was in 1981 that he first entertained "the possibility that space-time was finite but had no boundary, which means that it had no beginning, no moment of Creation" (p. 128). This possibility he has now come to believe is the actuality; an actuality which "has profound implications for the role of God in the affairs of the universe" (p. 158):

So long as the universe had a beginning, we could suppose it had a creator. But if the universe is really self-contained, having no boundary or edge, it would have neither beginning nor end, it would simply be. What place, then, for a creator? (pp. 156-157)

The suggestion embodied in that concluding rhetorical question cannot but appeal to the ungodly. Yet, however congenial that conclusion, anyone who is not a theoretical physicist is bound to be tempted to respond, like some character from Damon Runyon's Broadway: "If the Big Bang was not a beginning, still it will at least do until a beginning comes along."[7] It seems that Hawking himself would have at least some sympathy with such a response. For he says, "An expanding universe does not preclude a creator, but it does place limits on when he might have carried out his job!" (p. 10). And on the same page he goes on to say:

Hubble's observations suggested that there was a time, called the big bang, when the universe was infinitesimally small and infinitely dense. Under such conditions all the laws of science, and therefore all the ability to predict the future, would break down. If there were

---

[7]   See Damon Runyon, *Runyon on Broadway*, Constable, 1950.

events earlier than this time, then they could not affect what happens at the present time. Their existence can be ignored because it would have no observational consequences. One may say that time had a beginning at the big bang, in the sense that earlier times simply would not be defined. (p. 10)[8]

The consequence, therefore, seems to be that, even if it were to be allowed that the universe as we know it began with the Big Bang, still physics must always remain radically agnostic: it is physically impossible to discover what if anything caused that Big Bang.

In writing that "an expanding universe does not preclude a creator, but it does place limits on when he might have carried out his job" (p. 10), and elsewhere also, Hawking writes as if for him, or perhaps it is only for his readers, the problem is: not to discover whether there is sufficient or even any evidencing (as opposed to motivating) reason for believing in the existence and activities of a Creator; but instead to find some suitable cosmological employment for a God already known or believed to exist and to be active. So once Hawking is persuaded that, since the universe had no beginning, there is no room for God to serve as a First Cause "in the beginning," he starts to look elsewhere for suitable Divine employment.

This distinction between two conceptions of the problem is of crucial importance. For it is only in so far as you believe that you have sufficient evidencing reasons rationally to justify your believing in the existence and activities of God that it becomes reasonable for you to hypothesize that your God caused the universe to exist and the Big Bang to occur. Absent such a prior belief, physicists choosing to speculate about the nature of the possible but physically unknowable cause of the Big Bang would be bound to seek for a cause of the kind which they and their colleagues have discovered to be operating within the knowable Universe. Just about the last idea which would ever enter such unprejudiced heads is that of creation by an omnipotent, omniscient, incorporeal, personal Being. And, even if they did entertain such an idea, they would surely hesitate to add to it the idea that the Creator acts as a partisan within the creation, favouring some kinds of conduct and penalizing others.

Although of the greatest importance, this last point is almost always overlooked. The reason, surely, is that almost all those who have ever essayed

---

[8]   An earlier generation, tutored by P. W. Bridgman's *The Logic of Modern Physics*, Macmillan, 1948, would have said that expressions supposedly referring to such earlier times could not be given operational, physical meaning.

to seek evidencing (as opposed to motivating) reasons for believing in the Mosaic God of Judaism, Christianity and Islam have themselves been raised among what Islam knows as 'peoples of the Book'. Men and women raised in such environments have been, and most of us still are, prejudiced by the prophetic teachings of generations of parents and pedagogues, of priests and rabbis, of Imams and Ayatollahs, into accepting without question or surprise a conception of the hypothesized initiating and sustaining cause of the Universe as an omnipotent, omniscient, incorporeal yet personal Being who is at the same time a partisan approving and rewarding some sorts of human behaviour while disapproving and punishing others. But, to anyone who was for the first time and open-mindedly entertaining the idea of an omniscient and omnipotent Creator, it would surely appear obvious that everything that occurs or does not occur within a created universe must be expected to be precisely and only what its Creator wants to occur or not to occur. Certainly we are all members of a kind of creature who can, and cannot but, make choices between possible alternative courses of action. But an hypothesized omnipotent and omniscient Creator must be presumed (absent any supernatural revelation to the contrary) to ensure that we all are such individuals as will freely choose to make all the choices which we do freely choose to make in whatever senses that Creator wants those choices to be freely made.

In this perspective we may see the achievement traditionally attributed to Moses as possessing a truly world-historical significance. For it was he who is supposed to have produced the God of Mosaic theism by an extraordinary marriage of a limited, finite, tribal god with an omniscient, omnipotent Creator. Although hugely fertile, that was nevertheless a case of theological miscegenation. Tribal gods are naturally devoted to the values and the best interests of the tribe. That, after all, is what they evolved to become. But it is equally natural to characterize *a* or the Creator (as it is said that some Indian thinkers unprejudiced by any Mosaic commitments do characterize *a* or the Creator) as being, essentially and in the nature of the case, "beyond good and evil."

II. SO WHY DOES THE UNIVERSE EXIST?

At the very end of *A Brief History of Time*, as we have seen, Hawking does momentarily transcend the austere agnosticism which would seem to be the appropriate stance for physicists who do not assume that they have been vouchsafed some supernatural revelation. For he there entertains the possibility that one day everyone may be able to play an informed part in "the discussion of the question why it is that we and the universe exist" (p. 193). This possibility will, he believes, be realized "if we do discover a complete theory. For such a theory should in time be understandable in broad principle by everyone" (p. 193). But, as he has said before:

> Even if there is only one possible unified theory, it is just a set of rules and equations. What is it that breathes fire into the equations and makes a universe for them to describe? . . . Why does the universe go to all the bother of existing? Is the unified theory so compelling that it brings about its own existence? Or does it need a creator, and, if so does he have any other effect on the universe? And who created him? (p. 192)

We can get some further light on the mind of Stephen Hawking, if not of God, from his later book *Black Holes and Baby Universes*. There, in his interview for Desert Island Discs, he said that after all his theoretical work "You still have the question: why does the universe bother to exist? If you like, you can define God to be the answer to that question" (p. 159).

Indeed you can. But it is important to appreciate how little has been achieved by this verbal manoeuvre. You have simply stipulated that the word 'God' is to be equivalent to the expression 'the cause of the existence of the Universe'. And this verbal manoeuvre does nothing to establish even that there actually is or was a cause of the existence of the universe, much less that that cause was and is the Mosaic God of Judaism, Christianity and Islam.

It can be illuminating here to refer to Hume's *Dialogues Concerning Natural Religion*.[9] For in Part I of those *Dialogues*, Philo, who is usually taken to have been for the most part the mouthpiece of Hume himself, suggests that:

> where reasonable men treat these subjects the question can never be concerning the *being*, but only the *nature* of the Deity. The former truth . . . is unquestionable and self-evident. Nothing exists without a cause; and the original cause of this universe (whatever it be) we call God. (emphasis original)

---

[9] The standard edition is that by Norman Kemp Smith. This was originally published by the Oxford University Press in 1935, but reissued with a Supplement in 1947 by Thomas Nelson in Edinburgh.

Philo is thus making the same suggestion as Hawking: the word 'God' is to be defined as referring to the putative cause of the existence of the universe. Having defined the word 'God' in this extremely non-committal way, Philo would have had to allow that this God too would require a cause of its existence, and that cause also a cause of its existence; and so on to infinity. But, if people believe either that the universe had a beginning and that the God of Judaism, Christianity and Islam was the First Cause of that beginning or that the universe had no beginning and that God was and is and will be the First Cause of its existence, then they should dismiss the question "Who or what made or produced God?" as uncomprehending and improper. For their God is by definition the uncaused First Cause of everything else; a Being uncreated, eternal and without beginning.

In a lecture given in 1987, and printed as Chapter 9 of *Black Holes and Baby Universes*, Hawking said that "science . . . cannot answer the question why does the universe bother to exist," and confessed "I don't know the answer to that" (p. 90). But, if the universe had no beginning, why should we assume that there must be or have been a cause of its existence, even if neither Hawking nor anyone else knows what it was? Hawking himself, as we have seen, went on to argue in *A Brief History of Time* that if, as he now believes, "the universe is really self-contained, having no boundary or edge, it would have no beginning nor end: it would simply be. What place then for a creator?" (p. 157). But what place then for any other kind of cause? Why should we not simply accept the existence of the universe, as theists simply accept the existence of their God, as being itself the ultimately unexplained and inexplicable brute fact?   It is important here to recognize that any explanatory system has ultimately to end in something which is not, or some things which are not, themselves explained. This is a consequence which follows from the essential nature of explanations why something, which is in fact the case, is in fact the case. Suppose, for instance, that we notice and are puzzled by the fact that the new white paint above our gas cooker so quickly turns a dirty brown. The first stage is to discover that this is what always happens, with that sort of stove, and that kind of paint. Pressing our questioning to a second stage we learn that this phenomenon is to be explained by certain wider and deeper regularities of chemical combination: the sulphur in the gas fumes forms a compound with something in the paint, and that is what changes its colour. Driving on still further we are led to see the squalor in our kitchen as one of the innumerable consequences of the truth of an all-embracing atomic-molecular theory of the structure of matter. And so on. At every stage explanation is and has to be in terms of something or some things which, at least at that stage, has or have to be accepted as unexplained brute facts that is just how things are.

The conclusion, therefore, is that until and unless he can find sufficient evidencing reason rationally to justify him in believing that the universe is created and maintained by a personal Being having a purpose in so doing, Hawking ought to adopt the position which Hume in deference to Pierre Bayle called not Stratonian but Stratonician atheism. This position is named for Strato of Lampsacus, who was next but one after Aristotle as Director of the Lyceum. Strato's contention was that the existence of the universe and the subsistence of whatever may be discovered to be its most fundamental laws ought simply to be accepted as the explanatory ultimates for which no further explanation is either necessary or possible.

AFTERWORD

A PHILOSOPHER'S APOLOGY
(1996)

To yield to every whim of curiosity, and to allow our passion for inquiry to be restrained by nothing but the limits of our ability, this shows an eagerness of mind not unbecoming to *scholarship*. But it is *wisdom* that has the merit of selecting, from among the innumerable problems which present themselves, those whose solution is important to mankind. *Immanuel Kant*

Like, in this respect if no other, a remarkably high proportion of those whose names appear in the *Dictionary of National Biography*, I was a son of the manse. But my father was a minister of religion in the (originally Wesleyan) Methodist rather than the established Church of England. Although his heart remained always in circuit or, as Anglicans would say, in parish work my own earliest memories of him date back only to the period after he had been directed to become a Tutor in New Testament Studies at what would, after Methodist union, become the Methodist theological college in Cambridge. Later he succeeded the then Head of that college, and eventually he was to retire and die in Cambridge.

In addition to the basic scholarly and teaching duties of these offices he undertook a great deal of work as a Methodist representative on various inter-church, Christian-ecumenical organizations. During my time at boarding school my mother, who had for many years before her marriage served as a teacher at what was then called an Elementary School, and I (I was the only child) accompanied my Father when he attended international inter-church conferences held in Denmark, in Switzerland, and in Scotland. He also served one-year terms as President both of the Methodist Conference and of the Free Church Federal Council, while during World War II and for some years thereafter documents bearing the logo 'The World Council of Churches (in Process of Formation)' kept pouring into our post box. That said, I have in defence of my father's good name to protest that that gestating World Council of Churches was a very different animal from what the WCC was later to become.[1]

To grow up during the 1930s and 1940s in such a household was to be in Cambridge but not of it. (Any sociologically initiated reader will now begin to murmur 'marginality.') For a start theology was certainly not, then and there, accepted as the 'Queen of the Sciences.' Nor was a ministerial training college, especially one belonging to what the Royal Air Force (RAF) taught me to think of as one of the Other Denominations (ODs), any sort of mainstream university institution. And once I had begun to go away to boarding school I was in any case never in Cambridge in term-time for more than a very few days in any one year.

So, even had I possessed the talents of a Gwen Raverat, there was no possibility of accumulating sufficient materials for a rival to her supremely delightful *Period Piece: A Cambridge Childhood*.[2] Yet even she might have envied us our first Cambridge house. Erected on a site formerly used by the Hobson of Hobson's choice, number 31 Jesus Lane lies hard by Jesus College and the scanty ruins of the Nunnery of St. Radegund. It still glories in chimneys designed to accommodate nesting storks; notwithstanding that, within living memory, none have ever arrived to take up tenancies.

The school which I entered as a thirteen year old at the beginning of the academic year 1936-7 was Kingswood. Normally situated on Landsdown, a hill above Bath, but evacuated during the war years to Uppingham, it was founded by John Wesley for the education of, and in my time in the main still catered to, the sons of Methodist ministers. I began as a committed and conscientious Christian. But even then what was later to become one of my favourite epigraphic sentences applied to me: "He was religious, but without enthusiasm." For I never could see the point of worship, and have always been far too unmusical to enjoy or even to participate in hymn-singing. Going to chapel or church, saying prayers, and all other religious practices, were for me always matters of more or less weary duty. The only positive attraction of religion lay

---

[1] See, for instance, Bernard Smith, *The Fraudulent Gospel*, Covenant Publishing, 1991.

[2] Faber and Faber, 1952, and many subsequent paperback editions.

in the idea of God as (in Matthew Arnold's famous phrase) "something, not ourselves, which makes for righteousness."

Kingswood School was in my day an enormously lively place, presided over by a man who surely deserved to be rated one of the great Headmasters. In the year before I arrived it had won more open awards at Oxford and Cambridge than any other Headmasters' Conference school, notwithstanding that we were only a third or half the size of many of our competitors. It is scarcely surprising that once settled in this stirring environment I should begin to question the faith of my fathers. It must have been either not long before or not long after my fifteenth birthday that I reached negative conclusions.

My reasons then were, of course, inadequate. In the main they consisted, as I now recall, in two insistences: first that what theists call the Problem of Evil should instead be seen as a decisive disproof of the existence of a God who is at the same time both all-powerful and perfectly good; and, second that what I was later to christen 'the Free-will Defence'[3] cannot relieve an omnipotent Creator of responsibility for all (I should have said any) of the manifest ills of his Creation.

These juvenile insistences might perhaps charitably be construed as first gropings towards an important and still, it would seem, remarkably rare insight. It consists in recognizing the extreme a priori implausibility of the ethical monotheism presented in the Pentateuch. The difficulty in achieving this insight arises from the fact that almost all of those who have ever essayed to seek evidencing (as opposed to motivating) reasons for believing in the Mosaic God of Judaism, Christianity, and Islam have themselves been raised among what Islam knows as 'peoples of the Book'. Men and women raised in such environments have been, and most of us still are, prejudiced by the prophetic teachings of generations ot parents and pedagogues, of priests and rabbis, of Imans and Ayatollahs, into accepting without question or surprise a conception of the hypothesized initiating and sustaining cause of the Universe as an omnipotent, omniscient, incoporeal yet personal Being who is at the same time a partisan approving and rewarding some sorts of human behavior while disapproving and punishing others.

For to anyone who was for the first time and openmindedly entertaining the idea of an omniscient and omnipotent Creator, it would surely appear obvious that everything that occurs or does not occur within a created universe must be expected to be precisely and only what its Creator wants to occur or

---

[3] 'Divine Omnipotence and Human Freedom', in Antony Flew and Alasdair MacIntyre's (eds.) *New Essays in Philosophical Theology*, SCM Press, and Macmillan, 1955.

not to occur. Certainly we are all members of a kind of creatures who can and cannot but make choices between possible alternative courses of action. But an hypothesized omnipotent and omniscient Creator must be presumed (absent any supernatural revelation to the contrary) to ensure that we all are such individuals as will freely choose to make all the choices which we do freely choose to make in whatever senses that Creator wants those choices to be freely made.

It is one thing, and altogether reasonable, to expect a limited, tribal god to sustain the interests and values of the tribe: that, after all, is what tribal gods are for. But it is quite another, and a priori enormously improbable (enormously improbable, that is to say, absent some experienced Divine self-revelation) that an all-powerful and all-knowing Creator of an Universe should be thus acting as a partisan within that Universe. Such a Superbeing should be expected to be (as, I am told, some Indian thinkers have maintained) 'beyond good and evil.'

I have since my schooldays devoted a great deal of attention to possible reasons for or against reaching atheist and mortalist conclusions. But I have never found grounds to warrant any fundamental reversal. For the sake of domestic peace and, in particular, in order to spare my father I tried for as long as I could to conceal from everyone at home my irreligious conversion. But by at latest my return from war service the truth had, as it is said that it will, outed. It had progressively become manifest to all that I was both an atheist and a mortalist, and that it was now in the last degree unlikely that there would be any going back.

At Kingswood School I had developed various other philosophical or semi-philosophical interests. In the first place, like many of my contemporaries there, I read some of the expository writings of C. E. M. Joad. Those contemporaries would have been as astonished as I had it been known that I was (forty years on) to compose *Philosophy: An Introduction*,[4] a book intended to serve as the replacement for Joad's contribution to the 'Teach Yourself' series.

It was in part through reading Joad that I was led on to various best-selling but, as I have since learnt, lamentably unreliable books about psychical research, the subject now more usually known as parapsychology. This interest continued, although it has remained always much less than obsessional. It led to the production of my first, excruciatingly ill written book, entitled, with the brash arrogance of youth, *A New Approach to Psychical Research*.[5] This

---

[4] Hodder and Stoughton, and Prometheus, 1979.

[5] C. A. Watts, 1953.

treated both the putative facts and the philosophical problems of parapsychology. Decades later I summed up in numerous and sometimes extensive Editorial contributions to *Readings in the Philosophical Problems of Parapsychology*[6] what I believe that I had in the intervening years learnt of the solutions to those problems.

Two other philosophical interests arose from reading popular scientific writings, many of these being books in the old 'Thinkers Library' of the Rationalist Press Association or reprints in Allen Lane's then new Pelican series. The first was in the suggestion that evolutionary biology could provide a guarantee of progress. This suggestion was powerfully pressed in one of Julian Huxley's early *Essays of a Biologist*, a collection reprinted as one of the very first ten Pelicans. He pursued it, with increasing desperation, for the rest of his life. In *Time, the Refreshing River* and in *History is on Our Side*[7] Joseph Needham tried, as I myself also then wished, to combine this suggestion with a Marxist philosophy of history, an historicism in Sir Karl Popper's sense of a doctrine asserting natural laws of inexorable historical development.

It was partly, as Karl Marx himself used to say, in order "to settle accounts with" this literature that, when I was asked in the mid-1960s to contribute to a series of *New Studies in Ethics*, I undertook to produce a monograph on *Evolutionary Ethics*.[8] It was again partly for the same reason that, when in the early 1980s I was asked to contribute to a series on Movements and Ideas, I undertook to produce *Darwinian Evolution*.[9]

The second of the fresh philosophical interests aroused by reading a lot of popular scientific literature was in attempts to draw neo-Berkeleyan conclusions from twentieth-century developments in physics. The main source books here were the works of Sir James Jeans and Sir Arthur Eddington, especially the

---

[6]   Prometheus, 1987.

[7]   Since these two books were published by Allen and Unwin in London in, respectively, 1943 and 1946 I must first have read the first in 1943 while I was studying written Japanese at the School of Oriental and African Studies in London, and the second in 1946 after I had returned to Oxford on demobilization. After a false start in aircrew training my RAF service consisted in first acquiring and then employing for Intelligence purposes a very limited knowledge of Japanese. It concluded with a little over a year working in the Japanese section of the codes and cyphers centre at Bletchley Park.

[8]   Macmillan and St. Martin's Press, 1967. This and all the other slim paperbacks in the same series were in 1974 bound up as two hardcover volumes of *New Studies in Ethics*, edited by W. D. Hudson. *Evolutionary Ethics* occupies pp. 217-86 of Vol. II.

[9]   Granada/Paladin, 1984. To my regret, the first edition of that work seems never to have made it to North America. But now a second edition, supplemented with an aggressively topical new 'Introduction', is about to appear from Transaction Publishers of New Brunswick, New Jersey.

three which were reprinted as fairly early Pelicans: *The Expanding Universe* by the latter and *The Stars in their Courses* and *The Mysterious Universe* by the former. It was Susan Stebbing, whose *Philosophy and the Physicists* was reprinted as a Pelican in 1944, who taught me how to begin cutting my way out of this particular jungle.[10]

From what has been said so far it may seem that from well before going up to Oxford I was all set to become a professional philosopher. But in fact I was at school scarcely aware of the existence of such a kind of creatures. Even in the two terms which I had in Oxford during the first six months of 1942 before joining the RAF the nearest I came to philosophy was at occasional meetings of the Socratic Club. This had been founded by C.S. Lewis for the discussion of all manner of questions relevant to religious belief, some but only some of which questions were philosophical.[11] The truth is that at school my main interests outside my studies were political. That was still true at Oxford after January 1946, when the subjects studied began to include philosophy.

I arrived at Kingswood already a professing Communist, and remained a progressively less left wing socialist until, some time in the early 1950s, I resigned from the Labour Party. Shortly after that I became a regular Conservative voter. But I actually joined the party only after Margaret Thatcher had become its Leader, and shall certainly not continue a member unless the leadership takes an uncompromising stand against the project of making the UK one of the future United States of Europe. I still possess copies of all John Strachey's Communist books,[12] as well as Left Book Club editions of Edgar Snow's *Red Star over China* and Sidney and Beatrice Webb's *Soviet Communism: A New Civilization*.[13]

---

[10] This excellent and still salutary book was originally published in 1937 as a hardcover, was reprinted in 1944 as a Pelican paperback, and was much later reissued yet again in a third different pagination by the Dover Corporation in New York. Its Select Bibliography provides particulars of all the relevant works of Eddington and Jeans.

[11] For more about this organization see M. Diamond and T. V. Litzenburg (eds.), *The Logic of God*, Bobbs-Merrill, 1975, pp. 270ff.

[12] *The Coming Struggle for Power*, 1932, *The Nature of Capitalist Crisis*, 1935, and *The Theory and Practice of Socialism*, 1936, all published by Victor Gollancz.

[13] In 1990, during a visit to universities in Beijing, Nanjing, and Xi'an, my Chinese hosts were surprised to find themselves entertaining an old 'bourgeois philosopher', with no pretensions to sinological expertise, who nevertheless asked to be shown the memorial to Edgar Snow in the Beijing university in which he had taught, who already knew about the 1936 Xi'an Incident in which the forces of the Young Marshal (son of the murdered warlord of Manchuria) kidnapped Marshal Chiang Kai Shek, who knew that the Communist Eighth Route Army had been headquartered in that city, who had heard of the rape of (what was at that time still called) Nanking,

What saved me from eventually going on, as several of my Kingswood contemporaries did,[14] to join the Communist Party was the fact that after the German-Soviet Pact of 1939 that servile and treacherous organization started, in obedience to instructions from Moscow, to denounce the war against National Socialist Germany as 'imperialist,' and hence no business of the British people. These denunciations continued even through 1940, while the country was threatened with invasion. For members and fellow-travellers of that party the 'imperialist war' became a 'progressive, people's war' only but immediately after news arrived that German forces had invaded the USSR.

My interest in and sympathy with Marxist ideas, however, still continued. It must have been shortly after returning to Oxford in 1946 that I first met Lenin's *Materialism and Empirio-Criticism*. It was for me an exhilarating and emancipating read. For here Lenin (a professional revolutionary writing before World War I) was persistently maintaining something important and true; and something which I had not yet heard from professional philosophers.

Suppose that (like the Empirio-critics and their intellectual descendants, and indeed like most major philosophers in the three centuries subsequent to Descartes) you start from the position which he reached in the second paragraph of Part IV of *A Discourse on the Method*. Then there can for you never be any secure escape from that solipsistic and idealistic starting point; namely, that of an incorporeal subject enjoying only its own purely and inescapably subjective experience.

I reread this book of Lenin's in the early 1960s and wrote a paper which, after some alarms and excursions, was published in *Praxis* (Zagreb). A revised, extended and hopefully definitive version constitutes Chapter 10 of *A Rational Animal: Philosophical Essays on the Nature of Man*.[15]

---

and who had also long ago read and was still ready to discuss Friedrich Engels on *The Dialectics of Nature*.

[14] Among them Edward Thompson, the future historian of the English working class. We both came to Kingswood in the same term (he from the Dragon School, Oxford and I from St. Faith's, Cambridge) and became friends. Edward was preceded into the party by his idolized elder brother Frank, who was killed as a British liaison officer with the Bulgarian partisans. Formally Edward resigned in 1956 after the Soviet reconquest of Hungary. But his later labours for the pro-Soviet 'peace' movement suggest that his fundamental loyalties never changed. Frank Thompson is said to have been the first love of the philosopher-novelist Iris Murdoch.

[15] Clarendon, 1978. This was the first of several publications on Marxist themes to appear or reappear in book form. These included 'Russell's Judgement on Bolshevism', in G. W. Roberts (ed.), *Bertrand Russell Memorial Volume* (London: Allen and Unwin, 1979), and 'Communism: The Philosophical Foundations' and 'Comparing Marx with Darwin', in my *Atheistic Humanism*, Prometheus, 1994. Both 'Russell's Judgment on Bolshevism' and 'Communism: The Philosophical

As was emphasized earlier, I was certainly not set in a resolve to become a professional philosopher before going up to Oxford. Indeed I only began to see this as an attractive but remote career possibility a few months before taking Finals in December 1947. Had my fears of being placed in Class II been realized I should have proceeded, with the intention of concentrating on Psychology, to fulfil arrangements to read for a second set of Finals in the then new School of Philosophy, Psychology and Physiology. In the event I proceeded to work towards the then equally new-fangled B.Phil. (Bachelor of Philosophy) under the supervision of Gilbert Ryle, the Waynflete Professor of Metaphysical Philosophy.

It was, however, only in the last weeks of 1948, after being appointed to a probationary Studentship at Christ Church,[16] that I burnt my boats, by finally refusing an invitation to join the Administrative Class of the Home Civil Service. This decision seemed to have been vindicated when, a few days later, it was announced that I had won the John Locke Scholarship, the university prize in Philosophy, awarded annually on the results of a competitive examination. Some moral, but I do not know what, is perhaps to be drawn from the not necessarily unconnected facts: that all the other competitors contrived, throughout their entire working lives, to be based in one or other of the three 'golden triangle' universities of Oxford, Cambridge and London; and that they have all, as I have not, been elected to Fellowships of the British Academy.

I suffered rather bitter second thoughts about the decision to reject that offer of a Civil Service position when, at the end of my probationary year, 1949, to my shock and complete surprise, the Governing Body of the college, by a massive majority, decided not to admit me to a Studentship. I do not know what reasons members of that Governing Body had for their decision. I believe, not very confidently, that the main objections to my admission concerned trivial social faults, which could surely have been corrected had any friendly warnings been given. But perhaps none of those who might have given such warnings knew how strong the opposition was going to be. In any case it was all a very long time ago.

Regrets over not having taken that opportunity to join the Home Civil Service ceased when, some months into 1950, the University of Aberdeen offered me a Lectureship, five steps up the salary scale, to begin with the academic year 1950/51. Had I become a civil servant I might eventually have

---

Foundations' appear in the present volume (chapters ten and nine, respectively).

[16] 'Student' is that institution's peculiar synonym for 'Fellow'.

been, like two of my Christ Church pupils, a Treasury knight, one of the persons privy to the secrets of the Budget before the Chancellor communicates these to the House of Commons. But I doubt whether I could really have become either satisfactory or contented as a civil servant, much less (like one of those two) eventually Head of the Home Civil Service.

The four and a half years which I had in Oxford (two as an undergraduate, one as a graduate student, and eighteen months as a junior tutor) were during the heyday of so-called 'linguistic' or 'ordinary language' philosophy. They were also remarkable in that, during the two or three immediately post-war academic years, the male undergraduate population consisted almost entirely of ex-servicemen, including some with outstanding war records, and also including perhaps a majority of those surviving holders of scholarships who had originally matriculated (begun their university studies) in the years from 1938 to 1944.

This meant that we all had a quite exceptionally large number of contemporaries who had achieved and/or were going to achieve academic and/or other forms of distinction. Thus there were among my own immediate acquaintance two former Lieutenant Colonels: one who had served in an airborne division, was at Oxford a member of the Communist Party, and went on to a distinguished career in the film industry; and the other whose First Class Honours in the School of *Litterae Humaniores* enabled him to become a Keeper of Classical Antiquities in the British Museum.

Again, the recent publication of Richard Hernstein and Charles Murray's *The Bell Curve: Intelligence and the Class Structure in American Life*[17] has reminded me of a conversation with C. A. R. Crosland after a meeting at which Labour Party members had been plotting a coup to free the Socialist Club from Communist control. Crosland would within a few months be elected to a Fellowship in Economics. He later went on to hold cabinet offices in two Labour administrations. What we then discussed was the likelihood, indeed it seemed to us the certainty, that the extension of equality of opportunity would tend to produce an hereditary aristocracy of talent.

As an undergraduate the only teachers of philosophy whom I really got to know were my own tutors in St. John's College: John Mabbott and Paul Grice. The most memorable series of lectures which I attended during that period were given by Isaiah Berlin. A reviewer of his collection *The Crooked Timber of Humanity: Chapters in the History of Ideas*[18] said that "To read Berlin is to sit at an unlit window and see the landscape of European thought illuminated

---

[17]   The Free Press, 1994.

[18]   John Murray, 1990.

by a spectacular display of fireworks." To listen to Berlin is always captivating, and to have listened to him talking is to be enabled to appreciate reading him the more.

The most memorable philosophical occasion during my time as an undergraduate was Wittgenstein's visit to the Jowett Society. His announced subject was '*Cogito ergo sum*'. The room was packed. The audience hung on the great man's words. But the only thing which I can now remember about those words is that, whatever they were, they had absolutely no discernible connection with the announced topic. So, when Wittgenstein had finished, Emeritus Professor H. A. Prichard got up. With evident exasperation he asked what "Herr Wittgenstein" (the Cambridge Ph.D. was apparently not recognized) "thought about *Cogito ergo sum*." To this Wittgenstein's only response was to say, pointing at his own forehead with the index finger of his right hand as he uttered the first and third words: "*Cogito ergo sum*. That's a very peculiar sentence." I thought then and I still think that the most suitable riposte to Wittgenstein would have been an adaptation of one of the cartoon captions in James Thurber *Men, Women and Dogs*: "What do you want to be inscrutable *for*, Marcia?" or perhaps "Maybe you don't have charm, Lily, but you're enigmatic."[19]

As an undergraduate in the School of *Litterae Humaniores* philosophy occupied only a little more than half of my working time, the rest being devoted to Classical Greek and Roman history. The intensive study of Plato's *Republic* and Aristotle's *Nicomachean Ethics* was a major part of the work on the philosophical side. The history of philosophy has, therefore, for me always begun with Plato and Aristotle rather than (as for so many others it seems to do) with Descartes.

In consequence I have, for instance, never forgotten the warning issued by Plato's Socrates in the final sentence of Book I of *The Republic*: "For if I do not know what justice is I am scarcely likely to find out whether it is an excellence, and whether its possessor is happy or not happy." So in reviewing *A Theory of Justice*,[20] I was scandalized to discover that it was only on his five hundred and seventy ninth page that John Rawls thought to excuse his indifference to such warnings by saying that he was eager "to leave questions of meaning and definition aside and get on with the task of developing a substantive theory of justice." Again, I could not then fail to remember that Aristotle, who in his *Nicomachean Ethics* first introduced the notion of

---

[19] Hamish Hamilton, 1944.

[20] John Rawls, Harvard University Press, 1971.

distributive justice, did not assume, with Rawls, "that the chief primary goods
. . . rights and liberties, powers and opportunities, income and wealth" are "*at
the disposition of society*" (p. 62: emphasis added): an enormous collectivist
assumption of which no justification is even attempted, much less provided.

In the over twenty-five years since *A Theory of Justice* was first published,
I have again and again challenged Rawlsians to try to justify their crucial
assumptions: that all present holdings of capital and income are available for
redistribution in accordance with the supposed principles of 'social' justice, free
of any morally legitimate prior claims; and that Rawlsian 'social' justice is
indeed a kind of justice, as conceived either by the judicial tradition stretching
back to the writings of Ulpian and the Institutes of Justinian, or by such
classical social philosophers as David Hume and Adam Smith. I would
recommend others to do the same, and hope, but do not expect, that they will
be more successful than I have been. I refrain from exploring the significance
of such refusals even to attempt to meet radical objections. It is sufficient to
point out that it is only on the assumption that 'social' justice is indeed a kind
of justice, as traditionally conceived, that the militants of 'social' justice become
entitled to see themselves as the occupants of the moral high ground.

It was only after I became a graduate student that I began to get to know
philosophers in other colleges. Most of these acquaintanceships grew out of
attendance at graduate classes. These were customarily conducted by two tutors
cooperating. For me the most memorable were those of G.A. Paul and Gilbert
Ryle on Wittgenstein's *Tractatus Logico-Philosophicus* and of John Austin and
H. L. A. Hart on action and responsibility. (It was of course from the latter that
Austin's 'A Plea for Excuses' eventually emerged.)

Among the others whom I first met in this way were A. D. Woozley, J.
O. Urmson, R. C. Cross, Stuart Hampshire, Friedrich Waismann and H. H.
Price. Of all these others the person with whom I was later to have most
contact was Price. That was thanks to our shared special interests in both
parapsychology and the philosophy of Hume. The above list does not include
either R. M. Hare or A. J. Ayer because, for different reasons, neither was
involved in running a graduate class in Oxford during the period in question:
the one because he was settling down in his recent appointment to a Fellowship
at Balliol; and the other because he had moved to the Chair at University
College, London.

J. J. C. Smart, Geoffrey and the future Mary Warnock, Mary Scruton (the
future Mary Midgeley), David Pears and John Ackrill were among my graduate
student contemporaries. A. M. Quinton, Bernard Williams and Michael
Dummett graduated two or three years after I did. But they were already
prominent at philosophical occasions before I left Oxford. It was while we

were both junior Lecturers at Christ Church that Pears and I launched an exercise in underground publication.

At that time the typescripts of Wittgenstein's *Blue Book, Brown Book,* and *Lectures on Mathematics* were available only to in-group Wittgensteinians, and that only under vows of secrecy. But then one of us two (I forget which) got loaned, without having to make any vow of secrecy, one of those three works (again I forget which). Since that was long before the development of the photocopier, we hired a typist to retype it, taking the maximum number of carbon copies. Then we eventually managed to find two people who needed copies of the particular typescript we had had copied but who had access to one or other of the two typescripts which we had not yet been able to get copied. We then bought vow-free loans of both those other two at the price of one of the carbons of the first typescript copied, and hired our typist again to make the maximum number of copies of the further typescripts of which had thus managed to borrow. The remaining copies of all three newly made typescripts we sold to reward the typist for what, we feared, had been for her pretty weary work.

Thanks to this underground enterprise it became possible, long before these three Wittgenstein books were eventually published more conventionally, for anyone involved in or enjoying good contacts with Oxford philosophy who was really determined to read them to contrive to do so. The whole business of circulating these seminal typescripts only to members of an in-group and then only under vows of secrecy was one of the behaviors provoking outsiders' comments that Wittgenstein, who was undoubtedly a philosopher of genius, often behaved like a charlatan pretending to be a man of genius.

The dominant philosophical figures in Oxford during my time were Gilbert Ryle and John Austin. The one I was privileged to have as Supervisor of my B.Phil. studies. The other I saw most of when, after my appointment at Christ Church, I was able to become a regular attender at his now famous 'Saturday Mornings.'[21] About Austin I have nothing to add to what has been published by others already. But about Ryle there is something which has not, so far as I know, previously been put into print but which might perhaps be of interest to someone proposing to produce a doctoral thesis about *The Concept of Mind.*

That book was originally published towards the end of the calendar year 1948. I well remember that when I entered his rooms for my next supervision

---

[21] See Chapter III, 'Saturday Mornings', in Isaiah Berlin, et al., *Essays on J.L. Austin,* Clarendon, 1973.

Ryle greeted me with a characteristically mischievous boast: "And from cover to cover there is not a single footnote."

Some years later the BBC World Service put out a series of 'second thoughts' book reviews, of which I did the one on *The Concept of Mind*. The chief contention of my talk was that *The Concept of Mind* ought from the beginning to have been presented as an attempt to show the possibilities and the limitations of logical as opposed to methodological or metaphysical behaviorism. The metaphysical behaviorist maintains, or would maintain if he actually existed, that there is no such thing as consciousness. The methodological behaviorist insists only that introspection is an unfruitful form of psychological investigation, and that it is more profitable to concentrate upon studying behavior. The logical behaviorist contends that all psychological words and expressions can be completely analyzed in terms of actual behavior and dispositions to behave.

When I sent a copy of this talk to Ryle he agreed that it would have been better to present his material in this way. He also agreed: not only that, had he done so, Chapter VIII 'Imagination' would have had to contain a forthright admission that there are statements about mental imagery which simply cannot be analyzed in this logical behavioristic way;[22] but also that, had he done so, the whole book would have needed to be prefaced by some statement to the effect that even those psychological words and expressions which do not have any necessary reference to consciousness are nevertheless always applied to creatures who are assumed to be conscious at the time of their application.

Already, before leaving for Aberdeen, I had delivered to the publisher the materials for the first collection, *Logic and Language*, Series I. A second series followed.[23] So, soon after settling in Aberdeen, I found myself acting as the unappointed but nevertheless recognized spokesman in Scotland for 'Oxford linguistic philosophy.' When the Scots Philosophy Club, to which all those teaching Philosophy in Scotland belonged, launched a new journal, *The Philosophical Quarterly*, an early issue contained an attack on this Oxford school. To this the Editor asked me to respond. The result, 'Philosophy and Language', later became, in a modified form, the introductory chapter in a third

---

[22] See, for instance, Annis Flew, 'Images, Supposing and Imagining' in *Philosophy*, 1953, pp. 246-54, and J. M. Shorter, 'Imagination' in *Mind*, 1951, pp. 528-42; and compare Antony Flew, 'Facts and "Imagination"' in *Mind*, 1956, pp. 392-9.

[23] The First Series was published by Blackwell, 1951. The Second Series was also a Blackwell publication in 1953. After a very long run in hardcover and various paperback editions both series were in 1993 reissued in hardcover by Gregg Revivals of Aldershot, England.

collection of papers in the same genre as those of the two *Logic and Language* volumes.[24]

The most important and wide-ranging insight of that Oxford philosophy of the 1940s and the 1950s was the recognition that and why all philosophy, in so far as philosophy is a conceptual enquiry, must be concerned with correct verbal usage. This is because we have and can have no access to concepts save through study of the usage and, hence, the use of those words through which these concepts are expressed. When, as I was once most beneficially reminded by my father, Biblical scholars want to become seized of some peculiar Old Testament concept they do not strain after an introspective revelation. Instead they collect and examine, with as much context as they can find, all available contemporary examples of the employment of the relevant Hebrew word. We should never forget that Austin was a considerable Classical scholar before he began to apply this method to ordinary modern English usage.

It needs, however, to be emphasized that this New Look philosophy was neither so new nor so necessarily 'irrelevant' as it was often misrepresented as being. Nor, certainly, was it something utterly alien usurping the place of philosophy as traditionally conceived. For the Plato who wrote *Theaetetus* and the Aristotle of the *Nicomachean Ethics* would have been entirely at home in seminars run by Ryle or Austin; seminars which did in fact often attend directly to these and other works by Plato and by Aristotle.

But there were better grounds for the complaint that the practitioners were engaged in trivial and esoteric enquiries, enquiries the results of which, if any, could not possibly interest anyone outside the narrowest and most ingrown academy. For at least some of the practitioners, even if only very few, actually were devoted to trivial, esoteric and pointless enquiries.

Even 'the implacable Professor' J. L. Austin himself often trailed his coat, by making such provocative remarks as: "I propose, if you like, to discuss the Nature of Reality -- a genuinely important topic, though in general I don't much like making this claim".[25] To a question about "the importance of all this about pretending" he responded: "I will answer this shortly, although I am not sure importance is important: truth is."[26] And in concluding his William

---

[24] *Essays in Conceptual Analysis*, Macmillan, 1956. This was reissued by the Greenwood Press of Westport, CT in 1981. I read various versions of this same paper on 'Philosophy and Language' during several missionary journeys organized by the British Council. One of these versions was published in Portuguese in *Ciencia e Filosofia* of Sao Paulo, Brazil. 'Philosophy and Language' is included as chapter two in the present publication.

[25] *Sense and Sensibilia*, reconstructed by G. J. Warnock, Clarendon, 1962, p. 62.

[26] *Philosophical Papers*, edited by J. O. Urmson and G. J. Warnock, Clarendon, 1961, p. 219.

James Lectures, given at Harvard in 1955, he confessed: "I have as usual failed to leave enough time in which to say why what I have said is interesting."[27]

It was in vehement reaction against such actual or apparent triviality and pointlessness that I wrote, and read to the B.Phil. Club, a paper swingingly entitled 'Matter that Matters'. This argued that it was both possible and (all other things being equal) desirable to concentrate on those problems which even philosophically uninstructed laypersons could perceive as interesting and important; and this without abandoning, indeed while positively profiting from, insights obtained at Oxford.

In consistency with the principles proclaimed in that manifesto, the three papers which I produced while tutoring at Christ Church were very relevant to the first and third of what Immanuel Kant picked out as the great issues of metaphysics: God, Freedom and Immortality. The first of these papers, a Discussion Note on 'Selves' published in *Mind* in 1949, started from the observation that talk about 'a self', 'the self', or 'selves' is not colloquial but technical. This might seem to constitute a paradigm case of a philosophically irrelevant appeal to the conventions of ordinary, untechnical discourse.

But, on the contrary, it is in fact a paradigm case of the very opposite. For the paper which this Discussion Note was discussing had asked whether 'self' is a word for a substance; for something, that is to say, which could significantly be said to survive separately and to exist in its own right, as opposed to something which is only a quality or aspect or whatever of something else which actually is in this sense a substance. But (just so soon as it is realized that 'self' is indeed a technical term, for which no meaning has already been provided in our ordinary, non-technical vocabulary) it becomes obvious that those who wish to employ it are obliged themselves to explain what it is to be employed to mean and how it is to be used. When, but only when, this task has been satisfactorily accomplished it should become equally obvious whether or not 'self', according to that newly prescribed usage and meaning, is or is not a word for a substance.

It will, surely, prove impossible to explain the nature of selves save as being some sort of logical construction out of the desires, decisions, experiences, thoughts and so on of the persons whose selves they are. If that is so, then, manifestly, it can make no sense to speak of the selves of those persons existing apart from the persons themselves. If, therefore, anyone wants to hypothesize that people's minds or souls or personalities sometimes or always survive the deaths and dissolutions of their bodies, perhaps for ever,

---

[27] *How To Do Things With Words*, edited by J. O. Urmson, Clarendon, 1962, p. 162.

then he or she will need to introduce a viable new concept of (presumably immaterial yet in at least the present sense also substantial) minds or souls or personalities. If it is to serve the survivalist's purposes such an immaterial being not only has to be itself identifiable. It also has to be: both reidentifiable as one and the same individual immaterial being after the passage of time; and identifiable as the mind or soul or personality of some preexisting flesh and blood person.

It thus emerges that this brief Discussion Note of 'Selves', which was seen by several of my seniors as trivially and frivolously verbal and trifling, in fact had and has important, indeed crucial implications for that third great question of metaphysics, the question of a future life.[28]

The second of those three papers was 'Locke and the Problem of Personal Identity', first published in *Philosophy*, 1951.[29] Although this was once said to mark "a turning point in discussions of personal identity",[30] and although it has since been reprinted in four collections of articles, no one ever seems to have addressed its concluding contention that an adequate account of the present meaning of 'same person' (a solution, that is to say, of the philosophical problem of personal identity) does not have to provide, and indeed cannot provide, antecedently correct answers to all possible questions about what it would supposedly be proper to say in every conceivable puzzle case; such as (the imaginary instance there suggested) the case of a person who split like an amoeba to become a pair of identical twins.

The reason is of course that all our concepts, including the concepts of 'person' and of 'same person', were evolved to apply in those sorts of situations with which our forefathers and foremothers had to deal, and with which they expected to have to deal in the future. It is, therefore, not possible descriptively to define the present meanings of that word and of that expression and, by so doing, to construct a definition which provides for unequivocally correct

---

[28] As I wrote in the Preface to *The Logic of Mortality*, Blackwell, 1987, it was at the time of writing this paper, or not much later, that I first proposed that, if ever an invitation came to deliver the Gifford Lectures, they should be on this subject. When it did, they were.

It was no doubt a sign of the times that whereas my *God: A Philosophical Critique*, when it was first published in 1966 as *God and Philosophy*, won welcoming reviews in at least two serious weeklies, *The Logic of Mortality* was noticed only in specialist quarterlies, and in precious few of them.

[29] 'Locke and the Problem of Personal Identity' is also found as chapter five of the present collection. Please note the postscript added to that chapter.

[30] Godfrey Vesey, *Personal Identity*, Macmillan, 1974, p. 112.

answers to all conceivable questions about their proper and improper application.

Although 'Locke and the Problem of Personal Identity' explicitly eschewed the offering of any solution to that problem, the systematic insistence that person-words are all words for members of our peculiar kind of creatures of flesh and blood and bone surely made it obvious what the author would eventually offer as his solution. That solution emerges perhaps most clearly if we ask what would constitute the most powerful case which the prosecution conceivably could deploy in order to establish that the prisoner in the dock is indeed the same person as performed the action of which he is accused. The answer is that the ideal (an ideal which has presumably never been realized save perhaps in some old-fashioned Western movie) is a case in which the prosecution was able to call witnesses who had actually seen the action performed and who had thereafter never let the agent out of their sight until at the trial they were able to point to the prisoner in the dock and honestly assert: "That is the man!"

The third of the three pieces written while I was still tutoring at Christ Church was 'Theology and Falsification'. This was first published as the first item in the first issue of a new-founded and short-lived local journal called *University*. It has since, to my certain knowledge, been reprinted at least thirty-four times (counting the present collection); these reprints including translations into Italian (twice), German, Spanish, Danish and Welsh.[31]

A short piece of no more than one thousand words, 'Theology and Falsification' was a distillation from a longer paper which I had read to the Socratic Club. Discussions there had been tending to degenerate into sterile confrontations: between, on the one hand, Logical Positivists dogmatically asserting that theistic utterances are without literal significance; and, on the other hand, theists equally dogmatically denying that assertion. I was attempting to shift the discussions off onto fresh and more fruitful lines by asking the theists themselves to explain what they did mean. 'Theology and Falsification' therefore concluded with two challenging questions to theists: "What would have to occur or to have occurred to constitute for you a disproof of the love of, or of the existence of, God?"

---

[31] Published in 1950. It was also in Antony Flew and Alasdair MacIntyre (eds.), *New Essays in Philosophical Theology*, Macmillan, 1955. A 'Silver Jubilee Review' may be found in Flew, *God, Freedom and Immortality*, Prometheus, 1984. For a sympathetic account of its initial reception, see John Beversluis, *C. S. Lewis and the Search for a Rational Religion*, William Eerdman, 1985, pp. 124ff. 'Theology and Falsification' is included as chapter three in the present volume.

It has often and, as it seems to me, very perversely been assumed that I was offering a Falsification Principle as a criterion of meaningfulness, an alternative to the Verification Principle of the Logical Positivists. I was not. Instead I was presenting a Falsification Challenge as a means of forcing people to make clear (in the first instance perhaps to themselves) what they did mean. So far was I from contending that religious people utter nothing but meaningless verbiage that I concluded my second, summing up contribution to that first issue of *University* by suggesting that they sometimes maintain two mutually contradictory but equally meaningful propositions simultaneously:

> One final suggestion. The philosophers of religion might well draw upon George Orwell's last appalling nightmare *1984* for the concept of *doublethink*. "*Doublethink* means the power of holding two contradictory beliefs simultaneously, and accepting both of them. The party intellectual knows that he is playing tricks with reality, but by the exercise of *doublethink* he also satisfies himself that reality is not violated" (*1984*, p. 220). Perhaps religious intellectuals too are sometimes driven to doublethink in order to retain their faith in a loving God in face of the reality of a heartless and indifferent world.[32]

During my four years as a Lecturer in Moral Philosophy in the University of Aberdeen I married,[33] gave several radio talks and participated in three or four radio discussions[34] sponsored by the then newly founded and militantly highbrow (egghead) BBC Third Programme, served as a subject in various

---

[32] *Ibid.*, p. 108. Having since studied *The Koran*, in which every Surah begins "In the name of God, the Merciful, the Compassionate", while the first proceeds forthwith, as sooner or later do many of the rest, inconsistently to indicate that there is to be a Day of Doom on which the mercy and the compassion of the "All-Merciful, the All-Compassionate" will be revealed to be very strictly and very narrowly restricted, I am now inclined to give considerable weight to an observation made by Thomas Hobbes in Chapter XXXI of his *Leviathan*: "In the attributes which we give to God we are not to consider the signification of philosophical truth, but the signification of pious intention, to do him the greatest honour we are able."

[33] Since my wife and I first met at the beginning of her first and my last year in Oxford we were able to marry only after her graduation in the summer of 1952. For, as a last relic of the monastic origins of our ancient universities, women undergraduates were at that time still forbidden marriage, under penalty of expulsion.

[34] See, for example, Flew and MacIntyre (eds.), *New Essays in Philosophical Theology, op. cit.*, pp. 170-86.

psychological experiments,[35] and acquired a liking for Scotland and its university institutions. Afterwards for many years I hoped to conclude my career in a Scottish chair. But, when in the late 1970s it was suggested that I should put in an application, I realized that I had become unwilling to move so far from London and the social and political think-tanks with which I had become involved.

Five of the papers written in Aberdeen perhaps call for some comment here. First comes the one, mentioned earlier, which introduced the label 'the Free-Will Defence'. Although still as confident as ever that that defence cannot be sustained, I have over the years come to recognize that the key contrast is that between, on the one hand, being able (and therefore having) to choose between alternative possible courses of action, and, on the other hand, being inexorably necessitated to behave only in one particular way. It is not a contrast between acting of one's own freewill and, although subject to some kind of constraint or compulsion, nevertheless still acting. For the best which I am now able to do in this area, see Parts III and IV of 'Anti-Social Determinism' in *Philosophy*, 1994.

The second of these five papers was my contribution to the 1954 Aristotelian Society symposium 'Could an Effect Precede its Cause?'. It is noteworthy, as a sign of those times, that I was the sole symposiast to see this as a question of the philosophy of science, a question arising out of actual or possible findings in biology and parapsychology. I was later to develop my own negative answer to the question in 'Broad on Supernormal Precognition',[36] in the article on 'Precognition' in Paul Edwards' (ed.) *Encyclopedia of Philosophy*,[37] and elsewhere.

The third and the fourth of these five papers both dealt with questions about crime and punishment. One was 'The Justification of Punishment', first published in *Philosophy*, 1955, reprinted in two collections and excerpted in a third. I only returned to this subject decades later, in 'Retrospect and Prospect,

---

[35] These involved among other things my taking, after a psychiatric examination and under close medical supervision, the amount of LSD which had caused Aldous Huxley to see visions of the ineffable. Alas, it merely made me feel slightly sick. I left Aberdeen before we were able to try a stronger dose. All this happened years before the name of Timothy Leary became notorious on the campuses of the USA. Our purposes were purely scientific. (I was hoping to suggest useful extensions of the public vocabulary for describing the visions which I was never to have.)

[36] In P. A. Schilpp (ed.), *The Philosophy of C. D. Broad*, Tudor, 1959.

[37] Vol. 6, Macmillan, and The Free Press, 1967, pp. 436-41.

Retribution and Deterrence', a conference contribution eventually published in the *Israel Law Review*.[38]

The other member of this pair of papers was 'Crime or Disease?', published in the *British Journal of Sociology*, 1954. This was provoked by various items in *Probation* and similar journals found in the home of my Magistrate mother-in-law. The central contention of this article, which I went on to develop and illustrate in a book dedicated to her memory,[39] was that mental illness or disease, like physical illness or disease, can only be allowed to extenuate or to excuse what would otherwise constitute criminal action or criminal negligence to precisely and only the extent that that illness or disease is relevantly incapacitating. This contention may seem, indeed it certainly ought to seem, perfectly obvious. But, as that book showed, it has not always seemed so to many of the lawyers and psychiatrists most closely involved. This still continues to be the case not only in the USA but also in the UK.[40]

The fundamental source of the trouble is the reluctance of psychiatrists to employ as their criteria for mental disease and mental illness the discomforts and incapacitations rather than the eccentric or otherwise disfavoured actions and dispositions of their patients. My latest and presumably last incursion into this area was 'Mental Health, Mental Disease, Mental Illness: "The Medical Model"', Chapter 7 of *Atheistic Humanism*.[41] It ought to be noted much more often than it is that many psychiatrists, though well content to enjoy the high prestige and high incomes accorded to doctors, are nevertheless curiously reluctant to apply this model in their own professional thought and practice.

The fifth of the five Aberdeen papers was 'Motives and the Unconscious',

---

[38] Vol. XXV, No. 3-4, Summer-Autumn 1991.

[39] *Crime or Disease?*, Macmillan, 1973.

[40] Although I can vouch for the fact that it was forcefully put in 1973 to the Butler Committee on the Mentally Abnormal Offender, this point is still not taken in subsequent UK legislation. This legislation retains the confused definition of the old 1959 Mental Health Act. For it still stipulates that "'mental disorder' means mental illness, arrested or incomplete development of mind, psychopathic disorder, and any other disorder or disability of mind; and 'mentally disordered' shall be construed accordingly."

Psychopathy, which simply describes an anti-social kind of character, without carrying any implications of the inability of psychopaths to control their behaviour, is thus mistaken to be a condition excusing all actions of the sort characteristic of the people called psychopaths. So the very strength of the psychopaths' dispositions to and their persistence in misbehaviour becomes a legally acceptable excuse.

[41] Prometheus, 1993.

published in the first volume of *Minnesota Studies in the Philosophy of Science*.[42] Reading this paper, which was the first of several to treat problems arising from psychoanalysis, was the occasion of the first of many visits to the USA. (I recently calculated that it was the first of over 25 round trips across the Atlantic.) Along with two subsequent ventures into the philosophy of psychoanalysis, that Minnesotan paper provided most of the substance for Chapters 8 and 9 of *A Rational Animal*. Which offers occasion to mention and to recommend to others a practice which I began to follow just so soon as I felt that I could afford its economy. It is the practice of omitting from my lists of publications all papers the substance of which I have later incorporated into my own books, except for those papers which have been independently commended by their reprinted inclusion in other people's anthologies.

During the summer of 1954 I travelled from Aberdeen, by way of North America, to become Professor of Philosophy in the University College of North Staffordshire (UCNS), which later earned its charter[43] as the University of Keele. Keele, as we all called it even before that promotion, was, when I joined, and throughout the seventeen years which I spent in its service remained, the nearest thing which the UK has ever had to such US liberal arts colleges as Oberlin and Swarthmore. I quickly became devoted to it and left only when it began, slowly but irresistibly, to abandon its distinctiveness.

Spokespersons for university institutions often used to talk, and perhaps still do talk, about the cross-fertilization of teaching and research. I am pretty sure that what was and perhaps still is said is not equally true, or even true at all, of all university teachers and across all disciplines and indisciplines. But it most certainly did apply to me in my time at Keele. For it was the peculiar but welcome demands of teaching there which led me not only to a philosophical study of Darwin and Malthus but also to write a book about Hume's *Enquiry Concerning Human Understanding*. Previously that work (despite the protests of its author) was usually treated as a mere miscellany of afterthought essays,[44] a poor come-down when compared with the massive masterpiece he himself so testily dismissed as "that juvenile work".

---

[42] H. Feigl and M. Scriven's (eds.) *The Foundations of Science and the Concepts of Psychology and Psychoanalysis*, Minnesota University Press, 1956.

[43] The intended contrast is, first, with the so-called 'Shakespearean Seven', which were specially created as universities, and, second, with the remaining non-university institutions of tertiary education, which recently were all effortlessly and simultaneously renamed and accredited as universities.

[44] The sole known dissentient during my time at Oxford was Professor H. H. Price, to whom due credit is hereby given.

The first fruit of that study of *The Origin of Species* (1859) was an article published in 1959 in the centenary issue of *New Biology*,[45] on 'The Structure of Darwinism'. Eventually the substance of this article was incorporated into *Darwinian Evolution.*

The first fruit of that study of *An Essay on the Principle of Population* was an article on 'The Structure of Malthus' Population Theory', published in the *Australasian Journal of Philosophy.*

Eventually the substance of this article and considerably more was incorporated into the extensive 'Introduction' to my edition of that essay for the Penguin Classics series. It is noteworthy that this was the first edition of that enormously influential yet widely misunderstood and misrepresented work to supply Notes identifying the author's allusions and quotations and providing at least a minimum of biographical information about people mentioned. It should, therefore, until it is succeeded by a fuller and better version, be accepted as the standard edition.

The idea of writing an entire book about *An Enquiry Concerning Human Understanding* arose from experience of a peculiar UCNS institution, the Foundation Year Terminal Tutorial. In this a tutor met a group of, typically, eight students for one hour a week throughout a nine-week teaching term. The tutor's remit was to do something which would be worthwhile even for pupils who would never touch that particular subject again, yet at the same time providing a sample sufficient to enable them to make well-warranted decisions whether they should go further. Having tried various other classics, both ancient and modern, it soon became clear to me that this was the ideal set-book for such a course. It could be made to yield the right number of immediately intelligible and sharply distinguishable essay topics. And several of these are topics which might be picked out for attention by what Kant would have rated as properly responsible 'wisdom,' as opposed to self-indulgent 'scholarship.'

Hume's Philosophy of Belief[46] is the one book of mine to which I have wanted to make major corrections. But, although it remained in print for nearly thirty years, sales were never anything like sufficient to justify investment in producing a Revised Edition. The three chapters on 'The Idea of Necessary Connection', 'Liberty and Necessity', and 'Miracles and Methodology' all need to be radically rewritten in the light of a recognition that Hume was utterly

---

[45] This was an occasional journal, long since defunct, published by Penguin Books.

[46] Routledge and Kegan Paul, and Humanities Press, 1961. A reprint is forthcoming from Thoemmes Antiquarian Books of Bristol. It will be just that, a reprint. Chapter two of that work, 'Private Images and Public Language', is included as chapter six of the present volume.

wrong to maintain that we have no experience, and hence no genuine ideas, of making things happen and of preventing things happening, of physical necessity and of physical impossibility.

Generations of Humians have in consequence been misled into offering analyses of causation and of natural law which have been far too weak; while in Part II of Section VIII 'Of Liberty and Necessity' and in Section X 'Of Miracles', Hume himself was hankering after, even when he was not actually employing, notions stronger than any which he was prepared to admit as legitimate. In Part I of Section VIII Hume was able to deploy a Compatibilist resolution of "the most contentious question of metaphysics, the most contentious science", only because, having first presented the antinomy in stronger terms, he went on to construe natural necessitation as nothing more than regular succession.[47]

Having spent the academic year 1970-1 as a Visiting Professor in the USA, I resigned from what had by then become the University of Keele with effect from the end of calendar 1971. In January 1972 I moved to the University of Calgary. The intention was to settle there. But in the event, after only three semesters in Calgary, I transferred during May 1973 to the University of Reading.

That employment continued until the end of calendar 1982. But before requesting and receiving early retirement from Reading I had prudently contracted to teach for one semester each year in York University, Toronto during the remaining six years of my normal academic life. Half way through that period I resigned from York University in order to accept an invitation from the Social Philosophy and Policy Center, Bowling Green State University, Ohio to go there for the corresponding single semester each year for the next three years as, as the Center generously put it, a Distinguished Research Fellow. After that the invitation was extended for a further three years. The result was that I eventually became fully retired, and still reside in Reading, three years later than I would have done had I not in 1982 requested and been granted early retirement from the University of Reading.

These comings and goings were contemporaneous with, but were neither caused by nor a consequence of, a major shift in research interests; or, since

---

[47] For the development of these ideas see, for instance: 'Hume and Physical Necessity', in *Iyyun* (Jerusalem), 1990, pp. 251-66; 'What Impression of Necessity?' in *Hume Studies*, Vol. XVIII, No. 2, November 1992; and 'The Legitimation of Factual Necessity', in J. J. MacIntosh and H. A. Meynell (eds.), *Faith, Scepticism and Personal Identity*, Calgary University Press, 1994. 'What Impressions of Necessity' is included as chapter seven of the present volume.

there was no abandonment of any previous interests, perhaps it should be called a development or an expansion rather than a shift.

This shift or this development was towards the political, the social and the educational. What began to persuade me that I had to move in these directions was the events of 1968 ("the year of student revolutions") and the subsequent publication of the first collection of *Black Papers*[48] dealing with the progressive ruination of the UK maintained (public) school system. By the time that I returned to the UK from Calgary, I was already fully persuaded that I must devote a large share of my energies to what Sir Keith (later Lord) Joseph was going to christen "the battle of ideas" (against socialism and the ever growing state). This conviction was powerfully reinforced during the remainder of the 1970s, both by actions of the trades unions and the Labour Party in the UK,[49] and by various extensions of Soviet power outside the original Socialist Bloc.

The first book to result from this new turn was *Sociology, Equality and Education: Philosophical Essays in Defence of a Variety of Differences.*[50] It can be seen, and indeed by its author was seen, as an additional volume of *Black Papers*, but this time all by the same author and most of them considerably longer than any in the earlier collections. This book, like *The Presumption of Atheism,*[51] and like both *The Politics of Procrustes: Contradictions of Enforced Equality*[52] and *Equality in Liberty and Justice,*[53] consisted in the main of always revised and sometimes extended versions of pieces previously published. All these books were also furnished with indices and with both unified systems of notes and unified bibliographies.

The aim, which I commend as an example to be followed, where possible,

---

[48] C. B. Cox and A. E. Dysons (eds.), *Fight for Education: A Black Paper*, Critical Quarterly Society, 1969. There were four later collections using the title *Black Paper* followed by a number.

[49] Mainly because the Transport and General Workers' Union, then the largest in the free world, had recently been captured by the hard, Communisant left, both the Trades Union Congress (TUC) and the Labour Party had moved sharply in the same direction. One shameful sign of the darkness of those times is the fact that in 1976 the General Council of the TUC hosted a dinner for Alexander Shelepin, a former Director of the KGB whom the Politburo had recently put in charge of the Soviet 'trades unions'. These might have been characterized more aptly (borrowing the term favoured by the National Socialist German Workers' Party) as the Soviet *Arbeitsfront*.

[50] Macmillan, 1976. The fact that the form of the second of these essays, 'Metaphysical Idealism and the Sociology of Knowledge', was studiously modelled on that of Lenin has, so far as I know, been appreciated only by Sir Isaiah Berlin and by one Communist Party area organiser.

[51] Reissued in 1984 by Prometheus as *God, Freedom and Immortality: A Critical Analysis.*

[52] Temple Smith, and Prometheus, 1981.

[53] Routledge, 1989.

was to produce books with at least some appearance of unity rather than reprinted collections of idly assembled offprints. The reason why *Atheistic Humanism* was not similarly furnished with either an unified system of notes or an index was, simply and decisively, economic.

So what more might usefully be said? First perhaps that books in the genre of *Thinking about Thinking*[54] should ideally be written by native speakers of the languages in which they are to be published. But when no such work is available in some widely used language, as I am told was the case with Portuguese before *Thinking about Thinking* was translated and published in Sao Paulo, then, hopefully, the publication of a translation from a foreign language will stimulate some native speaker to attempt the same job, and to do it better. I hereby undertake to produce a suitably revised version of that book and to supply it on generous terms, or, if needs must, for free to anyone able and willing to translate and to publish it in another of the foreign languages in which no such work is available.

I have a similar missionary enthusiasm about *Thinking about Social Thinking*. But in this case the original 1984 edition published by Blackwell was in 1992 replaced by a revised and extended edition published by Harper-Collins.[55] The main additions are materials on the dishonesties of Marx as a social scientist and sections on the promise of the socialist project and on its failure to fulfil that promise.[56]

Finally, someone may protest that my latest book, *Shephard's Warning: Putting Education back on Course*,[57] is not a work of philosophy. Nor is it, although it does make devastating reference to the pervasively relevant yet persistently ignored logical link between the sincerity of purposes and the objective monitoring of success or failure in the achievement of those purposes -- a logical link which for those who are sincerely committed to the search for truth provides a compelling rationale for a Popperian critical approach. But, granted that *Shephard's Warning* is not a philosophy book, so what? I have never even been tempted invalidly to infer from the premise "I am only paid to know, teach and write philosophy" the conclusion "I am paid to know, teach

---

[54] Collins, 1975. This was published by Prometheus as *Thinking Straight*.

[55] This book is now out-of-print in the UK, and is now available only from Prometheus Books.

[56] I am told that the first edition has been translated into Chinese by colleagues at Shaanxi Normal University in Xi'an, and is now with the publisher and waiting its turn. The first rather than the second edition was chosen because the latter contains what the Imperial Japanese Police in the nineteen thirties knew as 'dangerous thoughts'.

[57] Adam Smith Institute, 1994.

and write *only philosophy, and nothing else*." And what could be more important, if not to all mankind then at least to the British people, than improving the at present wretchedly unsatisfactory overall performance of our state maintained school system?

For, to give a better employment to a phrase which used to be employed by Labour Party spokespersons of industries targeted for nationalization, it is "failing the nation". Not only are a substantial but unknown number of our children leaving school functionally illiterate and/or functionally innumerate after eleven years of tax-funded compulsory education, but international comparisons show that even our teenagers are up to two years behind their opposite numbers in economically competitive countries in mathematics and other subjects in which performance comparisons can fairly easily be made.

If an Afterword needs an epitomizing final paragraph then that paragraph should surely suggest that, if the young man who read a paper on 'Matter that Matters' to the Oxford University B. Phil. Club in 1948 had been able to foresee the subjects of the various publications listed above, then he would not have disapproved. And, though the author of this Afterword, who is in the primary, though of course forty-nine years later not in the secondary, sense the same person as that young man, is certainly not complacently satisfied with all the contents, he has no regrets about having tackled those subjects. On the contrary, he would as he should be ashamed if, when he believed that he had true and relevant things to say about such subjects (things which clearly needed to be said) he had not done so.

INDEX OF NAMES

ABOUT THE AUTHOR

Antony Flew is one of the United Kingdom's most renowned philosophers. He has held teaching positions at Oxford, Aberdeen, Keele, Calgary, and Reading. He is now professor emeritus of philosophy at Reading. His numerous books include *Hume's Philosophy of Belief*, *Thinking Straight*, *Thinking About Social Thinking*, and *Atheistic Humanism*. He has edited the influential *Logic and Language, Series I and II*, and several editions of Hume's writings. Professor Flew is also the editor of *The Dictionary of Philosophy*.

ABOUT THE EDITOR

John Shosky is adjunct professor of philosophy at American University. In 1997, he was a visiting senior member of Linacre College, University of Oxford. Currently, in 1998, he is a visiting professor at Charles University in Prague and a visiting scholar at the Academy of Sciences of the Czech Republic. He is president of Roncalli Communications, Inc., Alexandria, Virginia.